ECONOMIC LIFE OF MEXICAN BEACH VENDORS

ECONOMIC LIFE OF MEXICAN BEACH VENDORS

Alcapulco, Puerto Vallarta, and Cabo San Lucas

Tamar Diana Wilson

LEXINGTON BOOKS

Lanham • Boulder • New York • Toronto • Plymouth, UK

Published by Lexington Books
A wholly owned subsidiary of The Rowman & Littlefield Publishing Group, Inc.
4501 Forbes Boulevard, Suite 200, Lanham, Maryland 20706
www.rowman.com

10 Thornbury Road, Plymouth PL6 7PP, United Kingdom

British Library Cataloguing in Publication Information Available

Library of Congress Cataloging-in-Publication Data

Wilson, Tamar Diana, 1943–
Economic Life of Mexican beach vendors : Alcapulco, Puerto Vallarta, and Cabo San Lucas / Tamar Diana Wilson.
p. cm.
Includes bibliographical references and index.
ISBN 978-0-7391-7764-8 (cloth : alk. paper) — ISBN 978-0-7391-7765-5 (electronic) 1. Peddlers--Mexico. 2. Street vendors—Mexico. 3. Tourism—Mexico. I. Title.
HF5459.M58W57 2012
381'.180972—dc23

2012026501

∞™ The paper used in this publication meets the minimum requirements of American National Standard for Information Sciences—Permanence of Paper for Printed Library Materials, ANSI/NISO Z39.48-1992.

Printed in the United States of America

Dedicated to the beach vendors seeking a livelihood in tourist centers in Mexico and around the world.

Contents

Acknowledgments

A FEW YEARS AFTER I MOVED TO LOS CABOS, in 1994, I wanted to do a formal study of beach vendors in keeping with my continuing interest in the informal and semi-informal economy. This desire was enhanced when I spent two weeks each year, from 2002 to 2008, in Puerto Vallarta. Over the years, I informally interviewed beach vendors in both tourist centers and on the marina in Cabo San Lucas. In 2004, I also worked up an extensive interview schedule but never did formal interviews until 2010. This was because of my mistaken belief that I could lose my nonworking residence visa if I conducted a study of Mexican nationals. The truth was, as long as I was not earning a wage from a Mexican employer, I could interview anyone I liked without challenging my visa status.

At the end of 2009, I got to know Alba Gámez and Antonina Ivanova of the Department of Economics, Universidad Aútonoma de Baja California Sur (UABCS), La Paz. They were interested in the question of women's economic marginalization and women beach vendors as an instance of this marginalization. UABCS took on the responsibility of paying two young Mexican-born interviewers, Micaela Gozalishvili and Ekaterine Ramírez, for conducting thirty interviews with women vendors on the beach and on the marina in Cabo San Lucas. Meanwhile, I supplied the funds to pay the vendors for their time spent in answering the 40- to 50-minute interview. Four coauthored publications resulted from that preliminary study. Prior to the publication of the articles, however, I decided I wanted to continue the study in Puerto Vallarta and the long-time tourist center of Acapulco. Micaela Gozalishvili accompanied me to Acapulco and Puerto Vallarta.

I want to thank Alba Gámez and Antonina Ivanova for pushing me forward to do the study, and Micaela Gozalisvili and Ekaterine Ramírez for helping me to conduct the initial interviews in Cabo San Lucas, and Micaela for interviewing most of the women beach vendors in Puerto Vallarta and Acapulco. I also wish to thank Kuei-Hsaing Hseuh of the Department of Sociology, University of Missouri, St. Louis, for her statistical analysis of some of the data that was retrieved from the 166 vendors interviewed for this monograph. My dear friend Sheilah Clarke-Ekong of the Department of Anthropology, University of Missouri, St. Louis, was instrumental in introducing me, via e-mail, to Kuei-Hsaing Hseuh, and I thank her for that, as well as her continued support for all of my endeavors. I would also like to thank Jo Griffith, formerly with the Department of Geography, University of California, San Diego, for elaborating the two maps contained in this book.

I am beholden to Wendi Schnaufer, acquisitions editor for AltaMira Press, who handed on my book proposal to Amy King, acquisitions editor for Lexington Books. Amy King has shown great patience with my innumerable questions and helped to move the manuscript preparation along. I also want to thank Lindsey Frederick, production editor, for her valuable input and Bob Schwarz for his careful rending and professional indexing.

And most assuredly my thanks go to the beach vendors who lent me their time, patiently and willingly answered my many questions, and were interested in when the book would come out and if their stories and/or photographs would be included within it. Unfortunately, none can read English, and a few cannot read or write in any language. And unfortunately, as well, not all of their stories or all of my photographs of them could be included. This book, however, is dedicated to their lives and their struggles.

Introduction

The (Semi-) Informal Economy and Tourism in Mexico

RUFINA (ACA-11IC) IS A 50-YEAR-OLD MARRIED vendor interviewed in July 2010 on Icacos Beach in Acapulco. Born in Tlaxco, Guerrero, her father was and is a *campesino* (peasant farmer) in that *pueblo* (village). Rufina speaks Mixtec and a little Spanish, she says. Although she never went to school her 20-year-old son is in the last year of preparatory school (high school) and her 18-year-old daughter is in secondary school (junior high school). Rufina came to Acapulco 30 years ago and joined a paternal grandfather there. She has been a beach vendor since arriving. Her daughter is also a beach vendor on weekends and during school vacations. Her husband is an ambulant vendor on La Costera, the main boulevard running parallel to the beach in Acapulco Dorado. Rufina sells water pistols, sand buckets, and bracelets that she buys at wholesale prices in the Mercado Central (Central Market). She works daily from 10 a.m. to 5 p.m. but earns very little. She estimates that her profits on a good day are 50 to 60 pesos (between U.S. $4.50 and $5.00 during the year of the interview). Most beach vendors earn quite a bit more on a good day. Like the vast majority of beach vendors she earns nothing on a bad day. When asked if and how she has been affected by the current economic crisis, she replies, "Yes, sales have gone down, tourists are not coming or [if they come] they don't bring money" (*"Sí, bajó la venta, no viene turista, o no trae dinero"*).

Rufina is one among 166 beach vendors interviewed in Acapulco, Puerto Vallarta, and Cabo San Lucas in the course of 2010. In the following chapters many of their stories will be summarized. First, however, their work in informal or semi-informal self-employment in Mexican tourist centers must be put into context.

Pacific Coast of Mexico

A study of beach vendors must take into account several bodies of literature. First, because most are informally or semi-informally self-employed, there must be consideration of the informal economy and within it the case of self-employed vendors. Most work on self-employed vendors has looked at street or market vendors. Second, since the beach vendors sell to tourists, the development of tourism in Mexico must be examined, with special attention to the tourist destinations where they vend their wares. In this book, beach vendors were interviewed in Acapulco, Cabo San Lucas, and Puerto Vallarta. Below, in order to put this study in context, I will briefly look at definitions and characterizations of the informal economy, street and beach vendors in Mexico, the development of tourism in Mexico, and the history of tourism in each of the three tourist centers.

The Informal (or Semi-Informal) Economy

The informal economy has been defined in a number of ways. Early on, when called the "informal sector," it was conceptualized as a sector of last resort containing easy entry occupations filled by relatively uneducated rural to urban migrants with little capital or skills (ILO 1972). A more recent publication by the ILO (2002*a*) describes the range of employment found in the informal economy. Those in the informal economy include: own-account workers in survival-type activities, such as street vendors, shoeshiners, garbage collectors and scrap pickers and rag pickers; paid domestic workers employed by households; home workers and workers in sweatshops who are "disguised wage workers" in production chains; and the self-employed in micro-enterprises operating on their own or with contributing family workers or sometimes apprentices/employees (ILO 2002*a*, 2). The report holds that there are two central features in the informal economy: the lack of recognition or protection by law or regulations, and the high degree of vulnerability to which the informal workers and petty entrepreneurs are subjected (ILO 2002*a*, 3).

One widely cited definition conceives of the informal economy as involving "a process of income generation characterized by one central feature: *it is unregulated by the institutions of society, in a legal and social environment in which similar activities are regulated*" (Castells and Portes 1989, 12, italics in original). Thus those employed in the informal economy have no social security benefits, minimum wage guarantees, or coverage by other laws regulating labor conditions. Although this definition fits the beach vendors, it must be stressed that some are semi-informal, that is, in some tourist centers they are required to have vendor's licenses, and though some do, others do not. None have social security benefits attached to their jobs or any minimum wage they can count upon.

There are a number of theoretical approaches to the informal economy that have constantly developed and cross-fertilized one another since the time it was first called—in analyzing employment in Kenya and Ghana in the early 1970s—the "informal sector" (ILO 1972; Hart 1973). These include the dualist, the structuralist, and the legalist. Initially the ILO (International Labour Organisation) and its allied (but now defunct) organization, PREALC (*Programa Regional para Empleo en América Latina y el Caribe*, Regional Employment Program in Latin America and the Caribbean), were dualist in their analysis. Researchers such as Victor Tokman, past director of PREALC, early on held that the formal and informal sectors were distinct and failed to recognize linkages between them, though this position was later seen as untenable. Incorporating some of the arguments originally developed by modernization theory, researchers with these organizations initially held that with economic development this archaic, or traditional, sector would eventually disappear. The informal economy was seen as being populated by a labor force that could not find employment in the formal economy, and thus was marginalized from the rest of the national economy. Recently, the ILO (2002*a*) has recognized the linkages between both economies (see also Tokman 2001). It has also come to think of the informal and formal economies as existing along a continuum (ILO, 2002*a*, 4; 2002*b*, 12) thus allowing for the concept of "semi-informality" which encompasses occupations in which some labor laws are followed while others are not (see, e.g., Cross 1998*a*; de Soto 1989; Stillerman and Sundt 2007).[1]

The structuralists are informed by neo-Marxist insights. Early on they too endorsed the idea that the "reserve army of labor" would eventually be absorbed into the formal capitalist economy. More recently the informal economy has been analyzed as integral to capitalist development and global processes that impact on local economies (e.g., Portes, Castles, and Benton 1989; Portes 1995; Robinson 2008; Sassen 1998). They stress the linkages between the formal and informal economies: the latter is subsumed and exploited by the former (Wilson 2005, 41–45), and rather than gradually disappearing seems to be expanding in both developed and developing countries under neoliberal structural adjustment policies.

The legalists, associated primarily with Hernando de Soto (1989), on the other hand, hold that those in the informal economy are innovative but strapped entrepreneurs who are simply avoiding the distortions in legislation perpetuated by a mercantilist state. His case studies come from Lima, Peru. Notably both neoliberal de Soto (1989) and neo-Marxist Portes (1994) find the problematic of the informal economy in state legislation. For Portes the basic problem is imported, comprehensive labor legislation not adapted to the needs of the national economy; for de Soto it is due to legislation favoring elite groups. Both find "surplus labor" resulting from rural to urban migration as one of the root causes of the expansion of the informal economy. Both identify its continuance with the existence of bad (de Soto) or superfluous (Portes) laws. The neo-Marxists were most concerned with informalized wage laborers, while the legalists were focusing on the informal self-employed.

Although implicit in much of the early writing on the informal economy was recognition of its heterogeneity and its divisibility into sub-sectors, in the past two decades or so this division has become explicitly theorized. Thus researchers recognize the differences in dynamics between the informalized wage or salaried workers and the informal (or semi-informal) self-employed (e.g., ILO 2002*a*; Perry and Maloney 2007; Maloney and Arias 2007). Some scholars underscore even further divisions, such as employers, unpaid family workers, domestic workers, and homeworkers (e.g., Carr and Chen 2001; ILO 2002*a*; Sethuraman 1998). Importantly, while the informalized wage workers may be forced to take up informal employment due to the lack of opportunities for work in the formal economy (or by informalization processes in formal sector enterprises), many of the self-employed are attracted to such employment by factors such as autonomy (Maloney and Arias 2007, 74). Thus, though informal salaried work may be a refuge of last resort, self-employment may be voluntarily chosen. Whether this is the case among self-employed beach vendors, whether informal or semiformal, will be analyzed later in this book.

Among the questions addressed by the literature on the informal economy are the following. First, is informal wage work or informal self-employment actively chosen in preference to formal employment? Second, do the processes of globalization and neoliberalism augment a reserve army of labor that cannot be provided employment by the formal economy? Are they thus a marginalized population? Third, what are the linkages between the informal and the formal economy? Fourth, is the informal economy pro-cyclical, expanding in tandem with the formal economy, or countercyclical, expanding when the formal economy is contracting? These questions will be revisited, as concerns the beach vendors, in the concluding chapter.

Street and Beach Vendors

Street vendors, whether working from fixed or semi-fixed stalls or ambulatory, are found throughout the developing world and even in the advanced capitalist countries. Anthropologists and sociologists, for example, have written about street vendors in cities such as New York (Duneier 1999; Stoller 2002), Washington, D.C. (Spatler-Roth 1988), and Los Angeles (Bhimji 2011; Kettles 2007). The literature on street vendors in Mexico is large and includes, for example, studies by historians (Gordon 1997; Mendiola García 2008), sociologists (e.g., Cross 1998*a*, 1998*b*; Cross and Peña 2006; González et al. 2008; Silva Londoño 2010; Peña 1999) and anthropologists (Arizpe 1979; Martí 1994; Martínez Nova 2003). With a few exceptions most of these studies focus on street vendors in Mexico City. Other anthropologists, doing fieldwork in villages in Mexico, especially in Guerrero, have briefly described out-migration into beach vending, which can be considered a subset of ambulant street vending (e.g., Good Eshelman 1988; Good Eshelman and Barrientos López 2004; García 2007; Schryer 2007). Only a few have taken it upon themselves to interview beach vendors at destination (e.g., Gámez et al. 2011; González Chévez n.d.; Wilson and Gámez 2010).

Wherever in the world street vendors are found they seem to be subjected to harassment by local authorities. If they do not have licenses—if these are required—they may have their merchandise confiscated, be jailed, and/or forced to pay a fine. Even if street vendors comply with acquiring a license they may be forcibly removed in the interests of "modernizing" the city or under pressure from established retailers who resent their competition (ILO 2002*a*). As concerns the tension between the presence of street vendors and the drive to modernize, Bromley (2000, 12), for example, relates: "Right- and left-wing statists, modernists and authoritarians often describe street vending as a manifestation of both poverty and underdevelopment, so that its disappearance is viewed as progress toward the brave new developed world of universal prosperity." Modernist urban planning projects, which incorporate the interests of the powerful but usually ignore those of the poor, tend to make no provisions for street traders or marginalize them still further (Brown 2006; Cross and Karides 2007). In Mexico, national policies marginalizing street vendors in the interests of modernizing the state have existed at least as far back as the dictatorship of Porfirio Díaz, deposed in 1910 at the beginning of the Mexican Revolution (Martí 1994, 318–19). Modernization and "revitalization" projects in Mexico City often have as an aim the removal of street traders from historic centers and parks, plazas, and boulevards that may be visited by international tourists (Silva Londoño 2010). During the six years I lived in Mexicali (1988–1994), capital of the state of Baja California, and in Los Cabos (1994–2011), prior to visits by federal government officials or foreign dignitaries ambulant vendors would be removed from the streets. Beach venders, and street vendors as well, were removed during the June 2012, G-20 conference in Los Cabos.

Beach vendors also provoke an image of poverty and underdevelopment in a similar way, and many hotel and restaurant owners (as well as some tourists) resent their presence. Periodic checkups and crackdowns on those without a vendor's license are common in Cabo San Lucas and Puerto Vallarta, where, unlike Acapulco, a vendor's license is required to vend on the beach. On the political level, unions represent the interests of some of the vendors (in exchange for their dues and votes). On the economic level, license fees, amounting to a little over a one hundred dollars annually, are still an important source of income for the *municipios* (similar to counties in the United States). A further concern is that there exists little alternative employment for those who vend on the beach. Unlike some street vendors, beach vendors are not supplying merchandise that is vital for the sustenance or well-being of the buyer's household. They are primarily selling souvenirs to tourists who frequent the beaches on which the vendors ply their trade.

Tourism in Mexico

Contemporary tourism comprises Mexico's largest service sector and its third-largest source of foreign currency earnings, after oil export and migrant remittances (Wilson 2008, 37). At the close of the millennium Mexico had attracted more foreign tourists in the previous two decades than any other developing country (Clancy 1999, 9), partially because of its proximity to the United States from where most (approximately 85 percent) of the foreign tourists come. Mexico is the seventh most popular tourist destination in the world (Clancy 2001*b*, 129). Many books have recently been written that either focus on tourism development in Mexico or use Mexico as one of the case studies of tourism development in Latin America (e.g., Berger 2006; Berger and Wood 2010; Butler, Pick, and Hettrick 2001, chap. 10; Clancy 2001*a*; Evans 2008; Merrill 2009; Ward 2008). Although most scholars begin their investigation with relatively recent trends in tourism development in Mexico, Berger (2006, 4–7) argues that the government's emphasis on tourism development can be traced back to at least 1928, when Mexico's postrevolutionary administration established the Pro-Tourism Commission (CPT) in the interests both of presenting Mexico as a modern and modernizing state as well as fostering economic development more generally.

Tourism accelerated during and after World War II, primarily to Acapulco and Puerto Vallarta (Evans 1979, 307–8; González Romero, Pérez-Bourzac, and Rivera Borrayo 2008; Valenzuela Valdivieso and Coll-Hurtado 2010, 175–76). As early as in the 1950s FOGATUR (*Fondo de Garantía de Fomento de Turismo*, Fund for Tourism Guarantees and Promotion) was established to promote hotel development. Most scholars agree, however, that tourism development in Mexico received its biggest push in the course of the 1960s and afterward. A National Council for Tourism was established in 1961 with the idea that more federal involvement was needed to assure the continued development of tourist centers (Hiernaux-Nicolas 1999, 128). During the middle of that decade a study by Mexico's central bank, *Banco de México*, identified tourism as a major opportunity for earning foreign currency; and in 1969 INFRATUR (*Fondo de Promoción de Infraestructura Turística*, National Trust for Tourist Infrastructure) was established under the auspices of the bank (Clancy 2001*a*, 31, 51; see also Bringas Rábago 1999, 9). INFRATUR was merged with FOGATUR and became FONATUR (*Fondo Nacional de Fomento al Turismo,* National Fund for Tourist Development) in 1974. As FOGATUR, INFRATUR's mission, besides "building basic infrastructure" in sun and beach resorts such as Cancún, included "developing and selling land" (which could include expropriating those lands), and "promoting private investment" (Clancy 2001*a*, 51). Early on, five projected growth poles, located in low-income states with high unemployment rates, had been identified as places to promote tourism and tourism development. These included Cancún (Quintana Roo), Ixtapa-Zihuatenejo (Guerrero), Bahías de Huatulco (Oaxaca), and Los Cabos and Loreto (Baja California Sur) (Clancy 2001*b*, 132; Sernau 1994, chap. 7; Butler, Pick, and Hettrick 2001, 213). Some had no other prospects for economic development (Hiernaux-Nicolas 1999, 129). Government financial aid for infrastructural development was extended to traditional tourist centers such as Acapulco and Puerto Vallarta as well (Bringas Rábago 1999, 9; Evans 1979, 312). The World Bank and the Inter-American Development Bank soon began offering tens of millions of dollars in loans for tourism infrastructure, including hotels, roads, and recreational facilities (e.g., Clancy 2001*b*, 133–34; IADB 2004; World Bank 2004*a*, 2004*b*, 2004*c*).

The Mexican government had goals other than simply increasing foreign currency earnings in its drive to develop tourism poles. Among others, the country sought to alleviate unemployment and decentralize migration flows (Wilson 2008, 45). In-migration to tourist centers by Mexicans from rural areas within a state or from other states has been quite impressive, thus deflecting such flows from Mexico City, one of the most populated city in the world, the border cities, and state capitals such as Guadalajara and Monterrey. It has been noted that population growth through migration has been common in all Mexican cities, but "the growth has tended to be highest in the most dynamic tourist destinations, especially those centers which have been planned and promoted by the government. The populations of Cancún, Los Cabos, Ixtapa-Zihuatenejo, and Huatulco have grown considerably. The same has happened to a lesser extent in centers such as Cozumel, Puerto Vallarta, Manzanillo, and Acapulco" (Brenner and Aguilar 2002, 525). It is notable that 46.7 percent of the population of Los Cabos is composed of migrants from other states in Mexico, and 30.6 percent of Puerto Vallarta's population are in-migrants from outside of the state of Jalisco (Wilson 2008, table 6, 44). Acapulco, on the other hand, receives relatively fewer in-migrants from other states, but is a pole of attraction for migrants from its rural hinterlands in the state of Guerrero. In this way it resembles Cancún. In both cities many migrants come from the hinterlands and are indigenous peoples: Maya in the case of Cancún and Nahua in the case of Acapulco. Seasonal migration by *campesinos* (peasant farmers) is common in both, though in Cancún the Maya tend to be better educated and less involved in informal economic activities than are the Nahua in Acapulco (see Castellanos 2010).

Employment opportunities, both formal and informal, have burgeoned in Mexican tourist centers as well, primarily in construction of hotels, condominiums, and second homes and in services related to tourism. It has been noted that "Although the country has achieved significant levels of industrialization over the past half-century, more Mexicans work in the tourist sector than in any other except agriculture" (Clancy 2001*b*, 129). The quality of the employment, however, is often low. Most of the employment in tourism services, such as the work of hotel chambermaids and other hotel and restaurant staff, is low-paid and precarious. It is precarious both because of the seasonality of tourism and its negative growth during periods of economic recession, but also because hotels will often fire their unskilled or semiskilled staff to avoid paying social security and medical benefits that by law can be withheld until a three month trail period has elapsed. Thus in Los Cabos, at least, there appears to be a floating labor force that moves from one hotel to another every three months or so.

It seems that in most tourist centers in Mexico, whether traditional or preplanned, an expatriate community rapidly forms. They come to occupy condominiums, gated or other quasi-segregated communities, and even trailer parks, whether seasonally or permanently. These expatriates offer low-waged employment to domestic servants, gardeners, car mechanics, housepainters, construction workers, pool cleaners, and others. Besides providing this usually informalized employment, tourist centers on the Mexican coasts attract beach vendors, most of whom are informally or semi-informally self-employed and ambulant. They may number as much as one thousand or more on each major beach in some tourist centers. Many of the service workers, as well as the beach vendors, live in the most bleak of housing in squatter settlements on the periphery of tourist zones, as will be explored in the chapter on residential apartheid. In the next section I examine the growth of Acapulco, Puerto Vallarta, and Los Cabos as tourist centers, all of them being the sites of the interviews with beach vendors.

The Sites: Acapulco, Puerto Vallarta, and Cabo San Lucas

Each of the tourist centers to be discussed has its own unique history as regards the development of tourism. Acapulco is one of the oldest destinations and Cabo San Lucas one of the newest. Acapulco in recent decades has attracted primarily Mexican tourists, while Cabo San Lucas attracts primarily tourists from the United States. Most of the published work on these three tourist centers is in Spanish.

In 1991, of the top ten tourist destinations in Mexico, Cancún received the third-highest number of tourists (after Mexico City and Guadalajara) and Acapulco the fourth. For foreign tourists, however, Cancún was in first place, Acapulco in fourth, Puerto Vallarta in fifth, and Los Cabos in eighth (Propin Frejomil and Sánchez Crispín 2007, table 1, 151). By 2005 Acapulco had taken second place, after Mexico City; Cancún third; and Puerto Vallarta seventh out of the top ten receiving centers for all tourists. For foreign tourists Cancún came in second (again after Mexico City), Los Cabos third, and Puerto Vallarta fourth (Propin Frejomil and Sánchez Crispín 2007, table 2, 152). Acapulco no longer appeared among the top ten destinations for foreign tourists. Below is more information about each of the three sites where vendors were interviewed.

Acapulco

During the colonial period and until independence, Acapulco was the most important Mexican port city on the Pacific coast. Spanish galleons carrying merchandise from Asia and sailing from Manila arrived there annually. Since there were no paved roads, muleteers carried the ships' cargo along well-trodden dirt roads, across the Río Balsas (Balsas River) and over mountains to Mexico City and as far as the port of Veracruz on Mexico's east coast, from where some of the merchandise would be exported to Europe. Among these muleteers were Nahuatl-speakers from the Alto Balsas (Upper Balsas) region of Guerrero. Until the 1930s these indigenous people also traded agricultural products for salt in the Costa Chica of Guerrero, and sold it in the highlands (Schryer 2010*a*, 2010*b*).

Tourism to Acapulco became common after the construction in 1927 of a paved highway from there to Taxco that connected the port to Mexico City, and after the building of its first airport in 1928 (Bringas Rábago 1999, 16). Tourism in Acapulco became of interest to the federal government in 1934 (Sackett 2010, 166). The first tourist hotels were established in what came to be called *Acapulco Tradicional* (Traditional Acapulco), known more for its panoramic views than for its beaches. Nonetheless Caleta and Caletilla beaches, adjacent to one another and separated only by a naturally occurring pier, were an attraction and remain so today, though more for Mexican than foreign tourists. There are few if any hotels on the beach. Acapulco Tradicional grew during the 1930s and peaked as a tourist destination in the 1950s and 1960s (Valenzuela Valdivieso and Coll-Hurtado 2010, 184). Low-end tourist hotels shared space with low-income housing in this district. In the 1945 to 1954 period Acapulco came to be recognized internationally as a tourist destination. Veterans of World War II and later of the Korean War flocked to Acapulco, which along with Havana was pinpointed by the U.S. government as a place for their recuperation (Bringas Rábago 1999, 17). President Miguel Alemán (1946–1952) had a great hand in developing Acapulco as a tourist center during his presidency and after. He was interested in transforming what up to the mid-1940s had been an "informal tourist industry" into an international tourist resort (Sackett 2010, 166). Among other projects he backed the construction of the Avenida Costera Miguel Alemán (known as *La Costera*), which runs along the coast in the tourist and residential center known as *Acapulco Dorado* (Golden Acapulco), and also facilitated the building of a new airport (Valenzuela Valdivieso and Coll-Hurtado 2010, 175).

Under Alemán and afterward much *ejido* land (communally owned though often individually tenured) was expropriated in the interests of tourist development projects (Gomezjara 1979, chap. 10; see also Vázquez Castillo 2004). Such lands had been established under the authorization of Article 27 of the 1917 Mexican Constitution and distributed by a number of post-revolutionary presidents. The ejido program was meant to provide farmland to landless peasants.

Acapulco Dorado, established concomitantly with the appearance of the jet set in the 1955 to 1971 period (Bringas Rábago 1999, 20), boasts a number of luxury hotels belonging to national and international hotel chains, some of which were built in the 1950s (Sackett 2010, 178). It is located along a stretch of beaches that run for several kilometers and include Icacos Beach, Condesa Beach, and others, separated from one another by rock formations extending out into the sea. Part of Acapulco's draw after 1959 was due to the closing of Havana to American tourists after the Cuban Revolution that began in that year (Valenzuela Valdivieso and Coll-Hurtado 2010, 177–78).

Between 1972 and 1989 Acapulco began to draw national and foreign tourists of all social classes—not just the wealthy. It became known as the tourist center most accessible to residents of Mexico City, and by 1985, 67.7 percent of the tourists arriving in Acapulco were Mexican (Bringas Rábago 1999, 24). As lower-income people began to be drawn to Acapulco Dorado, as they had previously to Acapulco Tradicional, many of the more luxurious hotel chains moved to the more exclusive and newly opened up area to the south known as *Acapulco Diamante* (Diamond Acapulco). Acapulco Diamante is still under construction. It was planned to attract the more wealthy (and primarily foreign) tourists, in an effort to revitalize foreign tourism to this tourist center (Valenzuela Valdivieso and Coll-Hurtado 2010, 185). Many hotels offer time-shares to their visitors in an attempt to assure repeat visits. Acapulco Diamante encompasses a number of beaches including those identified by the vendors as Playa Diamante (on Punta Diamante) with stretches also known as Playa Revolcadero and Playa Mayan. In 2010, arrivals on international flights to Acapulco numbered only 72,612, down from a high of 146,642 in 2006. These numbers pale by comparison to tourist arrivals through international airports in Cabo San Lucas in 2010, which numbered 967,777 (down from a high of 1,064,003 in 2006) and in Puerto Vallarta, which numbered 973,675 in the same year (down from a high of 1,124,836 in 2006) (Datatur 2011).

Beach vendors are found in all three sections of Acapulco. Vendors came from the Nahua rural settlements in the Alto Balsas region (as well as from other places) to sell their wares to tourists in Acapulco beginning in the 1940s and 1950s. These Nahuatl-speaking vendors were originally known for making and selling hand-painted ceramic pieces and *amate* bark paintings, the bark being acquired from Otomí peoples in the neighboring state of Puebla (Good Eshelman 1988, 28–29; see also Schryer 2010*a*, 57–58). By the 1980s the sale of necklaces assembled from semiprecious stones became common among the Nahautl-speaking vendors in Acapulco and elsewhere. Some vendors became resellers of the artisan work carried out by residents of their villages or of neighboring villages (Good Eshelman 1988, 42–44).[2]

The length of time that Acapulco has hosted beach vendors is shown by the fact that only in this city were beach vendors found who had been born there. Thus 21 of the 55 vendors interviewed in Acapulco, including seven men and 14 women, had been born in that city. No vendors were interviewed or identified in Puerto Vallarta or Cabo San Lucas who had been born in the city in which they plied their trade. Although in Puerto Vallarta this may be due to a more diversified economy that offers employment outside of the tourist sector, in Cabo San Lucas it is partially due to the newness of this tourist destination. The parents of all but two of the Acapulco-born vendors had migrated to that city from rural *pueblos* (villages) and *ranchos* (unincorporated rural settlements) in Guerrero. One 37-year-old man, however, was born to parents who had also been born in Acapulco and who had worked as beach vendors. One 53-year-old woman born in Acapulco has been a beach vendor since 1969. An 85-year-old man from Amaltepac, in the municipio of Zumpango del Río, Guerrero, has been a beach vendor in Acapulco since 1965—prior to the increased governmental spending on tourist centers.

Vendor's licenses are not required to work on the beach in Acapulco. Theoretically anyone can enter and vend on the beach. Nonetheless there are informal controls. A beach vendor in Cabo San Lucas told me that if someone wished to sell their wares on the beaches in Acapulco, they would be run off if they did not have kin or friends who were vendors and who would sponsor their presence on the beach. On Playa Diamante a grassroots organization called *Organización de los Vendedores de Mayan* (Organization of Mayan Vendors) keeps all vendors who do not belong off their section of the beach known as Playa Mayan.

In Acapulco 21 of the 55 vendors interviewed were born in that tourist center and 31 more were born in rural ranchos and pueblos in the state of Guerrero. Of the three remaining, one was born in Oaxaca, one in Monterrey, Nuevo León, and one, whose parents are from Guerrero, in Veracruz.

Puerto Vallarta

Puerto Vallarta was a small agricultural and fishing village that had only 3,150 inhabitants in 1940 (Pérez-Campuzano 2010, figure 2, 154). The first dirt road was built connecting this isolated town to the state capital of Guadalajara in 1941 (Everitt et al. 2008, 90), and some adventurous tourists visited the small town. It was not until the 1950s, when Hollywood filmed *The Night of the Iguana*, starring Elizabeth Taylor, Richard Burton, and Ava Gardener, in Puerto Vallarta that the town began drawing in paparazzi and later wealthy and middle-class Mexican and foreign tourists (González Romero, Pérez-Bourzac, and Rivera Borrayo 2008, 27; Benchwick and Hecht 2009, 56).

As elsewhere the development of tourism attracted much internal migration. Puerto Vallarta grew rapidly between 1960 and 1970 from 7,484 to 24, 155 inhabitants and between 1990 and 2005 the population almost doubled from 43,503 to 177,830 (Pérez-Compuzano 2010, figure 2, 154). It has been noted that within Puerto Vallarta there are a multitude of traditional and modern hotels, the former locally owned and relatively inexpensive, and the latter often owned by international hotel chains and thus a "global industry" (Everitt et al. 2008, 94). The traditional hotels attract primarily Mexican tourists. Although most tourists are American, the number of Mexican tourists has grown steadily, especially since the turn of the millennium (Virgen Aguilar 2009, table 9, 19).

Puerto Vallarta is one of the places Nahuatl-speakers from Guerrero vend on the beach (García 2007, 3; Good Eshelman 1988, 37; Good Eshelman and Barrientos López 2004, 14; González Chévez n.d.). González Chévez (n.d., 30) estimates that indigenous peoples from only the villages of Temalac, Copalillo; and Xalitla, Guerrero; represent 70 percent of the beach vendors on Puerto Vallarta's *Bahía de las Banderas* (Bay of the Flags). She also estimates that there are 200 families, containing a minimum of 800 people, originating in Temalac alone, who now live in Puerto Vallarta and that the vast majority of these families have members who are beach vendors (González Chévez n.d., 31). The migrations from the three villages mentioned above peaked in the 1980s concomitantly with the increasing appearance of tourists in Puerto Vallarta (González Chévez n.d., 29). It can be expected that many of the children of the in-migrating beach vendors will themselves become beach vendors, as has been the case in Acapulco.

Beach vendors are required to have licenses in Puerto Vallarta, though some do not. For example, of the 51 vendors interviewed in Puerto Vallarta, two have licenses borrowed from another vendor and five have no license. The municipal government also urges them to join a union if they vend on the beach, but only 26, a little more than half of those interviewed, have done so.

In Puerto Vallarta 25 of the 51 vendors were from pueblos or ranchos in Guerrero, 10 from Oaxaca, six from the state of Mexico, primarily Toluca, three from Michoacán, two from pueblos in Jalisco, two from the Federal District, and one each from Monterrey, Nuevo León, Hidalgo, and Tlaxcala. Unlike the case in Acapulco, none of the vendors interviewed had been born in Puerto

Vallarta. Puerto Vallarta has a far more diversified economy than Acapulco or Cabo San Lucas, and people born there may have more formalized jobs.

Cabo San Lucas

The primary tourist zone in the municipality of Los Cabos encompasses the town of Cabos San Lucas, connected by a 33-kilometer-long tourist corridor to the municipal capital of San José del Cabo. Throughout most of the twentieth century Los Cabos was a region isolated both from the Mexican mainland and from the rest of the state of Baja California Sur. In the early 1950s, the only means of communication were by private plane or boat (López-López and Sánchez Crispín 2002, 56). At the behest of President Luís Echeverría (1970–1976) a highway connecting Tijuana—1,708 kilometers away—with Cabo San Lucas was begun in 1970 and terminated in 1973 (López-López and Sánchez Crispín 2002, 62). Immediately after the newly established FONATUR selected Los Cabos in 1974 as one of the five tourist poles to be developed, plans for building an international airport were put into effect: planes began arriving there three years later (López-López and Sánchez Crispín 2002, 59; footnote 6, 60). A maritime route connecting Cabo San Lucas and Puerto Vallarta was also initiated in 1974. It permitted access to the peninsula by Mexican tourists. The route was canceled in 1986 under pressure from private investors and FONATUR itself (López-López and Sánchez Crispín 2002, 56–57). Tourism became consolidated in Los Cabos in the late 1980s and early 1990s, when it became one of the most important tourist destinations in Mexico for American tourists (Ángeles, Gámez, and Ivanova 2009, 788).

As in most other tourist centers in Mexico, there was a rapid growth of American and often Canadian expatriates who bought homes there and lived in them seasonally or permanently. It has been estimated that over a million U.S. citizens live in Mexico, including those with permanent resident visas and those who enter on six-month tourists visas (Lizárraga Morales 2010, 77–78). If the 108,052 Americans who have residence visas, 13,905 live in the state of Baja California and 6,123 of those in the municipality of Los Cabos (Lizárraga Morales 2010, 79). Of those residing in this municipality, 80 percent are found in San José del Cabo and Cabo San Lucas (Lazárraga Morales 2010, 79). The American population of Los Cabos is highly underestimated in these statistics, however, as many who reside permanently there have tourist visas that they constantly renew, and those with second homes may only enter seasonally on tourist visas (Lizárraga Morales 2008, 100, 109). Lizárrage Morales (2008,109) makes the point that of a population of 164,162 in the municipio of Los Cabos in 2005, 6.57 percent were American. Of the 6,123 Americans registered in Los Cabos in 2009, 61 percent own their own homes, whether a condominium or a house (Lizárraga Morales 2010, 81).

As hotels were constructed on the beach in Cabo San Lucas and more recently in San José del Cabo, beach vendors arrived to ply their trade. They were initially found primarily in Cabo San Lucas, but due to increasing competition on that town's Medano Beach, as well as the opening of a plethora of new hotels after 2005 in San José del Cabo, many have moved on to that latter town. Since there is no public access to hotels on the tourist corridor, which include the Hilton, the Sheraton, and the Westin Regina, among many others, no beach vendors are found there.

Migrants from Temalac, Guerrero, have established themselves as beach vendors in Los Cabos, as previously they did in Puerto Vallarta (González Chévez n.d., 33). One of the first vendors from that town in Los Cabos arrived on the (now discontinued) ferry from Puerto Vallarta. Beginning by selling hammocks on the beach, he eventually opened several silver jewelry stores in Baja California Sur, from which he wholesales merchandise to the beach vendors from Temalac and elsewhere. He has only three years of education (González Chévez n.d., 33).

Among the beach vendors interviewed in Cabo San Lucas, only one has been a vendor there for more than 20 years. Of the eight vendors interviewed in Cabo San Lucas who have been vendors for more than 20 years, all had been vendors elsewhere prior to their arrival. Notably, six vendors in Cabo San Lucas had been born in Acapulco, and four in Mazatlán, where they began their careers. One vendor in Cabo San Lucas, who complained about the harassment from hotel security guards, pointed out that many vendors were selling on the beach prior to the construction of most of the hotels there, some of which have been built only in the past 10 to 15 years.

Beach vendors are required to have licenses in Cabo San Lucas and San José del Cabo, though many vendors complain of competition from those who do not. Twenty-eight of the 60 vendors interviewed in Cabo San Lucas do not have licenses, including all 13 women who vend on the marina. Thirty-three vendors belonged to a union or organization, including 27 of the 28 vendors who had licenses.

One of the benefits of union membership for the vendors is that the union will help them acquire and renew their licenses and sometimes aid them in the case of harassment by authorities (such as hotel or restaurant security guards or municipal tax collectors). In return, vendors pay union dues, attend meetings whenever union leaders call them (absence may lead to a fine or expulsion), and form a voting block whose votes can be directed as the union wishes.

There was a wide range of origins of vendors in Cabo San Lucas, though none interviewed had been born there. Thirty-six of the 60 vendors were from the state of Guerrero, including six born in Acapulco. Four were from Oaxaca, four from the state of Mexico, four Mazatlán, Sinaloa, three from Puebla, and one each from Querétaro, Colima, Chiapas, and La Paz, Baja

California Sur. The parents of the woman born in La Paz were from Temalac, Guerrero. As in Puerto Vallarta, no vendors were found who had been born in this tourist destination, though many had arrived with their parents at a young age. The increasing competition in Acapulco and Mazatlán may have driven the vendors born there to move to Los Cabos.

Methodological Note

The study of the beach vendors was a study in progress. After talking to beach vendors in Puerto Vallarta beginning in 2002 and in Cabo San Lucas, where I have lived since 1994, I knew I wanted to interview and write about their lives, their migration histories, and their work. I developed an interview schedule, but fearing (incorrectly) that I needed a professional visa, rather than my residence visa, to conduct a study in Mexico, I did not begin to interview them. When I met and spoke with Alba E. Gámez and Antonina Ivanova of the Department of Economics, Universidad Aútonoma de Baja California Sur, La Paz, about the study, they promised to supply me with interviewers. Both were interested in women's economic marginalization and women beach vendors as an example of this. Dr. Gámez modified two questions on the interview schedule and in January 2010, at the height of the tourist season in Los Cabos, Mexican-born Micaela Gozalishvili and Ekaterine Ramírez retrieved 30 interviews, 17 on Medano Beach and 13 on the Marina. To recompense the vendors for the 40 to 50 minutes each interview lasted they were offered 50 pesos (a little less than US $5) upon completing the interview. Our collective work resulted in several publications (Gámez, Ivanova, and Wilson, 2011; Gámez, Wilson, and Ivanova., 2011; Wilson and Gámez 2010).

After this first leg of the study I learned from an immigration official that I could indeed conduct interviews in Mexico as long as I was not being paid for my work by a Mexican employer or institution. I decided that I would continue the study in Puerto Vallarta and Acapulco, and retrieve a minimum of 50 interviews in each place. Micaela accompanied me to these two destinations and interviewed 25 women in each, while I interviewed the men, including 26 in Puerto Vallarta, 30 in Acapulco, and later 26 men and four women on Medano Beach, Cabo San Lucas. All the interviews in Puerto Vallarta were done on *Playa de los Muertos* (Beach of the Dead), a mile long-stretch along the *Bahía de las Banderas* (Bay of the Flags).

After analyzing the first 30 interviews in Cabo San Lucas it was found that several women mentioned increasing competition, low sales, and fewer tourists as reasons that they were less than very content with their work as vendors. I thus decided to add two questions. One was: "Has the economic crisis affected you? In what way?" The other was, "Are there more or less vendors this year than last?" The first was added in response to the observations about fewer tourists and lower sales, related to the economic crisis that has affected tourist numbers in Mexico, and the second in response to feelings about there being increased competition. These questions were asked of all vendors interviewed in Puerto Vallarta (N=51) in June of 2010, all vendors interviewed in Acapulco (N=55) in July of 2010, and all vendors I interviewed in Cabo San Lucas (N=30) in September of that year, for a total of 136 vendors.

After looking at the interviews from Puerto Vallarta it was found on the question asking whether the vendor had relatives who were vendors that quite a few had fathers and/or mothers who had been or presently were vendors. On the first 30 interviews in Cabo San Lucas, the interviewers had only annotated yes or no on the question, without inquiring into which family members were vendors. A third and fourth question were then added, asking for father's occupation and mother's occupation. These questions were asked of all the vendors interviewed in Acapulco and of the last 30 vendors interviewed in Cabo San Lucas, for a total of 85 vendors.

Vendors were selected by asking anyone who passed by if they would consent to be interviewed. Fifty pesos were offered in exchange for a completed interview, to reimburse them for their time. Most of the interviews took 45 to 50 minutes to complete. Interviews took longer if the vendor had many offspring or siblings or had been a vendor elsewhere (see Appendix I for the interview schedule). Some refused, giving as reasons that they still had not made a sale on that day and wanted to continue walking up or down the beach, that they were returning to a client that was waiting for them, or that they had promised to meet friends. Most of those asked answered in the affirmative. Many may have sent their friends, relatives, or *paisanos* (members of their communities of origin) to be interviewed as well, since vendors from several small towns in Guerrero, such as Analco, Tlamacazapa, Temalac, and San Juan Tetelcingo, as well as vendors from Mitla, Oaxaca, were well represented.

Although the short time that was spent formally interviewing and observing beach vendors (two weeks each in Puerto Vallarta and Acapulco and three weeks in Cabo San Lucas) might make this study what has been called "'drive-by' ethnography" (Sandstrom and Sandstrom 2011, 26), I had informally interviewed a number of beach vendors, and in Cabo San Lucas, marina vendors, over the years. I had especially long talks with vendors in Puerto Vallarta, where I had stayed in a beach hotel for two weeks each year from 2003 to 2008. I had also talked to beach vendors in Nueva Vallarta and in San José del Cabo, especially this latter town. Over the years I have lived in Los Cabos, I have visited three *colonias populares* (named working-class neighborhoods) where beach vendors live in Cabo San Lucas and one in San José del Cabo. In 2011 I visited the three *colonias* in Cabo San Lucas that will be described in this book. I also spent time in the houses of two couples who were vendors. One couple, in Lomas del Sol, was informally interviewed in 2009 and one couple in El Caribe was formally interviewed on Medano Beach in 2011. Both colonias are on the periphery of Cabo San Lucas, and both couples were originally from the state of Guerrero.

The Chapters in this Book

Chapter 1 examines the educational and employment aspirations of the beach vendors. It summarizes their responses to the questions "What would you study if you could?" and "What work would you like to do if you were not a vendor?" The high aspirations of most of the vendors show that there are differences between their marginal self-employment in petty commerce and what employment they might have had in a more egalitarian and developed economy. This finding shows that many are rural to urban migrants who are marginalized from the formal economy. Not all, however, would choose to work in salaried employment in the formal capitalist economy, and quite a few are very content with their work as vendors. Yet most would have sought a higher education than they attained. This was especially true among those who had never been to school but was also true of those who had attained some degree of education.

Chapter 2 attempts to measure the level of contentment as concerns their work as beach vendors. Although some are little content or not at all content, many are very content with their work. Data is presented to show what the vendors most like about their work and what they most dislike. The ability to set their own hours and work the days they wished was one of the things many liked about their work. This was true especially for women, but also for men. Notably, there was a tendency for more highly educated men and poorly educated women to be very content with their work in petty commerce.

Chapter 3 looks at beach vending as a family legacy. Almost all vendors had at least one family member who was also a beach vendor, and many had more than 10 family members who were. Family networks may draw relatives into beach vending and play a role in socializing them into the place of destination and of work. Family members may also help vendors to learn to add value to raw materials such as semiprecious stones and imported Indonesian cloth and advise them where to acquire merchandise. It is shown that "family social capital" as measured by the number of relatives who are also vendors is related to higher earnings on a good day.

Chapter 4 relates the presence and welfare of beach vendors to the forces of globalization. It is argued that neoliberal reforms have added to the numbers of beach vendors, and the current economic recession has affected their well-being. Vendors' views on how the economic recession has affected them and their opinions on whether there are more or fewer vendors in the past years are considered. It is shown that entrance into informal or semi-informal self-employment may be both pro-cyclical, expanding when the formal economy expands, or countercyclical, expanding when the formal economy contracts. The commodity chains in which the vendors are meshed are addressed: they may be local, national, or international; formal or informal. It is also argued that vendors in Mexican tourist centers occupy a transnational social space. Such spaces are found within a nation where advanced capitalism has penetrated and formed "zones of accumulation in the global economy" or "intense nodes of accumulation" (Robinson 2008, 203). Tourist centers are one type of these nodes.

Chapter 5 examines the residential apartheid between tourists and expatriates on the one hand, and the beach vendors on the other. The vendors tend to live in squatter settlements or other poor and working-class neighborhoods on the peripheries of the tourist cities, far removed from the central tourist zones. The housing in which they live, at least initially, is deplorable, with dirt floors and fragile construction materials being typical. These *colonias populares* (low-income named neighborhoods) are geographically isolated from the often-gated and well-planned communities where well-off Mexicans and foreigners live. Social apartheid is also apparent on the beaches in front of luxurious tourist hotels in places like the Tourist Corridor in Los Cabos, to which the vendors, as well as other poor Mexicans, are denied entry.

Chapter 6 is concerned with the indigenous vendors who have migrated to Acapulco, Puerto Vallarta, and Cabo San Lucas. Most of the indigenous vendors interviewed were Nahuatl-speakers who tend to come from poverty-stricken *pueblos* (villages) and *ranchos* (unincorporated rural settlements) in the state of Guerrero. Although some Nahua who have migrated from their places of origin at an early age are less than fluent in Nahuatl, Nahuatl speakers often maintain their language when they cluster in the same or nearby colonias on the peripheries of tourist cities. Among other indigenous language speakers there are also a number of Zapotec speakers from Oaxaca, primarily from the town of Mitla, which has a long history of sending vendors into villages and cities, even prior to the development of modern tourism. Although indigenous vendors may be marginalized by racism and poverty at origin, many are content with their vending activities and many have a family legacy of vending.

Chapter 7 looks at women beach vendors. They may be single women who contribute to their relatives' household economy, married women or women in free union whose economic contributions are central to household welfare, or single mothers—whether unmarried, widowed, or separated from their spouses—who are responsible for the care of themselves and their children. The single mothers may be heads of household or be incorporated into the households of relatives. In all cases their current economic situation forces them to earn an income. It is stressed that women have entered the informal economy in droves after the institution of neoliberal structural adjustment policies, in order to bolster a flagging household economy. Women, too, whether or not indigenous, tend to be marginalized. Their educational levels tend to be lower than men's though their earnings as vendors are roughly equivalent. Because they must care for their children, formal employment is often beyond their reach, and they are subjected to a double day of work.

A number of case studies of men and women vendors, both indigenous and nonindigenous, are presented in five of the chapters. To ensure their privacy the names of all of the vendors have been changed. It is hoped that the case studies will throw light on the reality of the lives of these (semi-)informal economy workers, and perhaps make those tourists who are antagonistic toward them a little less so. Although there is much literature on ambulant street vendors, of which beach vendors are a subset, I hope this book will serve to illuminate the struggles with which they are faced.

Notes

1. The existence of the "semiformal" self-employed has been considered in the literature on the informal economy in Latin America and elsewhere (e.g., Cross 1998*a*; De Soto 1989; Stillerman and Sundt 2007). In Chile, for example, Stillerman and Sundt (2007, 183), writing about street and flea markets in Santiago, point out that "local and national governments have partially regulated these markets, thus creating a distinction between formal, semi-formal, and informal markets. However, the formalization of these markets is incomplete in that vendors use family labor and verbal contracts, and often do not pay sales or social security taxes. They are legally and economically located between formal and informal actors."

2. Originally the *amate* bark in this region of Guerrero was painted with bird, flower, and animal motifs that had been commonly used on ceramic plates. By the end of the 1960s, representations of village life became common as well (Good Eshelman 1988, 31; see also Schryer, 2010*a*, 57–58). Initially, all of the bark paintings were original works by indigenous artists, but in the 1990s original designs began to be mass-produced on a printing press and "children filled in the colors" (Cowen 2005, 148). Some of these mass-produced amate bark paintings are still sold on the beach in all three tourist centers examined in this book.

1

Wasted Lives?

Aspiration of the Vendors

A large section of street vendors in urban areas are those with low skills who have migrated to larger cities from rural areas or small towns in search of employment. These people take to street vending when they do not find other means of livelihood . . .

There is also another section of the urban population that has taken to street vending. These people, or their spouses, were once engaged in better paid jobs in the formal employment sector. . . . Many of the displaced, or their spouses, have become street vendors to eke out a living.

—Bhowmik 2010, 8

THERE IS A DEBATE IN THE LITERATURE on the informal economy as concerns the circumstances of those who are employed in it. Some hold that informal employment is the survival strategy of a surplus population or reserve army of labor that exists in large part because of demographic factors and the differentiation of the peasantry. The resultant rural-to-urban migration of dispossessed landless peasants and circular migration of the semi-dispossessed with only subsistence or sub-subsistence agricultural plots leads to an inundation of cities that cannot provide sufficient formal employment opportunities. These workers of peasant origin are joined by the unemployed and underemployed generated by the erosion of formal work, which has been caused by economic restructuring and structural adjustment programs (e.g., Robinson 2008; Bhowmik 2010). They are considered a marginalized population, searching for any means of livelihood.

Nonetheless, some authors make a distinction between informal wage employment and informal self-employment, considering the former to be exploitative but the latter sometimes liberating (e.g., Perry et al. 2007). A study patronized by the World Bank, while recognizing the problem of a population surplus to the needs of formal enterprises, stresses that many, though not all, of the self-employed choose this option and are content with it (Perry et al. 2007). Maloney (2004, 1160) holds that as many as 60 percent of the men who are self-employed in Mexico "entered the sector voluntarily," giving "greater independence or higher pay as their principal motives." He cites Balán, Browning, and Jelin's (1973) findings that men in Monterrey gave being one's own boss and earning more money than in formal salaried employment as two motivations for entering informal self-employment (Maloney 2004, 1160). It must be pointed out, however, that though some self-employment may be relatively lucrative and satisfying, much, if not most, is low end and marginal (e.g., Roever 2010, 209). Both the marginalization and the liberation analyses throw light on the situation of street vendors, whether ambulant (as are the beach vendors in this book) or fixed.

This chapter will examine various findings from the interviews of the beach vendors that touch on the question of whether their self-employment is simply a survival strategy or an occupation they enjoy. These alternatives are not necessarily mutually exclusive, however. There is the possibility that men and women found themselves forced to take up informal income generating activities, but that once they did so they found such employment to have its positive aspects. The next chapter will consider what vendors found to be positive and negative about their work. In this chapter we will look at the educational levels of the vendors, what other work they might consider doing, and what—given the opportunity—they would like or would have liked to study.

Educational Levels of the Vendors

Although far more than half of the vendors had little or no education, there were some with relatively high educational levels. The following data are summarized in table 1.1. A total of 16.3 percent of the beach vendors had never attended school, with higher percentages of women (20.2 percent) having no schooling than men (12.2 percent). Thus, whereas a little over one in every 10 men had no schooling, two of every 10 women did not. Another 17.5 percent of the total sample had not finished the six years of primary school, whereas 25.3 percent had completed that schooling. The percentages for women completing primary school (27.4 percent) were slightly higher

TABLE 1.1
Educational Levels of the Beach Vendors

	Men (N=82)		*Women (N=84)*		*Total (N=166)*	
	No.	*%*	*No.*	*%*	*No.*	*%*
No schooling	10	12.2	17	20.2	27	16.3
Primary incomplete	15	18.3	14	16.7	29	17.5
1 year	2	2.4	1	1.2	3	1.8
2 years	4	4.9	4	4.8	8	4.8
3 years	4	4.9	5	5.9	9	5.4
4 years	2	2.4	1	1.2	3	1.8
5 years	3	3.6	3	3.6	6	3.6
Primary complete	19	23.2	23	27.4	42	25.3
Secondary incomplete	13	15.8	9	10.7	22	13.3
7 years	3	3.6	3	3.6	6	3.6
8 years	10	12.2	6	7.1	16	9.6
Secondary complete	12	14.6	13	15.5	25	15.1
Preparatory incomplete	4	4.9	4	4.8	8	4.8
10 years	3	3.6	0	0	3	1.8
11 years	1	1.2	4	4.8	5	3.0
Preparatory complete	6	7.3	4	4.8	10	6.0
>12 years	3	3.6	0	0	3	1.8
Totals	82	99.9	84	100.1	166	100.0

than the percentages of men (23.2 percent). Almost three-fifths (59.1 percent) of the beach vendors had primary school or less, including 64.3 percent of women and 53.7 percent of men. Thus over half of the men and over three-fifths of the women cannot reasonably expect to find many opportunities in the formal economy. At least some secondary school, with preference given to those who have completed the nine years of education, is necessary to work in the formal economy in Mexico. This includes, for example, work in the *maquiladora* (assembly) plants, as a cashier, or as a receptionist. The nine years of secondary school is also required for waiters or waitresses in tourist-oriented restaurants. Perhaps the only formal job that those without secondary school can find is housekeeping in a tourist hotel. Furthermore, completion of preparatory school is increasingly being called for in the formal economy, even for such jobs as being a cashier in Costco.

Only 28.4 percent of the sample had some secondary schooling or had completed secondary, including 26.2 percent of the women. Of those with some preparatory school, preparatory school completed, and post-preparatory studies, a little more than one of 10 (12.6 percent) had attained these higher levels, including 9.6 percent of women and 15.8 percent of men. Overall, more women than men showed lower levels of educational attainment, and at the higher end there were more men than women. It can be surmised that the almost 60 percent of beach vendors with primary school or less would have been forced into the informal economy. The 41 percent who have some secondary school or more could possibly find employment in the formal economy if sufficient jobs had been created there.

What Alternative Work Could Vendors Contemplate?

Although most vendors were very content with their work, as will be seen in the following chapter, the overwhelming majority could contemplate working at something else. Only 13.2 percent of the total sample indicated that they would not desire alternative work, and these included 15.5 percent of women and 11 percent of men (see table 1.2). Several mentioned that they wanted no other work because they liked being vendors, including 5.9 percent of the women. Several said they wanted to do no work at all. Five women (6 percent of women) didn't know and one man said that there was simply no other work available. Ten men (12.2 percent) would like to be *campesinos* (peasants, farmers) (See table 1.2).

TABLE 1.2.
Alternative Work Desired

Answers to "What work would you like to do if you were not a vendor?".

	Men (N=82)		*Women (N=84)*		*Total (N=166)*	
	No.	*%*	*No.*	*%*	*No.*	*%*
Nothing[a]	9	11.0	12	15.5	22	13.2
Informal	16	19.5	19	22.6	35	21.1
(Informal Self-Employment)	(10)	(12.2)	(9)	(10.7)	(19)	(11.5)
Formal	35	42.7	40	47.6	75	45.2
Construction	9	11.0	0	0	9	5.4
Campesino	10	12.2	0	0	10	6.0
Something else[b]	3	3.7	7	8.3	10	6.0
No other work available	1	1.2	0	0	1	0.6
Doesn't know	0	0	5	6.0	5	3.0
No information	0	0	1	1.2	1	0.6
Total	82	100.1	84	100.1	166	100.0

[a] Of these, two men and five women would do nothing else because they like being vendors.

[b] These vendors did not know what other work they would like to do but would exit from beach vending if they could find something else.

Of alternative work contemplated 21.1 percent of the sample (including 19.5 percent of men) mentioned work that was coded as informal, whereas 45.2 percent (including 47.6 percent of women) mentioned work that was coded as formal. This included being a waiter, waitress, or cook in a restaurant or hotel, which usually carried social security benefits, at least in Cabo San Lucas. Among the 21.1 percent who would choose informal work were 11.5 percent who would choose informal self-employment and 15 percent who would choose informal wage work. Construction is a case apart, as some construction workers have the package of security benefits, as mandated by law for their profession, and others do not. An architect in Cabo San Lucas estimates that only about half of the construction workers employed in building large tourists hotels are receiving social security benefits. The sub-contractor, he explains, will claim he has 50 workers for purposes of social security, but will actually be employing 100. Often, as well, when building houses, especially in the squatter settlements, construction workers will be informally self-employed. The desire for construction work was expressed by 1 percent of men, comparable to the 12.2 percent of men who wished to be campesinos.

Below are some snapshot summaries of those who would do nothing in the way of work if they could retire.

Among the men who would not seek alternative work was a 57-year-old vendor from a small town in Guerrero, who was interviewed in Acapulco. He has been a vendor for 10 years. He says he would not seek other work, because it is too expensive to be a campesino, which would have been his work of choice. He was referring to the need to pay for fertilizers, pesticides, herbicides, and other costs of farming. Both he and his father previously cultivated un-owned lands in the mountains near his village. A 59-year-old vendor from a small town in Guerrero, interviewed in Puerto Vallarta, would like to retire. He has been a vendor for 13 years and previously worked in a butcher shop. This work was informal wage employment, so he has no pension. This lack of a pension for those who worked the informal economy characterizes the situation of many of the older beach vendors.

Among the women is a 30-year-old vendor from a small town in Guerrero, interviewed in Acapulco, who would like to stay at home with her children. Another 40-year-old vendor from a small town in Guerrero, interviewed in Acapulco, is widowed and has two dependent children. She would like to stay at home with them but cannot because she is the household's breadwinner. There was a total of seven women who would prefer to be housewives, mentioning that they would like to be at home with their offspring. These cases can be seen as illustrative of poverty-driven self-employment and as an index of women's marginalization in a volatile economy characterized by deep inequalities.

Educational Aspirations

Among the questions asked on the interview were "What would you study if you could?". As many as 85.5 percent, including 92.7 percent of men and 78.7 percent of women, indicated that they would like to study or to have studied something (see table 1.3). Among those with no schooling (N=27), seven (25.9 percent) wished to learn to read and write and/or do math. Others among this group had higher aspirations, as will be discussed below. Wishes were expressed to complete primary school (3 percent), to complete secondary school (4.2 percent) and to finish preparatory school (5.4 percent). One

TABLE 1.3
What Beach Vendors Would Like to Study

Answers to question "What would you study if you could?".

	Men[a]		*Women*		*Total*	
	No.	*%*	*No.*	*%*	*No.*	*%*
Doesn't know	1	1.2	5	5.9	6	3.6
Nothing[b]	7	8.5	11	13.1	18	10.8
To learn to read, write, do math	3	3.7	4	4.9	7	4.2
To finish primary	3	3.6	2	2.4	5	3.0
To finish secondary	1	1.2	4	4.7	7	4.2
To finish preparatory	2	2.4	7	8.3	9	5.4
Technical school	12	14.6	10	11.9	22	13.2
(Computers)	(10)		(4)		(14)	
(Auto Mechanics)	(2)		(0)		(2)	
(Secretarial)	(0)		(2)		(2)	
(Beautician)	(0)		(0)		(4)	
English	24	29.3	10	11.9	34	20.5
Nursing	0	0	4	4.8	4	2.4
Accountant	6	7.3	2	2.4	8	4.8
Doctor	3	3.7	3	3.6	6	3.6
Engineer	8	9.8	1	1.2	9	5.4
Veterinarian	3	3.7	0	0	3	1.8
Teacher	1	1.2	9	10.7	10	6.0
Lawyer	3	3.7	0	0	3	1.8
Marine biology/ecology	2	2.4	0	0	2	1.2
Police work	0	0	2	2.4	2	1.2
Other[c]	5	6.1	3	3.6	8	4.8

[a] Some men expressed an interest in studying for more than one career. One would have liked to be an engineer or a veterinarian, and another would have liked to be a doctor or an engineer, for example.

[b] Those who did not want to study anything usually thought they were too old to do so or wanted to concentrate on their children studying.

[c] Among women one wished to study interior design, one to continue studying hotel science and gastronomy, and one to learn to be a cook. Among the men, one expressed interest in getting a master's degree in something, one a bachelor's degree, and one a degree in art.

out of five (20.5 percent), including 29.3 percent of men and 11.9 percent of women would like to learn English. Almost all specified that it would help them with their work with the tourists, though one man interviewed in Cabo San Lucas mentioned that it would help him get work in construction (including housing renovation) in the large expatriate community in that city. Technical school was the choice of 13.2 percent, including 10 (8.4 percent) who wished to learn computer skills, two men who wished to learn automobile mechanics, two women who wished to study to be secretaries, and two women who would like to be beauticians.

In terms of other careers, four women would have liked to be nurses; and three women and three men, medical doctors. One 48-year-old man would have liked to be a doctor because there was none in his village of origin in Guerrero. He wished to fill that void. Nine vendors, including eight men and one woman, would have liked to be engineers, including construction (one man and one woman), civil (three), automobile (one), agricultural (one) and with two unspecified. Eight would have liked to be public accountants, including six men and two women. The beach vendor who has studied to be a public accountant and worked in this profession for many years wished to study English for his work with tourists. Three men would have liked to be veterinarians. Nine, including one man and eight women, would have liked to be teachers; and seven, including one woman and six men, would have liked to study law.

Among those with no schooling (N=27), as mentioned above, seven would like to learn to read and write and/or do math (see table 1.4). One of the men would also like to learn English. Among them 18.5 percent would choose to study nothing, and 7.4 percent said they did not know. In total 79.3 percent expressed a desire to study something, including 80 percent of men and 76.8 percent of women. Two women expressed a desire to finish primary school and one man to finish preparatory school. Five vendors, including three women, in addition to the man who would also like to learn to read and write, would like to learn English to help them with their work as vendors. One man would have liked to be a doctor or engineer and another a *licenciado* (bachelor's degree holder) in law. One woman would like to study to be a cook. Few women would seek education higher than primary school, and none, other than the woman who desired to be a cook, expressed any interest in pursuing a career. The women with no schooling can be seen as not only marginalized because of their inability to read or write, but also subjectively marginalized in that their aspirations are low and greater opportunities and ways to achieve them not envisioned. Men, nine out of 10 of whom wished to study something, were less subjectively marginalized, though they are objectively so.

TABLE 1.4
What Vendors Without Primary School Completed Would Like to Study

	Men (N=15)		Women (N=14)		Total (N=29)	
	No.	%	No.	%	No.	%
What would study						
Nothing	3	20.0	3	21.4	6	20.6
Some sort of schooling	12	80.0	11	78.6	23	79.3
Total	15	100.0	14	100.0	29	99.9
Schooling desired						
Finish primary	3[a]	20.0	0	0	3	10.3
Finish secondary	0	0	2	14.3	2	6.9
Finish preparatory	1	6.7	1	7.1	2	6.9
English	6	40.0	1	7.1	7	24.1
Career[b]	2	13.3	5	35.7	7	24.1
Other[c]	0	0	2	14.3	2	6.9
Total	12	80.0	11	78.5	23	79.2

[a] One man also wanted to study English. Most who wished to study English indicated that it would help their work with the tourists.

[b] Among the careers mentioned by men were: civil engineering (1), construction engineering (1). Among the careers mentioned by women were: beautician (2), public accountant (1), and interior decoration (1).

[c] Other included one woman who wished to learn to sew better (she makes the sundresses she and her husband sell on the beach in Cabo San Lucas) and one who says she cannot study because she must care for her sick husband.

Case Studies

What Men with Less than Six Years of Education (N=25) Would Study (Other than English)

Case 1.1

Santiago (ACA-3PD) is a 36-year-old married vendor with eight children interviewed on Playa Diamante in Acapulco. He is from the village of Tlamamacan, Guerrero. He has three years of education speaks Nahuatl, Spanish, some English and a very little French and Italian. He learned the last three languages interacting with the foreign tourists. His father had a little land in the village and also worked as a sharecropper. He still cultivates land at the age of 86. Santiago has been in the United States twice, crossing in 1993 and staying two years, then crossing again in 1996 and staying for another two years. He worked in Santa Barbara, California, in construction, in remodeling houses, and as a gardener. He currently has a 46-year-old brother who is a construction worker in Santa Barbara. Santiago has three sisters and six brothers. A 54-year-old and a 56-year-old brother sell necklaces on the beach in Puerto Vallarta and a 50-year-old brother does so on the beach in Acapulco. Salvador's other two brothers cultivate lands in Tlamamacan. His three sisters aid their husbands on their agricultural lands.

Santiago estimates that he has at least 20 relatives who are vendors: most are offspring of his siblings. He and his children collect shells and shark spines on the beach, and then the family strings them into the unique necklaces he sells. He has been a vendor for 30 years, since he was six years old; and has also vended in Zihuatenejo for two years; in Manzanillo, Colima, for two months; in Puerto Vallarta for two weeks, and in Playa Azul, Michoacán for 3 years. He feels Acapulco is the best place to be a beach vendor because there are more tourists there. He is little content with being a vendor and would like to find better work ("*Quisiera tener otro trabajo major*"), such as a hotel receptionist. If he could study anything it would be languages, including Spanish, because he explains, his language is Nahuatl ("*Mi dialecto es Nahuatl*"), but also English and French because his clients speak those languages. Because of his low educational level, Santiago is constrained to work as a vendor if he wishes to stay in Mexico. He might have entered other informal employment, but his vast family network of vendors may have helped pull him into his present work.

Case 1.2

Clemente (ACA-18CA) is an 85-year-old vendor, interviewed on Caletilla Beach in Acapulco. He never went to school because his parents did not have enough money to buy him a school uniform. He has been widowed for 12 years and his 14-year-old grandson, also a vendor, accompanies him on his rounds of the adjacent Caleta and Caletilla beaches. His grandson is one of two children of Clemente's only daughter, who also works as a beach vendor. Clemente was born in Amaltepec, municipality of Chilpancingo, Guerrero. One of Clemente's two living brothers, now 70, is a sharecropper in that village. Clemente has also cultivated land in Amaltepec and worked as a field hand in the United States. Three of his deceased siblings painted clay figurines and sold them on the Caleta and Caletilla beaches in Acapulco.

Clemente has been a beach vendor since coming to Acapulco 45 years ago. He sells silver earrings from Taxco and shell earrings that he buys from wholesalers in Acapulco. He is very content with being a vendor because it allows him to earn a little money. If he had not been a vendor he would have liked to work in construction. He would have liked to attend a university, to be a licensiado, but couldn't because, he says, "We were very poor" ("*Estuvimos muy pobres*"). Clemente's lack of education, and lack of skills in anything other than farming, may have forced him to enter that subset of street vendors who work on the beach.

Case 1.3

Martín (ACA-26IC) is a 70-year-old married vendor who never went to school. He speaks Nahuatl and Spanish and is from the small town of Tlamacazapa, Guerrero. He has five daughters and three sons. Two of his daughters, ages 32 and 22, and one of his sons, aged 24, are living in Texas. He has not seen them for 14 years and does not know what work they are doing. He cannot read or write so has not been able to communicate with them. All seven of his siblings are now deceased. When alive they cultivated a vast stretch of land owned by his father, growing corn, tomatoes, and chilies. Martín has lived in Acapulco, where he was interviewed on Icacos Beach, for 36 years. Martín sells T-shirts with an Acapulco logo that he acquires from a wholesaler at 1,000 pesos for 20 shirts, and resells for anywhere between 80 and 150 pesos for each one. He says that previously he worked only as a campesino on his own lands. He is little content with being a vendor but asks, "What else can I do?" ("*Que más puedo hacer?*"). Martín says there is nothing he would study now, but when he was young he wished to be a doctor or engineer. When I ask what work he would like to do if not a vendor, he replies to the effect that since he has no schooling there is nothing else he can do. He says his main motivation for coming to vend on the beach is to pay for the medicines he requires. Martin, as Clemente, has few skills that would help him acquire formal employment, and is very aware of this.

Case 1.4

Roberto (PV-12) is a 49-year-old widower from Tlaxmalac, Guerrero, who was interviewed in Puerto Vallarta. He has completed the fifth year of primary school and speaks Nahuatl, Spanish, and a little English. He has been a vendor for 28 years, since arriving in Puerto Vallarta. Roberto previously worked cultivating lands on his father's small property in Tlaxmalac. He has four cousins, offspring of his father's siblings, as well as a 51-year-old brother, who are also beach vendors in Puerto Vallarta. Roberto sells hammocks that he weaves. He is very content being a vendor but asks, "If I did not like it, what am I going to do without studies?" ("*Sí no me gustaría, que voy a hacer sin estudio?*"). Roberto would have liked to study to be a construction engineer and explains that since he was a child he has always wanted to be something in life ("*Desde niño siempre quise ser algo en la vida*"). If he were not a vendor he would like to work in construction, although he has only done this for a week.

Case 1.5

Rodrigo (PV-13) is a 49-year-old married vendor from Tlamacazapa, Guerrero, interviewed in Puerto Vallarta. He finished the second year of primary school and says he speaks Nahuatl, Spanish, and almost no English. His 35-year-old brother comes and goes from the village to Puerto Vallarta so sell wooden bead necklaces on the beach. Rodrigo also sells wooden bead necklaces that are sold by a resident of the colonia where he lives in Puerto Vallarta to a number of vendors. He also sells handwoven name bracelets and applies temporary tattoos. Rodrigo has been a vendor in the state of Mexico for five years; in Iguala, Guerrero, for seven years; in Mexico City for two years; on the beaches in Zihuatenejo, Guerrero, for five months; in Mazatlán, Sinaloa, for three months; and in Puerto Escondido, Oaxaca, for three months. He has been a vendor for a total of 25 years. He previously worked cultivating corn on his father's lands in Tlamacazapa and if he were not a vendor would like to be a campesino. He would also have liked to attend and finish preparatory school. The men who would have liked to be campesinos are part of the dispossessed peasantry.

Men Who Would Like to Learn English

Case 1.6

Isidro (ACA-24IC) is a 54-year-old married vendor interviewed on Icacos Beach in Acapulco. He is a Nahuatl speaker from the town of Tlamacazapa, Guerrero. He never went to school and learned Spanish when he was a young man. He has three daughters and one son. His eldest daughter, age 23, and his wife make the woven palm-leaf handbags and sombreros that he vends. His 21-year-old daughter also makes these handbags and accompanies her husband to Cancún to sell them. Isidro's father and grandfather, as well as Isidro, cultivated corn on a small property belonging to his grandfather. He comes and goes to Acapulco every month, returning to Tlamacazapa to help make the handbags and sombreros (and sometimes masks) that he sells. He has been a vendor since he was 15 years old, and has also vended for two months or less in Mazatlán, Puerto Vallarta, and Cancún. In all three of these places he was forced to leave because he did not have a local vendor's license and was harassed by authorities. If he were not a vendor, Isidro would like to be a tourist agent, which he conceives as enabling him to go to the United States and bring tourists to Acapulco. If he could study anything it would be English because he likes to talk to the tourists. He is only a little content with his work, however, because "One does not earn much" ("*No se gana mucho*"). This is a case in which the tourists are not willing to pay much for the artisanry that goes into making the handbags and sombreros, not realizing they are unique.

Case 1.7

Oscar (PV-16) is a 42-year-old married vendor from Tenanguillo, Guerrero, who was interviewed in Puerto Vallarta and says he speaks only Spanish. He completed two years of primary school but has an 18-year-old daughter who is studying law in the university. Oscar has been a vendor for 15 years, including one year in Acapulco. He thinks Puerto Vallarta is a better place to be a vendor than in Acapulco because there are more tourists in the former city. He sells silver-plated bracelets from Taxco that he acquires from wholesalers in Puerto Vallarta. His only brother, aged 52, and a wife's brother both sell clothing on the beach in Puerto Vallarta. Prior to coming to Puerto Vallarta Oscar worked putting down cement for the PEMEX gas stations. He is very content with being a vendor, saying it is easy work. He complains only about the restaurant owners who put up ropes so that the vendors cannot enter. He would like to work in construction if not a vendor. If he could study anything it would be English, and finish primary school. In Oscar's case being a vendor might be chosen over other work opportunities.

Case 1.8

Jorge (PV-24) is a 57-year-old married vendor from a rancho called San Pedrito in the state of Michoacán. He finished the third year of primary school and speaks Spanish and a little English. Two of his eight sons, ages 33 and 30, are beach vendors in Puerto Vallarta. So are a mother's sister's son and daughter. His 29-year-old son works as a field hand in North Carolina, and his 20-year-old son is a waiter in Houston, Texas. Two of his five brothers and one of his three sisters are also in the United States. His 60-year-old brother works in a restaurant in Los Angeles, and his 29-year-old brother works in a factory in the same city. His 55-year-old sister sells leather boots and belts from her home in Denver, Colorado. Jorge has also worked as a field hand in the United States and for one year in construction in Puerto Vallarta. He has been a vendor for 15 years and sells silver jewelry made in Morelos and acquired from wholesalers who live in Puerto Vallarta. If he were not a vendor he would like to be a security guard in a large department store or in a hotel. If he could study anything it would be English because, he explains, he needs it for his work as a vendor. Jorge, whether or not he was forced into becoming a vendor because of lack of alternative work, has embraced vending and wishes to acquire skills that will make his vending activities more gainful. His family network of vendors shows that the younger generation (his sons, niece, and nephew) have sought employment in this semi-informalized work, despite the presence of relatives in the United States.

Case 1.9

Kevin (CSL-10) is a 19-year-old single vendor from Tlamacazapa, Guerrero, who speaks Nahuatl, Spanish, and a little English. He was interviewed on Medano Beach in Cabo San Lucas. He says he never studied. He went to school for 15 days but didn't like it. His father is a vendor in Oaxaca, selling handbags that Kevin's mother makes, and also a campesino. Most of Kevin's three brothers and five sisters are vendors as well. Two brothers, both of whom help their father farm his 15 hectares of private property, come and go to Cabo San Lucas to sell woven name bracelets they make, as does Kevin, on the beach. One sister makes woven palm-leaf handbags that her husband sells in Mexico City. Another sister makes handbags that she sells in Querétaro. Besides his siblings, five of Kevin's cousins, including four mother's sister's sons and one mother's sister's daughter, are vendors in Cabo San Lucas. Kevin has been a vendor since he was eight years old and has sold woven palm-leaf handbags in Oaxaca for four years, in Querétaro for three years, and in Aguascalientes for one year. He has also sold the woven name bracelets he makes in Acapulco for a year, in Tamaulipas for four months, and in Cabo San Lucas for the two years since he arrived in that tourist center. He says Cabo San Lucas is the best place to be a vendor because there are many gringos ("*Hay mucho gringo*"). If he were not a vendor he would like to be a campesino, and had previously worked with his father on his father's lands. If he could study anything it would be to learn to write and English—the latter because he likes it ("*Porque me gusta mucho*"). Kevin is a vendor who would have preferred to remain a peasant.

Case 1.10

Calistro (CSL-24) is a 46-year-old married vendor from the town of Acamburo, Guanajuato, interviewed on Medano Beach in Cabo San Lucas. He never went to school but taught himself to read by perusing comic books about cowboys. He explains that his father held school was a waste of time and preferred that his sons help him on his nine hectares of ejido land. Calistro speaks Spanish and a little English. He has four sons and three daughters. Two of his sons are agricultural day laborers, one in Puebla and the other in Jalisco. His 17-year-old married daughter sells necklaces on the beach in Puerto Vallarta and his 26-year-old son sells canvas bags with a Cabo San Lucas logo on Medano Beach, as does Calistro. Most of his 12 siblings help cultivate their father's land, though one 38-year-old sister sells sundresses on the beach in Puerto Vallarta, and two brothers, ages 31 and 34, work in construction in that city. Calistro says he has been a vendor for 15 years. He sold semiprecious stone necklaces on the beach in Puerto Vallarta for six years and in Nueva Vallarta for two years. If he were not a vendor he would like to be a gardener but explains it is hard for him to find a job doing this because he doesn't have a car. He is, however, very content with being a vendor. He would like to study English in order to understand the tourists ("*Para poder entenderme bien con los turistas*").

What Women with Less than six years of Education (N=31) Would Study (Other than English)

Case 1.11.

Lourdes (ACA-1PD) is a 56-year-old married vendor born in the state of Veracruz to parents from Arcelia, Guerrero. Her father worked on lands lent to him by ejidatarios in a small town in Veracruz. Lourdes was interviewed on Playa Diamante in Acapulco where she sells dresses made of Indonesian cloth that she buys ready made and wholesale from a downtown store. She finished five years of primary school and speaks only Spanish. Her two daughters have been in the United States for eight years, where one works in a restaurant and the other is a housewife. Lourdes herself previously cared for children in the United States. Her two sons live in Acapulco where one is a taxi driver and the other a beach vendor at Puerto Marquez. Lourdes's husband is also a beach vendor, selling silver on Playa Diamante. If she were not a vendor she would like to volunteer to take care of children in a child-care center. She would have liked to study to be an interior decorator. She is very content with her work as a vendor, however, and adds that one need not be rich to be happy ("*No necesita ser rica para ser feliz*").

Case 1.12

Magdalena (ACA-1pCA) is a 48-year-old single mother from Arcelia, Guerrero, interviewed on Caleta Beach in Acapulco. She speaks only Spanish. Although she finished only the second year of primary school, one of her two sons, age 21, is studying to be an engineer. Her 27-year-old son finished secondary school and is a taxi driver. Magdalena has lived in Acapulco for 35 years, joining her maternal grandmother and a mother's sister. She has been a vendor for 20 years and has never worked at anything else. She is little content with being a vendor when sales are low, as they were this year. She says that she has nothing in life besides her two sons, not even a house. She says "I came poor and poor I am going to die" ("*Vine pobre y pobre voy a morir*"). She says she finds little sense in life. Magdalena sells fried bananas in milk and has previously sold fish quesadillas. She has no relatives who are vendors. If she were not a vendor she would like to have a clothing store, and adds that previously she would have liked to be a nurse. When asked what she would study if she could, Magdalena answers to the effect that she cannot see well, so nothing, but earlier on in life she would have liked to study to be a beautician. Magdalena's situation is that of a woman who would have preferred doing something other than being a vendor, but due to her low educational levels could find little else.

Case 1.13

Lupe (CSL-26P) is a 50-year-old married vendor interviewed on Medano Beach in Cabo San Lucas. She is from a small town in the state of Michoacán and speaks only Spanish. She has completed the third year of primary school. Two of her five sisters and her only brother are living in the United States. Her husband and a husband's brother are beach vendors in Cabo San Lucas. She has lived in that tourist city for 15 years and has been a vendor for 13. She has never done any other (paid) work, and if she were not a vendor she would like to be a hotel housekeeper. What she likes about being a vendor, however, is the ability to set her own hours. If she could have studied anything it would have been to be a public accountant.

Case 1.14

Cecilia (PV-21) is a 32-year-old vendor with two sons and two daughters, who lives in free union. Interviewed in Puerto Vallarta, where she arrived a little less than a year ago, she is from the town of San Juan Copala, Oaxaca. She speaks Triqui and Spanish. Cecilia has finished two years of primary school. Her 17-year-old son sells chewing gum and candy on the beach in Puerto Vallarta. She previously lived in the Federal District, where six of her seven siblings are currently living. One brother, age 25, and one sister, age 23, are ambulant vendors there selling the same headbands that Cecilia makes and sells on Playa de los Muertos (Beach of the Dead), also known as Bahía de las Banderas (Bay of the Flags). They also sell necklaces and bracelets that they make, and Cecilia also sells magnets in the form of animals. Upon arrival Cecilia discovered that she had a female cousin in Puerto Vallarta who has a stall from which she sells clothing, handbags, and jewelry. Cecilia has no vendor's permit and complains about the harassment from the authorities who take away her merchandise. She points out that the fine she has to pay to recover the headbands and magnets, 250 to 300 pesos, is more than they are worth. Other than facing the threat of having her wares confiscated, Cecilia is very content being a vendor. She has previously worked cleaning houses in the Federal District. If she were not a vendor she would like to clean houses once again, because the work is more secure than vending. This means both that there is no harassment by authorities and that earnings are more predictable. If she could study anything she would like to be an accountant.

Women Who Would Like to Learn English

Case 1.15

Carla (PV-11) is a 27-year-old married vendor with three children from the town of Analco, Guerrero, interviewed in Puerto Vallarta. She speaks Nahuatl, Spanish, and a little English. Although she never went to school, her 15-year-old daughter is completing the last year of secondary school, her 13-year-old son is in the first year of secondary school, and her 10-year-old son is in the fourth year of primary school. All three of her siblings, including one sister and two brothers, are vendors on the Playa de los Muertos in Puerto Vallarta. Carla has been a vendor for 10 years, since arriving in Puerto Vallarta, and sells semiprecious stone necklaces that she makes. Her husband is also a beach vendor. She has never worked at anything else, but if she were not a vendor would like to be a hotel housekeeper. If she could study anything it would be English. She is very content with being a vendor, because she can earn some money, but complains about working under the hot sun, and the current lack of tourists.

Case 1.16

Flor (PV-7) is a 24-year-old married and pregnant vendor, who is also from the town of Analco, Guerrero, and was interviewed in Puerto Vallarta. She never went to school but speaks Nahuatl and Spanish. She has five cousins, offspring of her father's sister, as well as her husband, who are beach vendors in Puerto Vallarta. Her husband sells baseball caps, and Flor sells semiprecious stone necklaces that she makes. She has three children: one, age three; a daughter, age six, who is in kindergarten; and a son, age eight, who is in the second year of primary school. Flor has lived in Puerto Vallarta for eight years and been a vendor for five. She has never worked at anything else and when asked what work she would do if she were not a vendor, Flor replies: "I don't know how to read so I can't work anywhere else" ("*No sé leer entonces no puedo trabajar en otro lugar*"). If she could study anything it would be English. She is little content with being a vendor because there are almost no sales due to the low number of tourists. Flor's involvement in beach vending can be seen as necessary for her to earn an income, with few other jobs available because of her lack of education.

Case 1.17

Elvira (CSL-7P) is a 22-year-old single vendor from Chilpancingo, Guerrero, who was interviewed on Medano Beach in Cabo San Lucas. She has finished the third year of primary school and speaks Nahuatl, English, and, she says, enough English to make a sale. A number of her relatives, including aunts and uncles, are also beach vendors. Elvira sells semiprecious stone necklaces she makes and also braids hair. She is very content being a vendor because she earns money. No one helps her with her expenses. She has lived in Cabo San Lucas for eight years, and has been a vendor for three. She previously worked as a cook in a hotel and also took care of children. If Elvira were not a beach vendor she would like to have a stall or store. If she could study anything it would be English.

Conclusion

It is noteworthy that the majority of vendors would have liked to achieve higher levels of education than they actually did. In many cases, as those of Oscar and Magdalena given here, their offspring have far surpassed them in the educational levels they have attained. In other cases children followed their parents into low-skilled and precarious employment.

A number of the beach vendors, including Santiago, Clemente, and Lourdes have previously worked in the United States but chose not to continue doing so. Still others, including Martín, Jorge, Lupe, and Lourdes have siblings and/or offspring in the United States. Although they could possibly have taken advantage of these family network ties to cross the border, they have chosen to remain in Mexico and engage in informal or semi-informal self-employment. All are over 50 years of age, and it is doubtful they will leave vending to work in the United States. Martin's case was complicated by the fact that although he has offspring in the United States, he is unable to communicate with them because he cannot read or write.

Most vendors could contemplate working at something else, though many were content with their work as vendors, as the following chapter will show. Had they been able to achieve their educational aspirations, many would not be in petty commerce. Their inability to have achieved a higher education is an index of their economic and social marginalization. To better their lives as vendors, many would like to attain fluency in English. Although in some tourist centers, such as Cabo San Lucas, free classes in English are offered, they have two drawbacks as far as the vendors are concerned. First, the hours that such classes are given usually coincide with the hours the vendors work. Vendors may be on the beach as late as 7 or 8 p.m. Second, the schools that offer these English classes are often far away—an hour or more by bus—from the colonias (named neighborhoods) where the beach vendors live. To overcome these obstacles it would be of value to have English lessons in the local colonia schools, and early in the morning, since most vendors do not start work until 10 a.m. or noon. Such local school offerings would be of value not only to the beach vendors but also for those who aspire to work in any aspect of the tourist economy. Currently, English teachers are contracted by some of the hotels in Cabo San Lucas to help their employees upgrade their English skills, but the beach vendors have no access to such training.

Both the educational aspirations and the contemplation of alternative work show that the vendors are capable of envisioning a less marginal existence. This lends support to the idea that vendors are population surplus to the needs of the formal economy and are involved in make-work. There were a number of men who had worked as campesinos, and some would prefer doing so to being a vendor. They are part of the dispossessed peasantry that have come into being since the Green Revolution of the 1940s, and have been acutely affected by processes of globalization. They are also part of the peasantry that is differentiating into capitalist farmers and the landless, partially due to demographic pressures and partially due to the modernization of agriculture since the 1940s. It can thus be concluded that they are often vendors because no alternatives were or are open to them. This is despite the fact that, as we will see in a subsequent chapter, many come from a family legacy of vending.

2

Levels of Contentment among the Beach Vendors

[T]he nature of informal employment has been examined through two lenses: the "exclusion" and "voluntary" views. In the exclusion view, workers would prefer the benefits of formal jobs but are rationed out of these due to segmentation of the labor market . . . In contrast, the voluntary view suggests that informal jobs largely reflect workers' implicit choices given their preferences, skills, the costs and benefits of formality, and the availability of other means of social protection . . .

—Arias 2007, 88

THE LEVEL OF CONTENTMENT with one's work is an important component in understanding the quality of life and reasons for choosing informal self-employment. Although many of the beach vendors may be seen as marginalized because of their low educational levels as seen in the previous chapter, and as will be explored in future chapters, by their segregated residence, by their ethnicity, and by gender, many are also happy with their work. This is true despite the fact that many of the vendor's lives might have been improved if they could have achieved their educational aspirations. Notably, levels of contentment with one's work have been found to vary according to whether one is in informal salaried work or in self-employment, with the self-employed often being more satisfied with their work (Arias 2007). In this chapter we will look at the vendors' levels of contentment with their jobs, what vendors find positive about vending, and what vendors find negative about vending. To put their answers into context it is important to consider that the average age of male vendors was 42 years old, and that of women vendors 32.3 years old. The lower average age of women was affected by the interviews of three 15-year-old marina vendors in Cabo San Lucas. The higher age of men was partially due to interviews with an 85-year-old man in Acapulco and a 79-year-old man in Puerto Vallarta. The age range for women was from 15 to 70, with eight being over 50. The age range for men was from 16 to 85, with 23 being over 50.

Vendors' Levels of Contentment

As can be seen in table 2.1, 70.5 percent of the vendors were very content with their work, including 67.9 percent of women and 73.2 percent of men. The percentages of men and women who were little content with being vendors were 25.6 percent and 22.6 percent respectively. Only three women were not at all content as vendors and may be forced to earn an income in any way possible in order to help support their households. One is Rita (ACA-12IC), a 30-year-old Mixteco-speaking woman from a small town in Guerrero interviewed in on Icacos Beach in Acapulco. She lives in free union with a man who is also a vendor. Rita has finished preparatory school. Her father is a vendor on the main road, La Costera, in Acapulco. She has been a vendor for 20 years. She says she is sick and would like to stay at home and care for her children. Another is Sofia (CSL-19M), a 15 year old who vends on the marina in Cabo San Lucas. She speaks Nahautl and is from San Juan Tetelcingo, Guerrero. Sofia has finished seven years of secondary school and would prefer to work in a restaurant and study to be a doctor. Seven of her family members are vendors. The third is Alicia (CSL-20M), an 18-year-old vendor who lives in free union and has one child. She was born in Acapulco and interviewed in Cabo San Lucas. Although she is one of the highest earners in Cabo San Lucas, taking in 1,080 pesos (about US $90) on a good day, she likes nothing

TABLE 2.1
Level of Contentment with Being a Beach Vendor

	Men (N=82)		*Women (N=84)*		*Total (N=166)*	
How content	*No.*	*%*	*No.*	*%*	*No.*	*%*
Very	60	73.2	57	67.9	117	70.5
More or less	1	1.2	5	5.9	6	3.6
Little	21	25.6	19	22.6	40	24.1
Not at all	0	0	3	3.6	3	1.8
Total	82	100.0	84	100.0	166	100.0

about vending and would like to study to be a teacher. She has eight years of schooling and five family members who are vendors.

If the sample is differentiated by educational level (see table 2.2) what is striking is that 81.6 percent of men with more than primary school are very content with being vendors, as opposed to 43.3 percent of women with more than primary school. This suggests that relatively well educated men find informal self-employment to their liking whereas women may find themselves self-employed for lack of other opportunities or because they are forced by necessity into often part-time income-generating activities. Of men with less than primary school, only 65.9 percent are very content with being vendors, a lower percentage than men with higher educational levels. This suggests that the other 34.1 percent would have strongly preferred alternate work, but found themselves barred from it because of lack of education. In contrast, 81.5 percent of women with less than primary school were very content being vendors, a greater number, because they were enabled to earn some sort of income and do so with flexible hours. Because of their educational levels, few other opportunities except for housecleaning are open to them.

To summarize the findings: Forty-four men (of 82 men, 53.7 percent) and 54 women (of 84 women, 64.3 percent) had primary schooling or less. Thirty-eight men (46.3 percent) and 30 (35.7 percent) women had more than primary schooling. Sixty men (73.2 percent) were very content being vendors and 57 women (67.9 percent of women) were very content.

Of those 44 men who had primary schooling or less, 29 (65.9 percent) were very content being vendors. Of the 54 women who had finished primary school or less, 44 (81.5 percent) were very content being vendors. Of

TABLE 2.2
Level of Contentment with Being a Beach Vendor by Schooling

	Men (N=38)		*Women (N=30)*		*Total (N=68)*	
More than primary	*No.*	*%*	*No.*	*%*	*No.*	*%*
Very	31	81.6	13	43.3	44	64.7
More or less	0	0	3	10.0	3	4.4
Little	7	18.4	11	36.7	18	26.5
Not at all	0	0	3	10.0	3	4.4
Total	38	100.0	30	100.0	68	100.0
Primary or less	*Men (N=44)*		*Women (N=54)*		*Total (N=98)*	
Very	29	65.9	44	81.5	73	74.5
More or less	1	2.3	2	3.7	3	3.1
Little	14	31.8	8	14.8	22	22.4
Not at all	0	0	0	0	0	0
Total	44	100.0	54	100.0	98	100.0

those 38 men who had more than primary schooling, 31 (81.6 percent) were very content being vendors. Of the 30 women who had finished more than primary school, only 13 (43.3 percent) were very content with being vendors. This suggests that whereas more-educated men actively choose to be vendors, more than half of the more-educated women are vendors because there are few other job opportunities open to them.

What is Positive about Being a Vendor?

The vendors were asked what they liked and what they disliked about being vendors. Many gave more than one answer (see table 2.3). One in five enjoyed their work with the tourists, including 21.7 percent of the total sample, with 32.9 percent of men and 10.7 percent of women. To earn money (often specified as to earn their own money) was the reply of 32.1 percent of the women (almost one-third), but only 14.6 percent of men. Characteristic of informal self-employment and the reason it is often sought (Perry et al. 2007) are the flexible hours and the lack of a boss—or absence of factory-like discipline. Some studies of the the informal self-employed, including the self-employed in three Brazilian cities, street hawkers in Hong Kong, Irish jarveys in Dublin, and brickmakers in Mexicali, Mexico, suggest that they are actively resisting proletarianization (Despres 1990; Smart 1990; Wilson 2003, 2005, chap. 10, 2006). Though the vendors did not express their contentment in terms of resisting proletarianization, that aspect is suggested by the value placed on setting their own hours (and days) and of not having to take orders from a boss. Notably, a higher percentage of women (27.4 percent) than men (17.1 percent) found flexible hours the most positive aspect of being a vendor while

TABLE 2.3
Answers as to What Vendors Liked about Their Work

	Men (N=82)		*Women (N=84)*		*Total (N=166)*	
	No.	*%*	*No.*	*%*	*No.*	*%*
Nothing	4	4.9	6	7.1	10	6.0
To earn money	12	14.6	27	32.1	39	23.5
Flexible hours	14	17.1	23	27.4	37	22.3
No boss	18	22.0	10	11.9	28	16.9
Meeting tourists	27	32.9	9	10.7	36	21.7
Earns over minimum wage	4	4.9	1	1.2	5	3.0
Easy work	3	3.7	0	0	3	1.8

a higher percentage of men (22.0 percent) than women (11.9 percent) found having no boss an attractive aspect of their work. In total 39.3 percent of women and 39.1 percent of men (or almost two of every five vendors) found either flexible hours or not having a boss one of the more attractive aspects of their work.

Because self-employed vendors are often considered to be marginalized from jobs in the formal economy, it is worth considering the profiles of those six men and two women who mentioned that they liked being vendors only because there was no other work. Among the men are Fortunato (CSL-16P) a 55-year-old man from a small town in Guerrero, interviewed in Cabo San Lucas, who has previously and intermittently worked in construction. He has also intermittently worked as a vendor for seven years and has six family members who are vendors, among them his two sons, his wife, and his wife's mother. He says there is no work in construction at present. Two other vendors mentioned this lack of work in construction. Several men mentioned age-related factors. Among them were Hugo (ACA-28IC), a 60-old man from a small town in Guerrero, interviewed in Acapulco, who says that vending is easy work and there is no other employment available at his age. He finished primary school and previously installed air conditioners, but has been a vendor for 25 years. Another is Lázaro (ACA-12IC), the 70-year-old man from a small town in Oaxaca, who has been a vendor for 35 years. Interviewed in Acapulco, he was previously a stevedore in that port city, a job that he was able to get because his brother was head of the the local stevedore's union. Although he has never been to school, his reasons for liking to be a vendor are because there is no other work available at his age and that it is easy to do.

Gilberto (PV-8), a 79-year-old widowed vendor from a small town in Guerrero interviewed in Puerto Vallarta, who finished primary school and has been a vendor for 55 years, simply says there is no other work. Yet Clemente (ACA-18CA) the 85-year-old widower born in a small town in Guerrero and interviewed in Acapulco, who has been a vendor for the 45 years since he migrated to that city, does not relate his age to lack of alternative work but says he is very content being a vendor because he can earn a little money. He never went to school. Nine of his family members, including a daughter and two grandchildren, are also beach vendors. He says that if he could work at anything else it would be in construction.

As concerns men who related the absence of work as due to their lack of schooling, there is Santiago (ACA-3PD), a 36-year-old vendor from a small town in Guerrero interviewed in Acapulco, who has been a vendor for 30 years and has vended in a number of other cities, including Puerto Vallarta, Zihuatenejo, and Manzanillo. He says there is no other work because he does not have enough schooling. He completed the third year of primary school. He has approximately 20 relatives who are vendors. The high number of family members who are vendors suggests that his family and social networks are truncated and cannot aid him in a job search outside of vending.

Constantino (ACA-25IC), a 55-year-old man from a small town in Guerrero who was interviewed in Acapulco, has been a vendor for 41 years, also in Cuernavaca, Puebla, and Oaxaca. He says there is no other work available for him because he never went to school. His wife is also a beach vendor, as are seven other relatives. Palano (ACA-27IC), a 35-year-old vendor from a small town in Guerrero, also interviewed in Acapulco, says he has no schooling and he can find no other work because of that. Eight of his family members are vendors, and he has been a vendor since the age of 10.

Among the women who say there is no other work is Norma (CSL-25P), a 20-year-old single woman born in Puerto Vallarta and interviewed in Cabo San Lucas, who previously worked in a restaurant. She says no other work in available now. She completed eight years of schooling. She has no family members who are vendors.

Celestina (ACA-14IC), a 38-year-old married woman from a small town in Guerrero who finished primary school, has never worked at anything else and says no other work is available. Interviewed in Acapulco, she has five family members who are vendors. She has been a vendor for 20 years and has no other work experience.

What is Negative about Being a Vendor?

Even among those who were very content with being vendors, most could point out negative aspects associated with their work (see table 2.4). Especially in Cabo San Lucas and Puerto Vallarta where a vendor's license is required, those without licenses complained of harassment by the authorities, including restaurant and security guards, police, and tax collectors. Even those with licenses, and in Acapulco where no licenses are required, complained about harassment from hotel security guards and about the restaurant owners who roped off their premises so vendors could not enter. In one restaurant on Medano Beach in Cabo San Lucas, I saw one restaurant security guard threatening beach vendors who attempted to enter by walking toward them and shaking his club.

Although about one-fifth of vendors found nothing negative about being a vendor, harassment by authorities, including police, tax collectors, and hotel security guards, or restaurant owners, was mentioned by 13.9 percent, including 16.7 percent of women and 11 percent of men, well over one in every 10.

TABLE 2.4
Answers as to What Vendors Disliked about Their Work

	Men (N=82)		*Women (N=84)*		*Total (N=166)*	
	No.	*%*	*No.*	*%*	*No.*	*%*
Nothing	20	24.4	12	14.3	32	19.3
Being in the sun[a]	18	22.0	30	40.5	52	31.3
Tiring	7	8.5	10	11.9	17	10.2
Harassment[b]	9	11.0	14	16.7	23	13.9
Low sales	24	29.3	12	14.3	36	21.7
Few tourists[c]	4	4.9	8	9.5	12	7.2
Tourist behavior[d]	7	8.5	3	3.6	10	6.0

[a] Several vendors expressed the wish that there could be palapas where they could go to rest in the shade.

[b] Harrassment was by restaurant owners, managers, and waiters who wanted the vendors to move on. There was also harassment by police, tax collectors, and hotel security guards.

[c] The lack of tourists was often mentioned along with complaints about low sales.

[d] A few vendors pointed out that some tourists argue with, insult, or humiliate the vendors.

That tourists may insult or humiliate the vendors was mentioned by 6 percent of the total sample, including 8.5 percent of men and 3.6 percent of women. Women tend to be less aggressive in their sales techniques and thus less subject to verbal abuse, although I have seen tourists on the beach in Cabo San Lucas who treat vendors as intrusive and bothersome before they are even spoken to. A high 26.5 percent of the sample mentioned low sales, partially as a result of the current economic recession, and 7.2 percent mentioned that there were few tourists. Several vendors related the low sales to the lack of tourists.

Being in the sun and long treks back and forth on the beach are intrinsic to beach vending. Almost a third of the vendors (31.3 percent) mentioned being in the sun as a negative aspect of beach vending, including 40.5 percent of women and 22 percent of men. Several vendors expressed the wish for there to be palapas where they could rest and eat their lunches in the shade. One beach vendor in Cabo San Lucas also pointed out the lack of public bathrooms, which do exist in Acapulco. One in 10 (10.2 percent) said the work was tiring, including 11.9 percent of women and 8.5 percent of men. Hauling ceramic plates, ironwood statues, or two dozen T-shirts up and down the beach is more tiring than selling jewelry. In San José del Cabo, one vendor has solved the problem by placing his ironwood statues on a bed of sand just outside of a popular restaurant, thus erasing the ambulatory aspect of his work. Not all restaurant owners would permit such a presence. On Medano Beach in Cabo San Lucas the vendors must keep moving or will be harassed by hotel security guards or restaurant managers. They may be able to stand in front of the roped off section of the beach where chaise lounges are set up by hotel staff, but never for more than about 20 minutes. Some vendors sit in the sand and rest for a few minutes outside of these enclosures, hoping that those tourists inside the boundaries will notice their wares.

There are six women and four men among those who like nothing about vending (see table 2.3). Among the men are Emilio (ACA-5 PD), a 35-year-old vendor from a small town in Guerrero interviewed in Acapulco, who, despite having been a vendor for 20 years, says he is little content with vending but does it out of necessity ("*Por necesidad*"). His wife and two other relatives are vendors. He has completed primary school and occasionally works in construction. Among the women are Graciela (CSL-18P), a 27-year-old married vendor from a small town in Guerrero, who likes nothing about vending and also says she does it out of necessity. She has been a vendor for 11 years, one of these in the Federal District, and 10 in Cabo San Lucas where she will be interviewed. Although her husband is not a beach vendor, she has six relatives who are. She completed secondary school and would like to be a receptionist in a hotel. Another woman who likes nothing about vending is Alma (PV-9). Alma is a 32-year-old woman from a small town in Guerrero who was interviewed in Puerto Vallarta. She would like to stay at home and care for her three children. She has been a vendor for 12 years and has five family members, including her husband, who are vendors. If she could study anything it would be to learn to read, as she has never been to school. In the next section case studies of vendors who are very content with their work will be explored.

Case Studies of Those Very Content to be Vendors

It is very important to examine some of the cases of vendors who are very content with their self-employment in order to throw light on the characteristics of those who embrace such work. As mentioned previously, 44 of the 54 women (81.5 percent) who had finished primary school or less were very content being vendors. For men who had more than primary school, 81.6 percent were very content being vendors. Below are six cases of men and six cases of women who very much like their work as beach vendors.

Men Who Were Very Content Being Beach Vendors

Case 2.1

Mauricio (ACA-1PD) is a 27-year-old married vendor born in Acapulco, where he was interviewed on Playa Diamante. His parents were born in a small town in Guerrero, and after migrating to Acapulco his father, now deceased, worked as a waiter in a hotel. Mauricio helped him wash dishes there. He has three aunts and six of their offspring who work as vendors on Playa Diamante, selling semi-precious stone necklaces, as does he. He buys the stones in the Federal District, and he and his wife string them into necklaces. This is the most common pattern for those who vend necklaces. He finished seven years of schooling and says he speaks Spanish, a little Nahuatl, and very little English. What he likes about being a vendor is that no one orders him around. He can come when he likes and leave when he likes ("*No hay nadie que me está mandando. Aquí vengo cuando quiero y salgo cuando quiero*"). He finds nothing negative about being a vendor, saying "I like everything" ("*Todo me gusta*"). Mauricio has previously painted houses and worked in various aspects of construction. He has even washed cars he tells me. He has been a vendor for eight years. If he were not a vendor he would like to either work in construction or as a waiter in a hotel. Mauricio says that when there is not much work on the beach he will work building houses or putting down floors. If he could study anything it would be English. He explains, "I require it for my work. Many Americans and Canadians arrive" ("*En mi trabajo lo requiero. Vienen muchos americanos y canadienses*").

Case 2.2

Nestór (ACA-6IC) is a sixty-eight-year-old widower from a small town in the mountains of Guerrero where his father had 20 hectares of ejido land. He speaks Tlapaneco, Spanish, and a little English, French, and Italian. He finished 10 years of schooling. Nestór's only son and one of his six daughters are lawyers (*abogados*), two of his daughters are accountants, one is a nurse, and one is a psychologist. Only six of his 13 siblings are still alive. Two of his sisters work beside their husbands on their husbands' lands and one cleans houses in the Federal District. His two surviving brothers are ejidatarios. Nestór has lived in Acapulco since he was 13, having joined an elder brother who was a bartender in that city. He has been a vendor for more than 40 years. He owns a small piece of private property in his town of origin and occasionally cultivates it; previously he helped his father on his father's ejido lands. Nestór has no relatives who are vendors. Since becoming a vendor he has always sold silver jewelry from Taxco. What he likes about being a vendor is getting to know people, many people from all social classes ("*Conozco gente, mucha gente de todas las clases sociales*"). He says he likes everything about being a vendor but adds that he does not like it when he has no sales. When asked what he would like to do if not a vendor, Nestór replies that he wouldn't want to do anything else ("*No quisiera ser otra cosa*"). If he could have studied anything it would be to be a lawyer or political scientist. With his ejidatario father, Nestór has one of the most well-off origins of all the beach vendors. Yet it is the case that not all sons can inherit their father's lands, especially if the land is to be subsistence level or higher, a key factor in the differentiation of the peasantry.

Case 2.3

Leandro (CSL-12) is a 29-year-old married vendor with three children from the small town of Monte Alegre, municipality of Chilpancingo, Guerrero. He finished primary school and speaks Nahuatl, Spanish, and a little English. His father has 10 hectares of ejido land, and when Leandro was a child he helped his father on these lands. He came to Cabo San Lucas 15 years ago, joining a paternal uncle and a maternal aunt. He first worked in construction, then became a beach vendor eight years ago. He sells brightly colored tablecloths and has done so for four years; previously he sold ironwood statues. Leandro likes being a vendor because he has no set hours ("*No hay horario para venir*") and because he has no boss. What he doesn't like about being a vendor is the lack of a place to rest in the shade, such as a palapa, and because there are no public bathrooms. If he were not a vendor he would like to be a cook's helper in a hotel, because he likes cooking, but he points out that it pays very little. If he could study anything it would be English—so he could speak it better—to help him with his work.

Case 2.4

Eusibio (CSL-13P) is a 41-year-old married vendor from a very small town in the municipality of Arcelia, Guerrero. He explains that it is in the mountains and there are no roads or buses that reach it. He finished the second year of secondary school and then broke both of his legs in a car accident so had to drop out. When Eusibio's father, born in the state of Morelos, was young, he worked as an agricultural day laborer. His father later had a small souvenir store in Cabo San Lucas, but it went bankrupt. Eusibio's mother, born in the state of Michoacán, was a beach vendor in Acapulco for some years. Eusibio has lived in Cabo San Lucas for 18 years and been a vendor for 30, previously in Acapulco, Nueva Vallarta, Puerto Vallarta, Rosarito, and Ensenada. What he likes about being a vendor is that he can earn more money than he would working in a hotel or restaurant. He also mentions that he is his own boss, and works the hours he wishes, the days he wishes, and if he wants to take a day off he can. ("*Yo soy mi propio patrón. Vengo las horas que quiero, los días que quiero, y si quiero descansar un día puedo*"). He realizes the liberty his self-employment entails even though he has never been a waged worker. What he finds difficult about being a vendor is that the hotel staff regard the vendors as a problem. He points out that he arrived in Cabo San Lucas when many of the beach hotels had still not been built, with the implication that they are usurping his territory, not he theirs.[1] If he were not a vendor he would like to be a taxi driver. Eusibio tells me that his brother, who lives in Acapulco, owns two taxis that he bought with money he earned in the United States. If Eusibio could study anything, it would be how to use computers. He says he has a computer at home.

Case 2.5

Nathaniel (PV-21) is a 52-year-old widowed vendor living currently in free union. He was born in the Federal District, as was his mother. His father was from a small town in the state of Hidalgo. Nathaniel finished university studies in accounting, and is the most highly educated of all of the vendors interviewed. He worked as an accountant for a construction materials company in the Federal District for 10 years. He left that job because of the long hours and low pay. He also worked in a textile factor in the Federal District for five years, though not as an accountant. He came to Puerto Vallarta 22 years ago and has been a beach vendor since arriving. A nephew, son of his deceased wife's brother, and a brother-in-law, the husband of his deceased wife's sister, are also beach vendors, selling silver jewelry. Nathaniel sells fans, key chains, and a variety of bracelets, some made from copper and silver, others of semiprecious stones. He acquires these items from wholesalers, some of whom come to the beach to sell to the vendors. His adult son, age 32, and his 29-year-old daughter never reached Nathaniel's educational levels. His son is a waiter in a hotel in Nueva Vallarta, and his daughter sells pies and cakes on the streets in Puerto Vallarta. His 14-year-old son is presently in the second year of secondary school. Nahaniel is very content to be a vendor. He explains, "I am independent. I am not subject to the orders of another person. I work for myself. I do not have fixed hours with someone to tell me you enter at such and such an hour, leave at such and such an hour" ("*Me hago independiente. No estoy al orden de otra persona. Trabajo por mi mismo. No tengo horario que alguien me dice tu entras a tal hora, sales a tal hora*"). When I ask Nathaniel what he does not like about being a vendor, he replies, "The truth is that I have liked everything. If I hadn't liked it I would not do it" ("*La verdad es que todo me ha gustado. Si no me ha gustado no me lo haría*"). If he were not a vendor he would continue working as an accountant, preferably in a government office, but points out that most openings are for people under age 30. If he could study anything it would be to learn English well ("*Aprender bien el íngles*").

Case 2.6

Ariel (PV-25) is a 55-year-old vendor from Monterrey, Nuevo León. He is divorced from his wife. She lives near Grand Rapids, Michigan, with their four adult children, ages 21 to 28. Ariel now lives with a woman in free union. He finished secondary school and speaks Spanish and, he says, English very well. (All the interviews were conducted in Spanish, so I am unaware of the level of English fluency the vendors might have). Ariel came to Puerto Vallarta five years ago. He had previously been a vendor in Nuevo Vallarta. Prior to that he worked as a plumber in Colorado and as a field hand in various parts of the United States, including Colorado, Texas, and Michigan. He has no relatives who are vendors. He sells a unique item: tiles on which he paints pictures of flowers or scenes from Puerto Vallarta. He says he is extraordinarily content with being a vendor. He enjoys the people he meets and learns much from them, about where they are from ("*Aprendes mucho de ellos, de donde son*"). He finds nothing he dislikes about his work. He enjoys painting the pictures and notes that sometimes a client will ask for a larger painting or a smaller one than the tile size on which he usually paints. Ariel cannot imagine not being a vendor, if not on the beach, then with a stall on the street, perhaps selling fruit. But, he adds, he likes painting and selling the tiles. If he could study anything it would be art, to be a better painter. A large part of his great contentment with being a vendor is elaborating the merchandise he sells. Some of the stringers of necklaces, sewers of Indonesian cloth into sundresses, weavers of name bracelets and headbands, and painters of ceramic plates also mentioned this elaboration of their merchandise as a positive aspect of their work as vendors.

Women Who Were Very Content Being Beach Vendors

Overall, it was women with fewer years of education—though there were exceptions—who were very content with being vendors. Several mentioned the lack of a boss and the ability to set their own hours as positive aspects of their self-employment. Others, like some men with little education, said they did not know how to do any other work. Below are summaries of the characteristics of some of the women beach vendors who claimed to be very content with their work.

Case 2.7

Victoria (ACA-4PD) is a 37-year-old vendor living in free union who was born in Acapulco and interviewed there on Playa Diamante. She has finished the third year of primary school. Of her seven children, her eldest is an 18-year-old daughter who finished preparatory school. Karen (ACA-5PD) is currently a beach vendor but would like to continue studying to be a nurse. Victoria's 14-year-old son no longer goes to school because the family did not have enough money for him to continue his studies. He works with Victoria's husband cultivating borrowed lands just outside the city limits. Her mother and all four of her sisters are vendors in Acapulco on the Mayan Beach (also known as Diamond Beach, Playa Diamante). She also has cousins, father's sister's sons, who are beach vendors. The entire family sells shells that they buy from a diver who retrieves them. Victoria is very content with her work as a vendor because from the money she earns, she explains, she and her children can eat. She has been a vendor since she was six years old. What she does not like about vending is harassment by the police. She explains that if she wants to sit down awhile (in front of one of the hotels), they come and make her move on. (Although she calls them police, they are probably hotel security guards.) When asked what she would like to study, Victoria says that she wants her offspring to study, but there is no money to help them with higher education. If she were not a beach vendor, she would like to have a grocery or clothing store in her home.

Case 2.8

Monica (ACA-23IC) is a 37-year-old single mother born and interviewed in Acapulco where she sells coconut tanning oil on Icacos Beach. She finished primary school. Her 19-year-old son, the eldest of three children, finished secondary school and also sells coconut tanning oil, as do several of Monica's siblings, on Icacos Beach. All three of her sisters and all six of her brothers are beach vendors, as is her mother, a mother's sister, and 10 female cousins, offspring of mother's sisters. Her deceased father, born in Acapulco (as was her mother), was a beach vendor and sold leather sandals he made. Most of the family sells coconut tanning oil. They travel to the coconut orchards just outside of Acapulco where they buy the coconuts for 5 pesos each. Then they extract the oil and sell a small bottle of it for 15 pesos. When Monica has money she often buys clothing to sell on the beach as well. She is very content with being a vendor. She likes the ambience, to meet people, and to walk on the beach, though she complains about the hot sun. If she could study anything she would like to finish secondary school and study to be a nurse.

Case 2.9

Araceli (CSL-16P) is an 18-year-old single vendor born in Acapulco and interviewed in Cabo San Lucas. She came to Cabo San Lucas three years ago, to join an older sister and two older brothers who are also beach vendors. She finished primary school and speaks Nahuatl, Spanish, and enough English to make sales, she says. Araceli began vending when she was 10 years old and had been a vendor in Acapulco, Querétaro, and Cancún prior to coming to Cabo San Lucas. She thinks Cancún is the best place to be a vendor because there are more tourists and less competition. She thinks Acapulco is the worst city to vend in because there is so much competition and few foreign tourists. Araceli sells necklaces that wholesalers from Guerrero come to sell to the vendors. She is very content with being a vendor because she likes talking to the tourists and learning more English. What she does not like about being a vendor is that it is tiring work, and sometimes she makes no sales. (The vast majority of vendors said that on bad days they earned nothing). If she were not a vendor she would like to be a waitress or a hotel receptionist. If she could study anything it would be English and computers.

Case 2.10

Claudia (CSL-33P) is a 52-year-old married woman from a small town in Guerrero interviewed in Cabo San Lucas. She speaks no indigenous language. She speaks Spanish and a little English, enough to make a sale as well as colors, she explains. Although her husband Fortunato (9P-CSL), whose data were summarized in the previous chapter, never attended school, their 20-year-old daughter holds a bachelor's degree in law. In total they have three sons and four daughters. Two of their sons sell silver on Medano Beach in Cabo San Lucas but one sometimes work in construction. Claudia's mother is also a beach vendor and worked on the beach in Acapulco prior to coming to work on the beach in Cabo San Lucas. Claudia's only sibling, a 42-year-old brother, works in construction in Cabo. Claudia has lived in Cabo San Lucas for 25 years and been a vendor for 35, previously for 10 years in Acapulco. She points out that competition among vendors is very high in Acapulco. She sells women's and children's sundresses that she makes from Indonesian cloth bought wholesale from a downtown store. Claudia is very content being a vendor and would not do anything else. She says that she does not like taking orders ("*No me gusta que me manden*") and thus could not do any other work. Claudia explains that that is why, though she has thought of it in terms of alternate work, she does not clean houses: "Here I am my own boss" ("*Aquí soy mi propia patrón*"). If she could study anything it would be sewing, to better design the dresses she sells.

Case 2.11

Valery (PV-1) is a 31-year-old married vendor born in a small town in the state of Mexico and interviewed in Puerto Vallarta. She finished the second year of primary school, and speaks Nahuatl, Spanish, and a little English. All seven of her siblings, including three brothers and four sisters, are vendors at a *tianguis* (open air market) in Zapopan, Guadalajara, Jalisco. Her husband and a husband's brother are both beach vendors in Puerto Vallarta. Both she and her husband sell woven necklaces and bracelets that they buy from a woman beach vendor who makes them. Valery also braids hair, and this is what she likes most about her work on the beach. She has lived in Puerto Vallarta for 13 years and been a vendor for five. She says she is very content being a vendor because no one tells her what to do ("*Nadie me apura a trabajar. Yo trabajo como quiero*") But when asked what she does not like about being a vendor, Valery replies that being a vendor is the only thing she has done since beginning to work and she doesn't know anything else ("*Es lo unico que he hecho desde que empezé a trabajar. No sé otra cosa*"). She would like to finish primary and secondary school. If she could not be a vendor she would clean houses.

Case 2.12

Tomasa (PV-3) is a 38-year-old married vendor from the city of Ixtapa-Zihuatenejo, Guerrero. She speaks no indigenous language. Tomasa has completed a technical career in hotel science and gastronomy. She has three children and is living in free union with a man who works with her at a semi-fixed stall on the beach owned by his mother. They sell ceviche, shrimp and fish on a stick, and sodas. One of Tomasa's 4 siblings, a 43-year-old brother, lives in Oregon where he does maintenance work in McDonald's restaurants. Tomasa has lived in Puerto Vallarta for nine years and says she has been a vendor all her life. She is very content to be a vendor and likes being on the beach. When asked what she likes about the work, Tomasa answers, "Everything. If I didn't like it I wouldn't be here" ("*Todo. Si no me gustara no estuviera aquí*"). This kind of reply is available primarily to those with advanced education, as was seen in the case of Nathaniel (PV-21), the accountant. What Tomasa does not like about being a vendor is the envy and bad vibes ("*la invidia y mala vibra*") directed at her by some of the other vendors. If she were to study anything it would be to continue her schooling in hotel science and gastronomy. She has previously worked as a hotel receptionist, as a secretary in an accounting office, and as a cashier in a pharmacy. When asked what she would do if not a vendor, Tomasa answers that when there is no work on the beach, she looks for something else such as working as a cashier or cook. This lack of work on the beach, or lack of being able to sell anything, usually occurs during the low tourist seasons.

Conclusions

A study of the informal economy in various countries in Latin America showed that "Evidence from workers' reported motivations to be in their current occupation . . . and self-rated welfare assessments lends support to the view that the majority of independent workers are largely voluntary and attach significant value to the nonpecuniary benefits of autonomous work" (Arias 2007, 98). Those who were less content about vending usually pointed out lack of sales in the current climate of economic recession, excessive competition, or harassment by authorities when carrying out their work.

Whether the positive evaluation of autonomy is true of commission sellers is a debatable point. They have been characterized as "disguised wage workers" (Bromley 1978, 1165), who simply earn no fixed salary but must self-exploit for the money they earn. Of the 12 beach vendors who were commission sellers, three worked for and with relatives. These three can be conceived of as part of a family labor force paid on a commission basis. For the other nine, commission selling may be a way of entering into petty commerce when there is a lack of capital to acquire one's own merchandise. At least one beach vendor, who sells sunglasses made in China on Playa Medano in Cabo San Lucas, wished to save enough money to become an independent seller. He plans to vend the same merchandise but on his own account. He is motivated by the wish for greater autonomy. Notably, he had no vendor family members who could help him with raising capital or lend him merchandise to sell, although his wife vends sodas and snacks on the beach to help out the family economy.

Many beach vendors, as shown above, are quite content with their work. Even commission sellers pointed out that positive aspects of their work included flexible hours (i.e., they could work the hours and days they wished). Many of the independent vendors also stressed that an attractive factor of their work was that they had no boss, no one to tell them what to do. Even those who had never worked for a wage found these to be positive aspects of their work. In many cases this positive evaluation of autonomy may have been part of family lore. As we will see in the next chapter, many beach vendors have relatives who are also vendors and may be considered as keeping up a family tradition.

Typical Beach Vendor Wares

FIGURE 2.1
Ceramics seller Cabo San Lucas, Medano Beach, 2010

FIGURE 2.2
Handwoven palm-leaf handbags, Puerto Vallarta, 2010

FIGURE 2.3
Handwoven name bracelets, Acapulco, Caleta Beach, 2010

FIGURE 2.4
Silver from Taxco, Puerto Vallarta, Bahía de las Banderas, 2010

FIGURE 2.5
Imported Indonesian and domestic cloth dresses, Cabo San Lucas

Note

1. For the 19 vendors in Cabo San Lucas who have lived in that tourist center for 15 years or more, the newness of the hotels is apparent. For example, two hotels on the beach opened their doors to the public in 1989, one in 1991, and one in 1997 (*Dirección Municipal de Transparencia* 2011*b*).

3

The Family Legacy of the Beach Vendors

> In Latin America: *Evidence from workers' patterns of mobility, reported motivations, and self-rated welfare and job satisfaction indicate that (1) the majority of independent workers (approximately two-thirds, entered their jobs voluntarily, attach significant value to the nonpecuniary benefits of autonomous work, and choose to "exit" formal social protection systems; (2) on the contrary, the majority of informal salaried workers appear to be excluded from more desirable jobs, both as formal salaried and as independent workers, although voluntary motives are still significant for many of the people in this subsector . . .*
>
> Perry and Maloney 2007, 5

An article in a 2007 World Bank publication found that almost 9 percent of men and 3.6 percent of women who entered informal self-employment did so because it was a family tradition. Of males ages 19 to 34, 17.4 percent entered informal self-employment because it was a family tradition and 9.8 percent of women ages 15 to 18 did so for the same reason (Maloney and Arias 2007, table 2.7, 67). The well-known heterogeneity of the informal economy suggests that different types of informal (or semi-informal) self-employment may draw on family legacies in variable ways. The research conducted with the 166 beach vendors in Cabo San Lucas, Acapulco, and Puerto Vallarta showed that: 1) the overwhelming majority (86.2 percent) had family members who were vendors and more than 40 percent had five or more family members who were vendors; 2) of the 81 vendors who were asked specifically about father's occupation, more than 45 percent indicated that their fathers had been vendors; 3) more than 30 percent of the male and female vendors had spouses who were also vendors; 4) indigenous language speakers tended to have more family members who were vendors than those who spoke no indigenous language; and 5) high earnings on a good day were associated with having family members who were vendors.

Although the heterogeneity of the informal economy has long been recognized, recent and past studies underscore that it is divided into at least two subsectors. These include informal waged workers and the self-employed. Whereas the former are subjected to exploitative labor conditions and lack of benefits legislated for formal workers, the latter enjoy some degree of freedom and autonomy (e.g., ILO 2002*a*; Maloney and Arias 2007; Perry and Maloney 2007; Wilson 2005). Nonetheless, while some of the self-employed, including street vendors, may have earnings quite a bit higher than those of unskilled laborers, others are merely eking out a survival income (Bromley 2002). Portrayal of the subsector of the informally self-employed becomes more complicated when one considers the fact that many of them may be "semi-informal," that is, complying with some legislation while avoiding other. Thus, some street vendors—including the subset of beach vendors—may have procured a vendor's license but not pay taxes.

A recent World Bank publication included an article by Maloney and Arias (2007) that considered the reasons why people entered informal self-employment. It included the idea that some people were excluded, in the sense of being unable to find formal employment, while others voluntarily exited from the formal sector. In Mexico, using the 1994 *Encuesta Nacional de Micronegocios* (National Survey of Micro-Enterprises) they found that the top four reasons given by men for entering informal self-employment were: 1) obtaining a higher income that salaried workers (43.7 percent); 2) complementing family income from other sources (18 percent); 3) being unable to find a salaried job (12.4 percent); and 4) because it was a family tradition (8.9 percent) (Maloney and Arias 2007, table 2.7, 67). For women the top four reasons were 1) complementing family income (65.1 percent); 2) obtaining a higher income than in salaried work (12.2 percent); 3) lack of availability of a salaried job (6.1 percent); and 4) flexible hours (4.2 percent) (Maloney and Arias 2007, table 2.7, 67).

As has been seen in the previous chapter, a far higher percentage of men (17.1 percent) and women (27.4 percent) beach vendors mentioned flexible hours as a positive aspect of their work. Beach (and possibly street) vending may thus have a different dynamic than other forms of self-employment.

Although entering self-employment because of it being a family tradition included less than 10 percent of the informally self-employed in the Mexican sample looked at by Maloney and Arias (2007), I would argue that such a motivation is unevenly distributed across types of self-employment, and may even have an ethnic component. The informally self-employed may or may not employ waged workers, may or may not be subcontracted by a formal sector firm, and may or may not be satisfied with their work. The self-employed range from heads of small firms producing inputs for, or manufacturing on demand from, formal firms, to working as heads of small independent enterprises engaged in projects such as shoemaking, ceramic production, or vehicle repair, to street and beach vendors, whether working on a commission or independently.

Family Social Capital

From interviews with the 166 beach vendors, 81 of whom were asked their mother's and father's occupations, and all of whom were asked whether they had other relatives who were vendors, it can be concluded that family tradition played an important part in their selection of work. The high number of indigenous language speakers with five or more family members who are vendors, especially the Nahua from the state of Guerrero, suggests that there was also an ethnic tradition that underlay the family legacy of vending. The tradition of vending in the Alto Balsas region of Guerrero, for example, has deep roots. Peasants from that areas went to Acapulco to trade agricultural items for salt and returned to sell or trade it in the region's towns and villages until their trade was made superfluous with the building of a highway connecting Acapulco and Mexico city in 1927 (Schryer 2010*a*, 56; footnote 13, 76). An upsurge of craft vending occurred with the increase in tourism during World War II and thereafter (Good Eshelman 1988, 28–29).

Looking primarily at family social capital, it can be seen as important for a number of reasons for the informally, or semi-informally, self-employed beach or street vendor. It can, as Aliaga Linares (2002, chap. 3) showed in a study of street vendors in Lima, Peru, structure where vending takes place, where initial start-up resources are found (though in her sample most come from individual savings, and loans from family members only come in second), and what merchandise is sold. Having family members who are also vendors can also lead to the transfer of skills in selling strategies, in where the merchandise is acquired, in how one adds value to the initial merchandise (e.g., how to string beads into necklaces, cut and sew Indonesian or other cloth into skirts and sundresses, paint ceramic pieces, weave name bracelets), and to possible links with municipal authorities or to unions that can facilitate the process of acquiring a vendor's license. Although friends can also help in acquiring these skills and resources and this knowledge, family members represent the strongest ties in facilitating the processes necessary for relatively successful independent self-employment (Sanders and Nee 1996)—whether formal or informal.

It was not until 30 women vendors in Cabo San Lucas and 51 vendors in Puerto Vallarta had been interviewed and partially analyzed that the questions about father's and mother's occupation were added. They were added because when asked about relatives who were vendors, some answered that their fathers or mothers were. It was also becoming clear that a great number of vendors, most of whom were of rural origin, were sons and daughters of peasants, including *ejidatarios* (beneficiaries of communal property laws, or holders of ejido lands), small property owners, sharecroppers, those cultivating borrowed or unused lands, and agricultural day laborers. Father's occupations were subsequently identified for 80 vendors, including 26 men in Cabo San Lucas, 30 men in Acapulco, and 24 women in Acapulco. As table 3.1 shows, 42 percent of the sample had fathers who were peasants, including 46.4 percent of men and 32 percent of women. Furthermore, 37 percent of fathers were vendors, including fathers of 28.6 percent of men, and 56 percent of women. Fathers of vendors who were both peasants and vendors included 8.6 percent of the 80 vendors, all of them men. In total, then, 45.6 percent of the subsample had fathers who were full-time or seasonal vendors.

Seasonal Vendors

Seasonal vendors were common in Acapulco: although only three seasonal vendors were interviewed in that tourist center, several others mentioned that the number of vendors fluctuated throughout the year, because some went home to farm their lands during sowing and harvesting seasons. These seasonal vendors spend part time in their communities of origin and then come

TABLE 3.1
Father's Occupation

	Men (N=56)		*Women (N=25)*		*Total (N=81)*	
	No.	*%*	*No.*	*%*	*No.*	*%*
Peasant	26	46.4	8	32.0	34	42.0
Peasant & Vendor	7	12.5	0	0	7	8.6
Vendor	16	28.6	14	56.0	30	37.0
Other	7	12.5	2	8.0	9	11.1
No answer	0	0	1	1.4	1	1.2
Total	56	100.0	24	100.0	81	99.9

to Acapulco to vend their wares, especially during the high tourist seasons of Easter week and Christmas through New Year. Some of them are artisans who manufacture the goods they sell, or whose wives or other family members do so. The seven fathers who were both peasants and vendors were probably among these seasonal vendors. The fathers of the remaining 11 percent had jobs such as hotel waiter, miner, policeman, taxi driver, housepainter, and mason.

Two cases of seasonal vendors are illustrative.

Case 3.1

Palano (ACA-27IC), a 35-year-old married vendor who speaks Nahuatl and Spanish but never attended school, is from Tlamacazapa, Guerrero. He sells multicolored woven palm-leaf handbags that he and his wife make. His wife also sells them, as he does, on the Icacos Beach in Acapulco. His 15-year-old son sells woven name bracelets and his nine-year-old daughter (of three children) sells woven palm-leaf handbags during their vacations from primary school. One of his two sisters also weaves palm-leaf handbags. Three of his four brothers make woven name bracelets, which two sell on the beach in Cabo San Lucas, and one in Cuernavaca. His father, who cultivated corn on vacant lands in the mountains that have no owner ("*dónde no hay dueño*"), also sells woven palm-leaf handbags that Palano's mother helps to make. Cousins of his wife sell woven name bracelets on a variety of beaches in Acapulco. Palano comes and goes to his hometown of Tlamacazapa where he sometimes works as a mason.

Palano began working as a vendor when he was 12 years old. He first sold woven palm-leaf clothes hampers in Tepozitlán, near Cuernavaca, for five years, then woven palm-leaf handbags in the Zocalo of Mexico City for two years. He then moved on to Rosarito where he worked seasonally on the beach selling parachute dolls such as Spider Man and Superman, coming and going for four years, and then going one year to Ensenada to sell ironwood statuettes and serapes. He also sold handwoven sombreros as an ambulant vendor in downtown Mexicali for two years and in the beach town of San Felipe, two hours east of Mexicali, for two years. The merchandise Palano sells has changed over the years, though the woven palm-leaf clothing hampers, the handbags, and the sombreros are all artisan works typical of the town where he is from. Palano has an extensive family network of artisans and/or vendors, including his father, his mother, five of his six siblings, two of his offspring, his wife, and wife's cousins. His experience as a vendor in numerous cities in Mexico, as either an ambulant street or beach vendor, is also extensive, though there were some other vendors who had sold in multiple cities. He earns about 300 pesos on a good day, which he feels is about the same as he has earned elsewhere.

Case 3.2

David (ACA-29IC), a 16-year-old single vendor from Zumpango del Río, Guerrero, speaks Nahuatl and Spanish. He has finished the first year of secondary school and wanted to go on to study accounting, but says that his family's economic situation made it necessary for him to work, and thus he became a vendor on Icacos Beach, Acapulco. His mother, as David, sells shell and semiprecious stone necklaces. His father works seasonally on a small property—less than one hectare in size—that he owns, cultivating corn, watermelon, and melons. David helps him with this work. One of David's two sisters sells necklaces on Caleta Beach, Acapulco (the other is attending primary school) and one of his five brothers sells watches on Icacos Beach. His eight-year-old brother sells shells (as does his father) on Icacos Beach during school vacations.

The family's vending history began with David's paternal grandfather's arrival in Acapulco to work in construction. Finding the opportunity to sell shells on the beach, he transferred to this work. David reports that he has 12 uncles (including eight mother's brothers and four father's sisters), six aunts (including two mother's sisters and four father's sisters), and 15 male and 12 female cousins, sons and daughters of his aunts and uncles, who sell merchandise throughout the many beaches in Acapulco. Among the things they sell are shells, necklaces, sunglasses, and watches. In sum, David's family social capital as a vendor is quite extensive. He likes being a vendor: he likes stringing the shells and stones into necklaces and being friendly ("*amable*") with the tourists. He also points out that he has an obligation to work as a vendor to help out his parents. On a good day he earns 400 pesos in profit, though nothing on a bad day.

Vending as a Family Tradition

As the two cases above show, vending as a family tradition may be quite extensive, including many other relatives besides father and mother. Table 3.2 shows the number of family members who are vendors for the entire sample of 166 vendors, and for males as compared to females. Only 13.8 percent of vendors had no family members who were vendors. If those who have five to nine family members who are vendors (33.1 percent) are added to those who have 10 or more family members who are vendors (12 percent), it can

TABLE 3.2
Number of Family Members Who are Vendors

	Men (N=82)		Women (N=84)		Total (N=166)	
	No.	%	No.	%	No.	%
None	12	14.6	11	13.1	23	13.8
1–4	32	39.0	36	42.8	68	41.0
5–9	25	30.5	30	35.7	55	33.1
10 or more	13	15.8	7	8.3	20	12.0[a]
Total	82	99.9	84	99.9	166	99.9

[a] 45.1 percent of beach vendors have five or more relatives who are vendors.

be seen that those with more than five family members who are vendors adds up to 45.1 percent, including 46.3 percent of male vendors and 44 percent of female vendors. Furthermore, 41 percent had one to four family members who were vendors. Those with over five family members who are vendors show the influence of family tradition on being a vendor to an overwhelming extent.

Vendors with One to Four Family Members Who are Vendors

Case 3.3

Álvaro (PV-11) is a 40-year-old married man with three children, ages 16, 19, and 23. Álvaro finished primary school and speaks Nahuatl, Spanish, and enought English to be able to vend, he says. He was born in the pueblo of Temalac, Guerrero, to parents who migrated there from Acatlán, Guerrero. He, his wife, and eldest son moved to Puerto Vallarta in 1989, 21 years prior to the interview in 2010. He has been a beach vendor since his arrival. Álavaro has owned his own house for 15 years. His only relatives who are vendors are three wife's brothers who sell serapes, blankets, and tablecloths on the beach. They had preceded him in their move to Puerto Vallarta. Prior to being a vendor Álvaro had worked on his father's lands, a small property in Temalac that was left to his eldest brother. Another brother, who lives in Puerto Vallarta, makes wooden statues of fish, dolphins, and other sea creatures, and wholesales them to beach vendors. Álvaro sells blankets and tablecloths that he buys from wholesalers from Puebla and Tlaxcala who bring their merchandise to the colonia where he lives. He earns 300 to 500 pesos on a good day, nothing on a bad day. Álvaro is somewhat satisfied with his work as a vendor, noting that there are not many tourists until November and December, months in which his sales will be higher. If he were not a vendor Álvaro would like to work in construction or as an automobile mechanic. His family is not bad off as his 23-year-old son, who has a stall in a tianguis from which he sells secondhand clothing from the United States, and his 19-year-old daughter, who is a waitress in a beach restaurant, both contribute to the household economy. His 16-year-old son has completed secondary school and will continue his studies. Álvaro has a vendor's license and belongs to CTM (*Confederación de Trabajadores de México*, Confederation of Mexican Workers), the largest union in Mexico, which was founded in 1936 under President Lázaro Cardenas (1934–1940). He says the union helps the vendors if they have problems with work or if the municipality cancels their licenses.

Case 3.4

Karen (ACA-5PD) is an 18-year-old single vendor born in Acapulco to parents born in Acapulco. Her father farms on borrowed lands on the periphery of the city. Karen has four family members who are beach vendors, including her mother and three mother's sisters. All sell shells or ornaments they make of shells. Karen finished preparatory school and would like to continue studying for a career in nursing. She had been a beach vendor for less than a month when she was interviewed on Playa Diamante in July of 2010. She finds her sales to be low and tells me that the economic recession has affected her family so much that there is no longer enough money to pay for her studies. She is an only child. She likes vending because she can help her mother pay the household expenses. What Karen does not like about vending is the police harassment to which she is subjected despite belonging to the local vendors' association (*Organización de Vendedores de Mayan*, Organization of Mayan Vendors). Licenses are not required in Acapulco, but Karen has a credential from the organization that encompasses only vendors on one section of Playa Diamante. On a good day she earns 200 pesos, receiving about 30 pesos for each shell or shell ornament she sells, after buying the shells from a diver. On a bad day she earns nothing. Notably, all of her family members who are vendors are women.

Vendors Married to Vendors

Many of the vendors who have only one to four family members who are vendors are married to vendors themselves. For the total sample, broken down into male and female components and town of vending, it can be seen in table 3.3 that 31.3 percent of all vendors (52 of 166) have spouses who are vendors, approximately the same as in Acapulco, Cabo San Lucas, and Puerto Vallarta. Far more female vendors (41.7 percent) than male vendors (20.7 percent) have spouses who are vendors, suggesting that men pull their wives

TABLE 3.3
Spouses of Vendors Who are also Vendors

	Acapulco (N=55) M=30 W=25		Cabo (N=60) M=27 W=34		P. Vallarta (N=51) M=27 W=25		Total (N=166) M=82 W=84	
Spouses also vendors[a]	*No.*	*%*	*No.*	*%*	*No.*	*%*	*No.*	*%*
Men	7	23.3	2	7.4	9	34.6	52	21.9
Women	11	44.0	15	45.5	9	36.0	35	41.7
Total	18	32.7	17	28.3	18	35.3	53	31.9

[a] Of the total sample, 11 men were single and six widowed; nineteen women were single and three widowed.

into vending when the family comes under economic pressures. Importantly 53 women (63.1 percent) and 63 men (76.8 percent were married or living in free union. Of these, 38 women were legally married and 55 men were as well. The following two cases summarize the histories of female vendors whose husbands are vendors.

Case 3.5

Antonia (PV-16) is a 32-year-old married vendor living in free union. She never went to school but speaks Nahautl, Spanish, and a little English. She has three children, ages six, nine, and 12. All are in school. Born in Analco, Guerrero, Antonia migrated to Puerto Vallarta 12 years ago and has been a beach vendor since arriving. Her husband is also a beach vendor and sells dresses. Her three brothers and one sister, all older than Antonia, are beach vendors in Acapulco. Antonia was never a vendor in that city. She sells semi-precious stone necklaces, buying the stones from a wholesaler from Taxco, Guerrero, who comes to the house she and her husband rent to sell his wares. Despite having lived in Puerto Vallarta for 12 years, she and her husband do not own a house but pay 1,000 pesos a month in rent for lodging. At times they find it difficult to pay, but Antonia says the señora who rents to them will wait for 15 days past the due date. As many other vendors from Analco, she returns to her pueblo each year for the Fiesta de la Resurrección (Festival of the Resurrection) in March. She says she likes nothing about being a vendor and that if she had the money she would be at home with her children. Antonia says she earns 200 pesos on a good day, receiving 30 pesos in profit on each necklace. As the vast majority of the vendors, she reports that she earns nothing on a bad day. If she could study anything it would be to learn to read. She has a vendor's license that cost her 20,000 pesos (initial fees are common in procuring a license) and also pays the usual annual fees of about 1,200 pesos. She does not belong to a union or organization.

Case 3.6

Isabel (CSL-4P) is a 25-year-old married vendor with two children, who comes from San Juan Tetelcingo, Guerrero. She finished primary school and speaks Nahuatl, Spanish, and a little English. All five of her siblings are beach vendors, as is her husband. Isabel came with her parents to Cabo San Lucas 15 years ago and has been a vendor for 10 years. She sells semiprecious stone necklaces, as is most common among all women beach vendors from San Juan Tetelcingo. She earns 300 pesos on a good day, receiving a profit of about 20 pesos for each necklace. (This is quite low.) If she could study anything it would be English. Isabel is little satisfied with her work as a vendor because sales are low. If she were not a vendor she would like to stay at home and take care of children, including her own. It is apparent Isabel is working as a beach vendor because her family needs the money. Isabel and her husband rent a house in the partially invaded colonia El Caribe (see chapter on residential apartheid). She belongs to a union (though she does not specify which) and has a vendor's license.

Despite a general pattern of wives following husbands into vending, it is sometimes also the case that a female vendor will pull an otherwise unemployed husband into vending.

Case 3.7

Fortunato (CSL-16P) is a 55-year-old married vendor with three sons and four daughters, ranging in age from 20 to 38. Although he never attended school, his youngest son is studying for a bachelor's degree in law. Fortunato came to Cabo San Lucas with his family of orientation 25 years ago after hearing from a friend in Acapulco, where they were living, that construction work was available. Both he and his wife Claudia (CSL-T33), were originally from the pueblo of Ahuatitlán, Guerrero, where Fortunato's father cultivated corn, beans, and peanuts on his three hectares of private property as well as working as an agricultural day laborer. The family initially migrated to Acapulco so Fortunato could find work in construction. Claudia's mother, who took up work as a beach vendor in Acapulco, followed them to Cabo San Lucas and is a beach vendor on Medano Beach. Claudia and two of their sons are also beach vendors. Fortunato prefers construction work but has worked as a beach vendor on and off for 17 years, including nine years in Acapulco, during periods of the year when he could not find employment on a building site.

When the economic recession began to be felt in Los Cabos toward the end of 2008, and half of the approximately 20,000 construction workers there found themselves unemployed (*elijuarez*, 2008), Fortunato began to vend full time. He had the example of his mother-in-law and of his wife to follow as well as of two of his sisters who sell sundresses on the beach in Manzanillo, Colima.

Fortunato sells the sundresses that his wife, Claudia, sews from the Indonesian cloth she buys at wholesale prices from a downtown store. She also sells her hand-sewn sundresses on the beach. Two of their three sons are also beach vendors and sell silver jewelry from Taxco. Fortunato says he can earn up to 500 pesos on a good day, but he would prefer to work in any aspect of construction. His last steady construction job was helping to build the modern Puerto Paraíso mall in downtown Cabo San Lucas. If he could study anything it would be English to help him get work building and remodeling homes for American and Canadian expatriates. He is little content with being a vendor because some days there are no sales. He and his wife have owned a house in Los Cangrejos for 12 years (see chapter on residential apartheid).

Both Fortunato and Claudia have vendor's licenses for which they pay 1,300 pesos in annual fees. Both belong to an organization affiliated with the PRI (*Partido Revolucionario Institucional*, Institutional Revolutionary Party) called 26th of November. It is a *colonia*-based, not a vendor-based organization, but helps them if they have problems at work. Their son Juan Carlos (CSL-7P), age 35 and married with five children, also lives in Los Cangrejos, in two rented rooms. He had previously worked in construction and has no vendor's license. He is anxious to find work in construction once more, despite having been an occasional vendor for 16 years. Their son Marcos (CSL-8P), is 30 years old and recently separated from his common-law wife. He, like his brother Juan Carlos, was born in Acapulco. Marcos lives in a laminated tin house that he self-built in the colonia Lomas del Sol (see chapter on residential apartheid). He has never worked at anything but vending and has a vendor's license. Both brothers belong to CNOP (*Confederación Nacional de Organizacions Populares*, National Confederation of Popular Organizations). It is notable that not all of the family members have vendor's licenses, and that not all belong to the same union or organization. Having one family member who belongs to a union means that the family interest may be represented through him or her, however.

Vendors with Five or More Family Members Who are Vendors

Those vendors who speak an indigenous language tend to have far more family members who are vendors than those who do not speak an indigenous language, suggesting a stronger element of family tradition among the former.

TABLE 3.4
Number of Family Members Vendors by Indigenous Language Speakers

	None		*1–4*		*5–9*		*10+*	
	No.	*%*	*No.*	*%*	*No.*	*%*	*No.*	*%*
Indigenous language speakers (N=81)	8	9.9	25	30.9	36	44.4	12	14.8
No indigenous language (N=85)	15	17.6	43	50.6	19	22.3	8	9.4
Total (N=166)	23	13.8	68	41.0	55	33.1	20	12.0

Of the indigenous language speakers, 59.2 percent had five or more family members who were vendors as compared to 31.7 percent of the vendors who spoke no indigenous language.

As table 3.4 shows, whereas 17.6 percent of those who do not speak an indigenous language had no vendor family members, only 9.9 percent of indigenous language speakers did so. Nonetheless, 50.6 percent of those who do not speak an indigenous language had one to four relatives who were vendors. Among those who had five or more relatives who were vendors, 31.7 percent of non-indigenous language speakers but 59.2 percent of indigenous language speakers had such extensive family social capital. Indigenous language speakers comprise 49.4 percent of the sample (82 of 166): most (77.8 percent or 63 of 81) spoke Nahuatl, with 12 (14.6 percent) speaking Zapoteco, three Mixteco, two Tlapaneco, and one each Triqui and Otomí. Palano, David, Álvaro, Antonia, and others are all indigenous language speakers. More of the indigenous vendors' stories will be considered in a subsequent chapter.

Below I will summarize the stories of three beach vendors, all of whom are indigenous language speakers, two from Guerrero and one from Oaxaca, and have an extensive network of family members who are also vendors.

Case 3.8

Gabriela (ACA-6IC), a 37-year-old vendor from the municipality of Xalpatlahua, Guerrero, never went to school. She speaks Mixtec and Spanish but does not mention speaking any English. Separated from her husband since he crossed to work in the United States eight years ago, she has to support two of her three children. The eldest, an 18-year-old son, crossed the border to join his father. Gabriela has no idea where either of them are—just somewhere in the United States. Her two younger children are currently in primary school. Although only one of her eight siblings, a sister, is a beach vendor, Gabriela has a number of other family members who are vendors. Her father sells water pistols and sand pails and her mother necklaces on Icacos Beach. Her sister sells beachwear there. In addition, a father's brother and three of this uncle's daughters are beach vendors, as is a father's sister and three of her offspring—all in Acapulco. In total, Gabriela has 11 family members who are beach vendors. Gabriela sells bathing suits and sundresses that she buys wholesale and previously has sold necklaces from a fixed stall downtown. She lives, along with three of her siblings, in her parents' house and has been a vendor for 16 years. She would like to finish primary school and if she were not a vendor to become a secretary. She earns 180 to 200 pesos on a good day, and claims to receive five to 20 pesos for each sundress or bathing suit she sells. Although her family social capital is high, her earnings are relatively low, and a necessary input to the support of her children.

Case 3.9

Victor (PV-10) is a 65-year-old married Nahuatl speaker born in Temalac, Guerrero, and interviewed in Puerto Vallarta. He has three sons and three daughters, ranging in age from 22 to 42. Most work in employment carrying formal sector benefits. For example, one is a cook in a tourist hotel. His only living brother plants corn on a small property he owns in Temalac and also works as a sharecropper. If Victor were not a vendor he would like to cultivate corn or work cleaning a hotel. Victor has lived in Puerto Vallarta for 25 years and been a vendor since then. He accompanied *paisanos* (community members) to Puerto Vallarta and then brought his wife and children. He has a number of cousins, including two sisters' sons and four sisters' daughters as well as nieces and nephews of his siblings (two) and wife's siblings (four) who work as beach vendors in Puerto Vallarta. Though in Victor's case his relatives are not immediate family members, they do provide information about vending possibilities and strategies. Victor sells bedspreads, made in Tlaxcala, that he acquires from a wholesaler who lives in Puerto Vallarta. He says he earns 200 pesos on a good day but often goes for days without selling anything. He works various hours every day of the week, entering the beach between 10 and 12 and leaving between four and seven. Victor has a vendor's license that cost him 500 pesos 25 years ago. It has a 1,200 peso annual renewal fee. He belongs to CTM, which he points out is affiliated with the PRI (*Partido Revolucionario Institucional*, Institutional Revolutionary Party), the ruling party in Mexico until the election of President Vicente Fox in 2000. Victor previously worked for 23 years as an agricultural day laborer, cutting cane in Veracruz, picking cotton in Sonora and Sinaloa, and harvesting chilies and tomatoes in Nayarit.

Notably, although indigenous peoples comprise less than 10 percent of the population of Mexico, 37 percent of the agricultural day laborers who originated from ejidos between 1994 and 1997 were indigenous language speakers (Davis, Stecklov, and Winters 2002, 296). Taking the indigenous population as a whole, whether coming from ejidos or not, Arroyo Sepúlveda (2001, 112) estimates that in 1998 almost 40.5 percent of agricultural day laborers were indigenous and that 27.9 percent of the total were from the state of Guerrero, which surpassed the state of Oaxaca in this rural-to-rural migration for the first time in that year. These percentages far outnumber their proportion of the population. Agricultural day laborers tend to be less educated than rural-to-urban migrants and international migrants (Davis, Stecklov, and Winters 2002, table 1, 296). Victor, however, was the only vendor interviewed who had previously been an agricultural day laborer.

Case 3.10

Federico (PV-20), born in Mitla, Oaxaca, is a 55-year-old married vendor with seven daughters and one son. He finished the fifth year of primary school and speaks Zapotec and Spanish and not much English, he says, only enough to make sales. Federico has recurrently migrated to Puerto Vallarta for 25 years and has been a vendor for that time. Previously he made the Oaxacan-style clothing he now sells on the beach. His wife, with the help of a daughter, and one of his brothers are the only ones in his family who now make the blue, green, and yellow blouses they sew from cloth that they buy. They also weave the pants that he sells. Six of his cousins, offspring of his father's sisters, are beach vendors in Puerto Vallarta. Federico has never vended elsewhere in Mexico. He estimates that he earns 300 pesos on a good day, receiving 30 to 40 pesos for each item of clothing he sells. He rents a room for 1,000 pesos a month while in Puerto Vallarta and returns to his family in Mitla every six to eight months. He says that presently there is little business so it is difficult to pay the rent. Federico offers that he has been unable to save up the money he needs to repair the family house in Mitla. He has a vendor's license and belongs to the CTM. He says the union helps the vendors if they have problems with the authorities.

The Importance of Family Social Capital

What is the importance of having other family members who are vendors? There are at least four advantages, the first regarding where selling takes place, the second regarding what merchandise is sold, the third involving links to unions or municipal authorities which enable the acquisition of a vendor's permit or license, and the fourth involving skills passed on that can lead to higher earnings.

Where selling takes place, in terms of the various tourist beach towns in Mexico, depends, as does all migration with the exception of pioneering migrants, on where an individual or family has network ties. It may also take place in stages, as natives of Guerrero go first to nearby Acapulco, then may move on to Cabo San Lucas or Puerto Vallarta or to any one of a number of destinations. Once within the tourist city, if there are multiple beaches, such as in Acapulco and Los Cabos, or in the Vallarta complex—including Puerto Vallarta, Jalisco and Nuevo Vallarta, Nayarit—which beach the vendor chooses to vend on often depends on where other family members work. Thus David, his mother and father, and his siblings work on Icacos Beach in Acapulco, though aunts, uncles, and cousins may work there or on other beaches such as Caleta, Barra Vieja, or Marquez.

Second, as concerns merchandise sold, there are two aspects. The first concerns links with suppliers who, if family members sell the same merchandise, may sell to the entire family or to members of the family. One family member may lead others to an initial supplier and/or to subsequent ones. This was the case with Marcos and Juan Carlos, for example. The second concerns the manufacture and/or value added to the merchandise sold. In the case of handwoven palm-leaf handbags and sombreros, ceramic bowls and plates, hammocks and wood carvings, the vendor or members of the vendor's family are often the artisans who manufacture them. Value may be added to the original merchandise. Thus the coral, pearl, turquoise, onyx, or wooden beads and shells may be bought from a wholesaler and strong into necklaces unique in some ways to each vendor or each vendor's family. Lengths of cloth may be cut and sewn into women's and children's sundresses, an endeavor carried out by both men and women. Plain ceramic bowls and plates may be acquired and painted by the vendor with the help of his or her family members. Thread is bought and woven into name bracelets. Clothing is woven or sewn. Cotton candy, doughnuts, and other pastries are manufactured in the home with the help of the spouse. Both original manufacture and value-added are artisanal skills that can be passed on to a family member, a case in which family social capital adds to human capital.

For those who sell merchandise such as key chains, T-shirts, canvas bags with a local logo, sunglasses, or Cuban cigars, among other wares, there is no artisanal work involved by the vendor, but s/he may have seen the success of other family members (or other vendors) in selling these wares and may be led to a supplier through either familial or extra-familial advice. Strategies for selling, part of the vendor's portfolio of skills, may also be learned from family members, as well as basic English needed to deal with American and Canadian tourists.

Family members as well as others in the vendor's social network may be able to provide information about who to contact in the municipal offices or what union or association to join in order to obtain a license, if that is required, as it is in Cabo San Lucas and Puerto Vallarta. Possession of a license usually means that the beach vendors are protected from undue harassment and confiscation of their merchandise by local authorities; union membership means they have someone to turn to in case they are harassed or have their merchandise taken from them.

Last, the vending skills that are transmitted though family ties may lead to higher earnings. T-tests run by Ivonne Gómez on the data from 30 women vendors in Cabo San Lucas show that the highest predictor of high earnings on a good day (at 0.52) was the number of family members who were vendors. This is compared to a lower 0.29 correlation between human capital, as measured by years of formal education and earnings on a good day (Wilson and Gámez 2011). Hsueh Kuei-Hsaing, who ran t-tests on the entire sample of 166 vendors, concluded that there are significant differences in earnings on a good day between those who have fewer than family members who are vendors and those who have five or more family members who are vendors (T=4.25, P< 0.5). She sustains that the finding indicates that on a good day, those with five or more family members who are also vendors earned significantly more money (N=75, mean=1128.93 pesos) than those with fewer than five family members who are vendors (N=91, mean=411.43 pesos).

Although the official minimum wage in Mexico is 60 pesos or less a day, most unskilled or semiskilled workers, such as construction laborers, gardeners, and domestic servants, earn approximately 300 pesos a day, at least in Los Cabos. Although the vast majority of beach vendors admitted to earning nothing on a bad day—one of the vicissitudes of working in informal self-employment—quite a few earned more than 400 pesos on a good day. As can be seen in table 3.5, whereas 43.4 percent of those with no family members who were vendors earned 400 pesos or more on a good day, 69 percent of those with one to four family members who are vendors earned 400 pesos or more on a good day and 50 percent of those with 10 or more family members who are vendors earned that much. Why approximately the same percentage of those with five to nine family members (41.7 percent) earned 400 pesos or more on a good day as those who had no family members who are vendors (43.4 percent) is a bit of a mystery and may be due to the fact that those with extremely high numbers of family members who are vendors are especially marginalized economically and must send more family members into income-generating activities. Nonetheless, while 65.1 percent of those with no family members earned more than 300 pesos a day, 78.1 percent of those with five to nine family members did so, and whereas 33.7 percent of those with no family

TABLE 3.5
Earnings on a Good Day by Number of Family Members Who are Vendors

	None		*1–4*		*5–9*		*10+*		*Total*	
	No.	*%*	*No.*	*%*	*No.*	*%*	*No.*	*%*	*No.*	*%*
Pesos[a]										
<200	3	13.0	7	10.3	2	3.6	1	5.0	13	7.8
200–299	5	21.7	11	16.2	10	18.2	5	25.0	31	18.7
300–399	5	21.7	3	4.4	20	36.4	4	20.0	32	19.3
400–499	3	13.0	9	13.2	8	14.5	2	10.0	22	13.2
500–599	2	8.7	23	33.8	8	14.5	2	10.0	35	21.1
600+	5	21.7	15	22.0	7	12.7	6	30.0	33	19.9
Total	23	99.8	68	99.9	55	99.9	20	100.0	166	100.0
<300	8	34.7	18	26.5	12	21.8	6	30.0	44	26.5
300+	15	65.1	50	73.4	43	78.1	14	70.0	112	73.5
400+	10	43.4	47	69.0	23	41.7	10	50.0	90	54.2

[a] There were approximately 12 pesos to the dollar in 2010 when the vendors were interviewed.

members earned under 300 pesos on a good day, only 21.8 percent of those with five to nine family members did so.

Conclusions

From the high percentage of beach vendors who have one or more family members who are vendors—143 of 166 or 86.1 percent—self-employment in beach vending can be seen as a family tradition. Family members pass on information, knowledge, and skills to other family members. This includes information about what town to sell in and on what beach as well as about what merchandise to vend (though this may change over time), knowledge about suppliers and how to acquire a license or the benefits of joining a union and what union to join, and skills concerning dealing with clients and how to manufacture, or add value to, the merchandise they sell. Not only does family social capital add to human social capital, but it also seems to have some influence on increasing earnings. Indigenous vendors, some from villages with a long tradition of ambulant and beach vending, tend to have far more family members who are vendors than others. This too suggests that such vending is a family tradition. Although some vendors have engaged in no previous income-generating work, and have most probably been pulled into vending by other family members, some indeed have had other employment. Others have been pulled into vending later in life but may be aided in this employment by family members who are vendors.

Thus, in this subsector of informal self-employment having relatives who are also vendors is extremely important. The existence of five or more family members who are vendors means that a vendor will most probably have higher earnings on a good day. The better earning capabilities can be attributed to family social capital that embodies a lore or "culture" of vending. Given lack of employment opportunities in the formal economy, family members may network unemployed relatives into beach vending. Part of the problem of unemployment, coupled with the dispossession of the peasantry, is related to the processes of globalization, as will be seen in the next chapter.

Beach Vendor Families

FIGURE 3.1
A family of beach vendors, Acapulco, Icacos Beach, 2010

FIGURE 3.2
A couple with two sons who are also beach vendors, Cabo San Lucas, 2010

4

Globalization and the Increase of Beach Vendors

The penetration of capitalism into the countryside results in an ongoing and massive displacement of the peasantry. A major story of globalization—worldwide—is the agonizing death of the peasantry. Where have the peasants, the displaced workers, and the middle classes gone? First, they have turned to transnational migration. Second, they constitute the new labor force for new agribusiness farms, factories, and service sectors [among them tourism] of the global economy. Third, they have shifted en masse to the informal sector?

—Robinson 2008, 169

THE CONTINUING DECLINE OF THE PEASANTRY in Mexico has been well documented over more than five decades. The differentiation of the peasantry into capitalist farmers on the one hand, and subsistence, sub-sub-sistence, and disposed peasants on the other, became clear in the 1960s when analyzing the effects of the post–World War II introduction of the Green Revolution to Mexican corn farmers. The Green Revolution package included genetically modified corn (that could not reproduce itself, thus necessitating that new seeds be bought each year), fertilizers, and pesticides that some peasant farmers could cover the costs of and others not. Expansion was the destiny of those who successfully adopted Green Revolution technologies and contraction or decline the fate of those who could not (Hewitt de Alcantara 1976). Thus the peasantry differentiated into successful capitalist farmers at one extreme and landless peasants who worked on borrowed or unowned lands, as sharecroppers, or as day laborers, on the other.

In the 1980s economic crises and the imposition of structural adjustment programs, closely followed by the adoption of neoliberal reforms under President Salinas de Gortari (1988–1994) led to the erosion of subsidies to small farmers (Rivera and Whiteford 2009), and more of them were marginalized and uprooted. After the implementation of NAFTA in January of 1994, Mexico's small farmers, especially corn farmers, were bludgeoned once again, as heavily subsidized corn coming from the United States undercut prices for corn grown in Mexico—of which, in any case, there was an insufficiency to fulfill demand (Rivera 2009; see also Harvey 2005, 101–3). In all three periods, many subsistence and sub-subsistence peasants were forced to find a supplementary income through seasonal migration to the United States or elsewhere in Mexico. Even relatively successful small farmers entered the migration stream, primarily to the United States, as "target earners" (Massey et al. 1987, chap. 7) to earn income to buy a tractor or other capital goods necessary for their agricultural enterprise. Demographic pressures as well the ongoing differentiation of the peasantry led the dispossessed to migrate permanently, whether to the United States or to urban centers in Mexico.

Many peasants/farmers under economic stress have entered the informal economy in Mexico. Among them are street vendors in a multitude of Mexican cities and beach vendors in most Mexican sun and beach tourist centers. The interviews with beach vendors in Acapulco, Puerto Vallarta, and Cabo San Lucas revealed that 81 (48.8 percent) were from rural areas in the poverty-stricken state of Guerrero, and that 58 (71.6 percent) of these were speakers of Nahuatl. Several seasonally migrate from their subsistence plots to vend on the beach during the high tourist seasons: this is a pattern typical in Acapulco. Some, who were born in Acapulco and who are sons and daughters of indigenous vendors, have lost their ability to speak Nahuatl. The vast majority of the Nahuatl speakers are offspring of peasants or of beach vendors. There were vendors from rural pueblos and ranchos in other states as well: Oaxaca (five), the state of Mexico (four), Puebla (three), Michoacán (two), Jalisco (two), as well as one each from Querétaro, Colima, Chiapas, and Morelos. Even at least half of those born in cities had parents who were born in pueblos or on ranchos. Thus 14 of the 27 vendors born in Acapulco had parents born in rural areas of Guerrero. Another 12 of these vendors had parents born in Acapulco, and one had a father born in the Federal District. The numbers of beach vendors are constantly rising, resulting in competition that is lowering their earnings. This is one reason that vendors from older tourist centers such as Acapulco and Mazatlán, where competition has been high for many years, are moving to newer tourist centers such as Cabo San Lucas. For example, six of the vendors, including four women and two men interviewed in Cabo San Lucas, were born in Acapulco, and four men were born in Mazatlán. In this chapter I will first address how globalization and Mexico's dependence on tourism in this time of economic recession is viewed by the vendors. Then I will consider conceptualizing the tourist centers as transnational social spaces.

Globalization

Although some scholars find the roots of globalization to lie in world-systems processes that began over half a millennium ago (e.g., Milanovic, 2003; Robinson 2007; Schuerkens 2008, 2–3; Staven 2005), others stress its recent manifestations as occurring in the 1970s in alliance with neoliberal economic policies such as the structural adjustment programs and free trade initiatives implemented in the 1980s and 1990s (e.g., Chossudovsky 2003; Harvey 2005; Robinson 2008, 2004; Rothstein, 2007, 113–14; Sassen 1998). Robinson (2008, chap. 1; see also Robinson 2004, chap. 1) conceives of present-day globalization as representing an "epochal shift in world capitalism." This shift has, among other things, led to an ever more-massive dispossession and dislocation of the peasantry and an ever more-massive swelling of the informal economy, including both informalized wage laborers and the informally (or semi-informally) self-employed, primarily though not exclusively in urban centers. Tourism development is an integral part of the processes of globalization (Robinson 2008; Hannam 2002; Merrill 2009; Mowforth and Munt 1998), and tourist centers such as those discussed in this book can be conceived of, following Robinson's (2008, 203) analysis, as "nodes of intensive or specialized accumulation." Multinational hotels and airlines, among other transnational businesses, perform an integral role in this accumulation (Clancy 1998).

Contemporary globalization means the unfettering of capitalism from nation-state boundaries and capital becoming global in its reach (Robinson 2008, 15). The handmaiden of globalization has been neoliberal reforms, most often in the guise of structural adjustment programs imposed by the World Bank, the International Monetary Fund (IMF), the World Trade Organization (WTO), and other international financial institutions. These neoliberal reforms include privatization of state-owned enterprises, reduction or elimination of tariffs on international commodity flows, austerity programs (involving cutbacks in funding for education, health, and welfare), lowering of taxes on the well-to-do, deregulation and flexibilization of labor markets, openness to foreign direct investment, and export-oriented production (e.g., Chossudovsky 2003; Harvey 2007, chap. 3; Portes and Roberts 2008, 16; Robinson 2008, 16; Rothstein 2007, 30–31). The North American Free Trade Agreement (NAFTA), initiated in 1994, is part of this neoliberal package as it involves reducing tariffs on imports, promulgating further export-oriented production and encouraging foreign investments.

There are at least two results of the implementation of neoliberal policies throughout most of Latin America, including Mexico. First, there has been a growing inequality between the rich and the poor. Second, there has been a swelling of the informal economy as small- and medium-sized formal enterprises went bankrupt because of foreign competition. This foreign competition was apparent both in international commodity flows and as a result of foreign direct investment in local competing businesses. For example, in Los Cabos, the opening of WalMart, Costco, and Home Depot has led to the bankruptcy of many locally owned grocery stores and small businesses supplying household and electronics goods, among other things. The informal economy also expanded in part because formal enterprises began cutting back on legally instituted workers' benefits in the interests of employing a cheaper and more flexible labor force (Portes and Roberts 2008; see also Robinson 2008, chap. 1). Many people sought out a niche by becoming self-employed. Robinson (2008, 244) notes that for Latin America, "There has been an explosion of people who scratch out a living through the provision of whatever service they are able to market since the informal sector has been the only avenue for millions of people thrown out of work by contraction of formal sector employment and by the uprooting of remaining peasant communities by the incursion of capitalist agriculture." The petty commerce engaged in by street and beach vendors is encompassed within this explosive growth of the informal economy.

The forces of globalization and a world ever more interlinked through trade agreements can be seen in terms of the wares some beach vendors sell. Globalization has also affected those vendors' fathers who were peasants, as well as the vendors themselves who continue farming. They are also apparent in the ways the economic recession that began at the end of 2008 has affected the vendors.

Commodity Chains and the Beach Vendors

Commodity chains may provide links between informal activities or between formal and informal enterprises, whether nationally or internationally. Informal artisans may provide merchandise to the beach vendors, or beach vendor families may themselves be the artisans. The research on beach vendors in Cabo San Lucas, Puerto Vallarta, and Acapulco showed that many of the Nahuatl-speaking beach vendors from Guerrero did indeed sell traditional artisan crafts, including woven palm-leaf handbags and sombreros, and occasionally masks—all a specialty of Tlamacazapa; hand-painted pitchers, plates, and bowls, usually ceramic but sometimes of wood; hand-painted ceramic fish assembled into mobiles; hammocks, and a very few—though none of these were formally interviewed—selling amate bark paper paintings of relatively low quality. Several also sold cut fruit, prepared meals, and sodas; and, particularly in Acapulco, shells, ornaments and necklaces made from shells; and starfishes. Many of the women, but also some of the men—and overwhelmingly from the town of San Juan Tetelcingo, from where 12 vendors were interviewed; and Analco, from where 10 vendors were interviewed—sold semiprecious stone necklaces. The semiprecious stones were most usually beads made of coral, turquoise, and pearl, sometimes interspersed with shells, black onyx, or amber. The vendor would buy the beads from wholesalers—some in towns such as Taxco or Iguala when they went back on visits to their home villages, and some from wholesalers who came to the beaches or to their homes in the colonias where they resided in these tourist cities. They would then string the beads, usually with a pendant, into patterns of their own choosing. The origin of the stones could be Mexico, Asia, or Eastern Europe (Cowen 2005, 148).

Other vendors resold goods they had bought from stores in towns near origin or at destination at wholesale prices or from wholesalers who sought them out at home or at work. Hence they were the ultimate link in a chain passing from formal or informal manufacturers to wholesaler to retailer. This was especially true in the case of T-shirts, each carrying a local logo, such as Acapulco or Cabo San Lucas. The vendors held that these T-shirts were manufactured in Mexico City and subsequently sent out to each tourist city to be imprinted with the local logo. This was also true of canvas beach bags. Other goods that were resold without any value added on the part of the vendor or the vendor's family were tablecloths from Guadalajara, silver jewelry from Taxco—this being widely available through beach vendors in all three tourist centers—and bedspreads, blankets, or serapes from Tlaxcala. Another widely sold item was elaborated from cloth imported into Mexico from Indonesia, showing the complicated trade networks that exist in this era of globalization. Both Nahuatl speakers and those who spoke no indigenous language would buy lengths of this cloth and refashion it into women's and children's sundresses. By 2010 this had become the most common way of selling Indonesian cloth. Earlier on, in the 2002 to 2007 period in Puerto Vallarta, a higher-quality Indonesian cloth, embossed with typically Mexican themes such as Pancho Villa riding a horse and Frida Kahlo backed by themes from her paintings, was being sold as a single, non-value added piece. Other vendors worked these lengths of cloth into simple muumuu type dresses: using two separate pieces they would sew them together at the sides. As with other items, vendors acquire the cloth from in-town stores at wholesale prices or buy from merchants who came to the beach or to their colonias to sell it.

Thus, there are at least three types of value chains: vendors working with indigenous materials, such as palm leaves, clay, hammock thread, ironwood, and amate bark paper and making their own handicrafts for sale, or selling those crafts made by extended family or community members, illustrated a local (and usually informal) value chain. Vendors selling wares like T-shirts, canvas bags, silver from Taxco, some precious stones, and serapes and blankets from Tlaxcala were involved in national level inter- or intrastate formal or informal value chains. Vendors selling semiprecious stones imported from Asia and Eastern Europe that they strung into necklaces, and sundresses made from Indonesian cloth, were involved in international value chains, though both types of merchandise had value added by the vendors and/or his or her family. Vendors of Indonesian cloth imprinted with Mexican designs in Indonesia, sunglasses made in China, and a nonindigenous vendor's sale of Chinese fans bought in a Chinese-owned store in Puerto Vallarta, as well as another's sale of blouses from India acquired in Acapulco, show their role in the retail of internationally produced goods to tourists visiting Mexican beach cities.

Father's Occupational Marginality

Having a father or a mother who was a vendor was actually more frequent among nonindigenous language speakers than among indigenous language speakers and their subset of Nahuatl speakers from Guerrero. Thus 36.9 percent (31 of 84) of the nonindigenous language speakers, as compared to 29.2 percent (24 of 82) of the indigenous language speakers and 31.7 percent (19 of 60) of the Nahuatl speakers from Guerrero had either a father or mother or both who were vendors. Having a parent who was a vendor shows the length of time that those of rural, and peasant, origins have been dispossessed.

A question as to father's occupation was not added until the interviews of the vendors in Acapulco, numbering 55, and male vendors in Cabo San Lucas, numbering 26, were being taken. Earlier there had only been a question as to whether the vendor's father or mother had also been a vendor. Of the 81 vendors whose father's occupation was asked, 45.1 percent (23 of 51) of the nonindigenous language speakers, 61.3 percent (19 of 31) of the indigenous language speakers, and 65.2 percent (15 of 23) of the Nahuatl speakers from ranchos and pueblos in the Guerrero subsample mentioned that their fathers had been campesinos. They ranged from being relatively well-off ejidatarios and less well-off small property owners, to being sharecroppers or cultivating unused lands on the sides of mountains, to being agricultural day laborers. In several cases they alternated between vending and cultivating subsistence plots. This was especially true in Acapulco, and several vendors mentioned that campesinos flocked to the beaches during the agricultural off-season and the corresponding tourist high season.

Notably, this kind of circular migration, with long absences of the breadwinner from his family, used to be typical of undocumented migrants from Mexico to the United States. The pattern was disrupted in the 1990s when Operation Hold-the-Line in El Paso (1993), Operation Gatekeeper in San Diego (1994), Operation Safeguard in Nogales, Arizona (1996), and Operation Río Grande in Southeast Texas were put into effect. At least two consequences of these deterrence efforts were seen: first, an increasing number of deaths among undocumented border crossers as they were channeled into more dangerous border crossings, especially the Arizona desert; and second, an end to the pattern of circular migration in favor of a more permanent settlement as more people decided not to risk crossing the border regularly (Cornelius 2001; Massey, Durand, and Malone 2003). Now a similar pattern of circular migration is occurring to the tourist zones or nodes of capital accumulation within Mexico. The beach vendors can easily return to their hometowns, and many who work in Puerto Vallarta and Acapulco do so intermittently or annually, as their hometowns are often less than a day's bus ride away. Few beach vendors in Cabo San Lucas visit their *pueblos* so often because of the Baja peninsula's isolation from the mainland and thus a much longer travel time and expense.

There are several other factors related to globalization that impinge on the lives of the beach vendors. Those of peasant background have been affected by neoliberal structural adjustment policies imposed in the early 1980s and by provisions of NAFTA in 1994—both of which led to the withdrawal of subsidies to small farmers (Rivera, Whiteford, and Chávez 2009; see also Harvey 2005, 101–3). This fomented a rural surplus of workers, many of whom sought independent self-employment as vendors in Mexico's cities, whether permanently or temporarily. They constitute the supply side for informal economic activities. Tourism growth has been portrayed as a index of globalization and a creator of internal transnational spaces (e.g., Torres and Momsen 2005). The World Bank and the Inter-American Development Bank, for example, have funded tourism development projects in Mexico various times in the past four decades (Clancy 2001*a*, 52 passim). The tourism growth poles represent what can be conceived of—at least in beach vendor consciousness—as the demand side. The vendors perceive that they can, in other words, find employment opportunities in those tourist cities that, building on Robinson's (2008) analysis of Latin America and global capitalism, can be conceived of as internal "core capitalist nodes." The profound influence of globalization on local spaces means that any conurbations in core capitalist countries will reverberate around the world.

Effects of the Economic Recession

The beach vendors, for example, have been victims of the economic recession that began in the United States at the end of 2009 and had repercussions around the globe—and thus can be seen as integral to the effects of globalization. The first 30 vendors interviewed were all women beach or marina vendors in Cabo San Lucas. The effects of the recession were reflected in their answers to two questions, one about what they did not like about vending and the other about how content they were with their work as vendors. Several women responded that they had good days and bad days, and at times could not sell anything, or very little. A 29-year-old Nahuatl-speaking woman from a village in Puebla who has lived in Cabo San Lucas for 19 years and been a vendor for the same time mentioned that one of the disadvantages of being a vendor is that there were not as many tourists as previously. Inspired by these responses, two questions were added to the interview schedule and asked of 136 vendors. They were: "Have you been affected by the economic crisis?" and "Do you think there are more or less vendors this year as compared to previously?".[1]

Many of the answers given were quite instructive. A 43-year-old Nahuatl-speaking man from Ahuehuepan, Guerrero (PV-7), interviewed in Puerto Vallarta, pointed out that there were many more vendors this year (2010) than in previous years, a response echoed by many other vendors, male and female, in all three tourist cities. They generally attributed it to the lack of available employment in other occupations. A 40-year-old Nahuatl-speaking man (PV-11) from Temalac, Guerrero, interviewed in Puerto Vallarta as well, elaborated on this theme. He said: "Each year more vendors arrive and there is more competition, one sells less, we have to sell more cheaply" ("*Cada año entra más vendedores y hay más competencia, se vende menos, tenemos que vender más barato*)." As concerns how the economic crisis has affected him, Álvaro says: "It affected us a lot. There were no people, there was no tourism, there were no sales. It affected us very badly" ("*Nos afectó mucho. No hubo gente, no hubo turismo, no hubo ventas. Nos afectó muy feo*)." The declining numbers of tourists was mentioned by a number of vendors in all three tourists centers as well.

In Puerto Vallarta a 42-year-old Nahautl speaker from Tlamacazapa, Guerrero (PV-10), offered an explanation for why there were more and more vendors, many without permits to vend, on the beach: It was "Because of the crisis. There is no work and they come to look for a way of surviving" ("*Por la crisis. No hay trabajo, y vienen a buscar [una manera de sobrevivi]*"). This reflects the fact that with the economic recession alternative informalized or only occasionally formalized work, such as that of construction, has dried up and that many of the workers in hotels and other tourist attractions were laid off due to declining tourist numbers. Others echoed his observation about the unemployed seeking work as vendors, though some felt that the numbers of vendors had remained steady.

A 40-year-old Nahautl-speaking man from Tlamacazapa, Guerrero (CSL-2P), who has been a vendor for 25 years, the past 12 in Cabo San Lucas, opines that, "Three years ago there were fewer vendors and now we have tripled, and there are few tourists" ("*Hace trés años hubo menos vendedores y ahora nos triplicamos, y hay pocos turistas.*") Thus both fewer tourist arrivals and more competition were identified as problems related to economic recession. Another problem the vendors identified was that the tourists who did arrive had less money to spend. Thus a 35-year-old man born in Acapulco (CSL-7P), whose mother, father, and brother are also beach vendors in Cabo San Lucas, pointed out: "Sales are low. Here there is no money, there are no sales, the tourists do not want to spend (money)" ("*Son bajas las ventas. Aquí no hay dinero, no hay ventas, los turistas no quieren gastar.*") His words are echoed by many of the vendors in Cabo San Lucas. For example, a 36-year-old Nahautl-speaking man from Copallilo, Guerrero (CSL-11P), who has been a vendor for 18 years, five of them in Cabo San Lucas, says that with the economic crisis, "All the tourism disappeared and there is no one to sell to and those who come do not buy because they say there is no money (to do so)" ("*Se fué todo el turismo y no hay con quien vender y los que vienen no compran porque dicen que no hay dinero.*") A 26-year-old Nahuatl-speaking woman from a village in the municipio of Chilpancingo, Guerrero (ACA-20IC), interviewed in Acapulco, mentioned that at times sales were so low that she did not have money to buy more merchandise. She sold semiprecious stone and shell necklaces that she assembled. Another Nahuatl-speaking man from Tlamacazapa, Guerrero (ACA-3PD), interviewed in Acapulco showed empathy for the tourists' low spending. He felt the economic crisis had affected him, "Very, very much. There is no money, there are no sales. People don't buy—because of the crisis. How are they going to buy if there is no money? People come but do not spend—they guard the little money they have" ("*Muchíssimo. No hay dinero, no hay venta. La gente no compra—por la crisís. Como van a comprar si no hay dinero? La gente viene pero no gastan—cuidan el poquito dinero que tienen.*")

An analysis of the interviews shows that beach vendors conceive of at least three ways in which the economic recession has affected their welfare and earnings. First, the numbers of vendors have multiplied, leading to increased competition and the driving down of prices for their wares. Second, a decrease in the number of tourists has caused a shrinking of their market for potential clients. Third, the unwillingness of the tourists who do arrive to spend as much as they did previously affects their sales potential. One of the problems exacerbating competition is that there are large numbers of vendors selling similar merchandise. This is especially the case with Taxco silver, semiprecious stone necklaces, hand woven name bracelets, and sundresses cut from Indonesian cloth. Unfortunately, the mass tourism market is not discerning enough to be willing to pay the higher prices that indigenous handicrafts should command—and fewer and fewer vendors are making and selling such handicrafts (see, e.g., Cowen [2005] on the decline in original amate bark paintings).

To summarize, due to supply side factors shaped by forces of globalization, more people are turning to beach vending in order to survive, driving up competition and lowering the prices of the merchandise sold. The economic recession, with its global reach, has also affected the demand side as tourist numbers fall and the tourists who do arrive in these centers have less money to spend.

Transnational Social Spaces

As concerns migrants, the concept of transnational migration was originally and most commonly applied to those people who cross national borders and who "develop and maintain multiple relationships—familial, economic, social, organizational, religious, and political" that bind sites of origin and destination (Basch, Glick Schiller, and Szanton Blanc 1994, 7). The focus of most literature on transnational migration has been on those who cross borders from one sovereign state to another (e.g., Basch, Glick Schiller, and Szanton Blanc 1994; Glick Schiller, Basch, and Blanc-Szanton 1992; Smith and Guarnizo 1998; Levitt 2001; and many others). It is stressed that "Transnationalism is a process by which migrants, through their daily life activities and social, economic, and political relations create social fields that cross national boundaries (Basch, Glick Schiller, and Szanton Blanc 1994, 22). Transnational migration has been viewed as "one of the constitutive processes of globalization today" (Sassen 1998, xxi). Portes (2000, 254) argues that one of the working-class responses to globalization has been transnational migration: what "common people have done" is "to create communities that sit astride political borders that in a very real sense are 'neither here nor there' but in both places simultaneously."

More recently there has been a theorizing of "border zones" that argues that these may exist within nations, at a "subnational" level (Sassen 2005, 523; see also Sassen, 2000). Part and parcel of processes of globalization these interior border zones are created though "legislative acts, court rulings, executive orders, policy" that permit the penetration of global capital into local spaces within the nation" (Sassen 2005, 526). Tourism development policies in Mexico, with the creation of entities such as FONATUR designed to develop tourism infrastructure often hand in hand with foreign capital, as well as other policies that permitted funding of tourist projects by international lending institutions and promoted investment by multinational hotel and restaurant chains, can be seen as indexes of the appearance of the global in subnational spaces. These nodes and zones of capitalist accumulation that tourist centers come to represent can be seen as constructing a kind of internal border zone separating less-developed regions of the nation from the more developed (except in the case of the squatter settlements and other colonias where the poor reside) tourist centers.[2] As Robinson (2008, 44, 203 passim) has pointed out, zones of accumulation can exist in the old core or in the old periphery: the global reserve army of labor may migrate to these nodes either internally or internationally.

Writing on the theme of internal migration to tourist centers, Torres and Momsen (2005, 378) argue that, "The concentration of capital in Cancún as a center of tourism production has served as a catalyst for the rural-to-urban exodus of impoverished populations in search of improved income earning opportunities." They propose that tourist centers in general "may be conceived as transnational spaces" where affluent international tourists are serviced by a local labor force composed primarily of rural-to-urban migrants (Torres and Momsen 2005, 321). Tourist centers are transnational in the traditional sense because of the constant circulation of tourists, some of whom arrive in a circular migration pattern to occupy time-shares for a week or two annually, and some of whom settle out and buy condominiums or houses that they occupy permanently or seasonally (Torres and Momsen 2006, 65). They also include expatriate professionals and entrepreneurs who service the tourist industry and the expatriate community (Torres and Momsen 2006, 64). But the tourist centers are also transnational in the sense that internal migrants from rural ranchos and pueblos arrive to engage in various types of employment that bring them into contact with tourists and expatriates and cross cultural, ethnic, and linguistic borders to do so. Tourists, expatriates, and internal migrants are crossing into a hybrid cultural space. As an approximation of the degree of hybridity and thus the transnational character of the tourist centers, it has been found that in 1995 there were 5.34 foreign tourists per resident population in Cancún, 0.55 in Acapulco, 2.4 in Puerto Vallarta, and 5.5 in Los Cabos (derived from Propin Frejomil and Sánchez Críspin 2002, table I). Clearly, the influence of foreign, mainly American, tourists in Cabo San Lucas, as in Cancún, is very high, whereas in Acapulco, where there are proportionally more national tourists, it is relatively low.

It has been held that a transnational social field exists when multistranded social relationships link people who are "exposed to a set of social expectations, cultural values, and patterns of human interactions shaped by more than one social, economic, and political system (Glick Schiller 2003, 107–8). Tourist centers have social and economic dynamics that differ markedly from the rural ranchos and pueblos from where most of the beach vendors come. They are also politically different, as state and local governments must shape policies concerning tourist development and in some cases policies on licensing, taxation, and use of space as concerns the beach vendors themselves. Tourist centers are essentially subnational nodes of accumulation, or as Appaduri (1990) would have it, deterritorialized spaces.[3] Because of the presence of numerous foreign visitors and expatriates and services directed to attracting them and enhancing their stays, in-migrants can be seen as transmigrants entering "zones of accumulation in the global economy" (Robinson 2008, 203).

Transnational Social Space and the Beach Vendors

The importance of learning English for their work with tourists, as has been seen earlier, has been stressed by slightly over one-fifth of the beach vendors. The desire to learn English to help them with their work shows that the tourist centers are hybrid spaces requiring more than knowledge of the national language in order to earn a livelihood. The fact that the overwhelming majority of beach vendors speak at least a little English, often phrased as "enough to make sales," attests to this hybridity as well. It also shows than an internal boundary of subnational social space in which a second or third language is needed for economic success, unlike the linguistic situation in their regions of origin. Many vendors also report that one of the things they best like about their work is interacting with tourists. A large number return occasionally to their places of birth, and others are involved in an annual seasonal and circular migration between their hometowns and the tourist centers.

Interacting with tourists

Thirty-six of the vendors (21.7 percent), including nine women and 27 men, mentioned getting to know and/or interacting with tourists as one of the most positive aspects of their work. Those who responded to this effect included 12 of the 51 vendors interviewed in Puerto Vallarta (23.5 percent), 14 of 55 of the Acapulco vendors (25.4 percent), and 10 of the 60 Cabo San Lucas vendors (16.7 percent). In Cabo San Lucas, 35-year-old Juan Carlos (CSL-7), who was born in Acapulco, is very content to be a vendor because he can converse with the tourists, some of whom, he says, return annually and seek him out. Matias (ACA-10IC), a 63-year-old widower from Valle de Galeano, Guerrero, enjoys his work as a commission seller of sodas, beer, and food on Icacos Beach in Acapulco, because of the conversations he has with his tourist-clients. He often came to talk to me between interviews each day I came to the beach and often tried to recruit vendors who were passing by for me to interview. Maribel (ACA-2PD), born in Acapulco and interviewed on Playa Diamante, likes her job as a vendor because she can interact with the foreign and Mexican tourists with whom she says she sometimes makes friends. Jorge (PV-24), born in San Pedrito, Michoacán, and interviewed in Puerto Vallarta says the thing he likes most about vending is "the people, you learn much from them, about where they are from" ("*la gente, aprendes mucho de ellos, de donde son*"). Socorro (PV-24), a 54-year-old vendor born in the Federal District and interviewed in Puerto Vallarta, likes being a vendor because she can meet people, including tourists and other vendors. Women's place in México has ideally been in the home, where opportunities to meet others was severely restricted.

There are vendors, however, who object to their treatment by the tourists. For example, Sylvestre (PV-3), born in Toluca, state of México, and interviewed in Puerto Vallarta notes that "There are people that do not talk to you in a nice way, they only say 'no, go away, go away' instead of saying 'no thanks'" ("*Hay gente que no te hablan bien, no más dicen 'no, véte, véte' en vez de decir 'no, gracías'*"). He adds, however, that while there are people who are very rude, there are also people who are very nice and very friendly, too" ("*Hay gente muy grosero pero hay gente muy buena, muy amable también*"). Omar (PV-23), born in Arandas, Jalisco, and interviewed in Puerto Vallarta, mentions that one thing negative about being a vendor is "when there are very aggressive people, who are bothered that we approach" ("*cuando hay gente muy agresivos, que se molesta que arrimamos*").

The desire to know and interact with tourists represents what has been identified as the tourists' embodiment of "soft power" (Merrill 2009). Soft power has been defined by Nye (2004, x) as the ability for a country to get what it wants through attraction of others to its values, ideals, culture, and politics. The concept has been adapted to the understanding of the influence of tourists in receiving areas. Merrill (2009) argues that tourists come to represent a portion of the soft power of the sending country, a soft power that engages the cultural other, and spreads U.S. cultural and normative practices throughout the tourist destinations. But this is not merely "cultural imposition": the "transnational discourses" that result from tourism tend to generate "difficult-to-predict combinations of cultural clash, cultural negotiation, and hybridization" (Merrill 2009, 13). Merrill (2009, 15 passim) thinks of tourist centers not in terms of borderzones, but in terms of "cultural contact zones," which may very well be, in terms of transnationalism, part of the same thing. He underscores the fact that, on the one hand, although some tourists act as "goodwill ambassadors" (see also Berger 2010), thus extending the soft power of the United States, others do not respect or wish to enter in negotiations with other cultures (Merrill 2009, 12–13). On the other hand, he stresses that the local population "possess their own soft power and no less than tourists seek to make tourism work in their interest" (Merrill 2009, 16). The learning of English and finding positive interactions with tourists can be seen as part of the outreach of the local population of vendors to tourists, and thus part of their soft power.

It is difficult to predict in which way cultural negotiations will go. I have lived in Mexico since 1988 and have become aware of the conservative sexual morality in many places in México. Thus, I was somewhat ashamed at some of the behavior I saw in mixed groups on the beach. When I was talking to a vendor born in Mazatlán whom I formally interviewed and conversed with a number of times on Medano Beach, I mentioned that it was a bit embarrassing how a rowdy bunch of drunken college-age tourists were behaving. Adrián (CSL-14P) immediately defended them, saying essentially that young people often behaved that way and soon they would have responsibilities that would not let them do so. Although 32 and married, Adrián seemed to empathize with these young people (in a way that perhaps their parents would not). It is impossible to predict whether such normative values as displayed by tourists will be adopted or disparaged by the vendors or by others in the local population.[4] Wearing bikini tops and shorts on the downtown streets was introduced by tourists and has been adopted by some of the Mexican women who live in Cabo San Lucas, for example, while even wearing less than shorts and T-shirt to go swimming or even wearing a sleeveless blouse on the street is looked upon with disfavor in the interior regions of the country from which most of the vendors come.

Tourist centers are evident as transnational social spaces, as border zones, and as cultural contact zones in some of the vendors' desire to learn English to help them with their work and others vendors' enjoyment at conversing and interacting with the foreign tourists. These often foreign-dominated centers are linked in space to the hometowns where many of the vendors continue to maintain dense familial and friendship relationships.

Ties with the Hometown

Several of the beach vendors, especially those who work in Acapulco, are engaged in a circular migration, which, as previously seen, was once common in work-seeking behavior among those who migrated across international borders. The cases of Palano and David, given in the chapter on the family legacy of beach vendors and the case of Manuel given in the chapter on indigenous vendors, illustrate this pattern. Several vendors in Acapulco mentioned that it was a common pattern for some vendors who were campesinos to come to Acapulco during the agricultural low seasons, which coincide with the tourist high seasons. The case given below is another illustration of this pattern.

Case 4.1

Cipriano (ACA-13IC) is a 57-year-old married vendor from Tlamacazapa, Guerrero. He speaks Nahuatl and Spanish. His father was a campesino who cultivated unowned lands in the surrounding mountains, a practice that Cipriano says many people from Tlamacazapa engage in. He formerly also cultivated unowned lands with corn and beans but says he has recently stopped doing so because he does not have sufficient income to pay for the fertilizer or to hire the workers necessary to clear the land. Cipriano comes to Acapulco primarily during the high tourist seasons and rents a room for 400 pesos plus electrical and water expenses. His two brothers continue to cultivate unowned lands in the mountains, and his only sister makes and sells woven palm-leaf handbags in Tlamacazapa. That is the merchandise Cipriano also sells, though he buys the handbags from wholesalers in Acapulco. Cipriano says he is very happy in Acapulco because it never gets as cold there as it does in Tlamacazapa. He is less content with his work as a vendor because, he says, sometimes he sells nothing and cannot even buy a soda. He says there is much competition now because the economic crisis has had an effect everywhere ("*la crisis está por dondequiera*"). All three of his living offspring have migrated from Tlamacazapa. His only son, age 36, works on commission at a stall in Cancún and weaves name bracelets. His 21-year-old daughter sells T-shirts and shorts on the beach in Acapulco. His 26-year-old daughter, who is a housewife, lives in Morelia, Michoacán.

Notably, it is relatively cheap and easy for those from Guerrero to migrate seasonally to Acapulco, though a vendor in Puerto Vallarta also did so. Cipriano, in explaining why competition has increased, noted that it cost only 200 pesos (less than US $20) to take a bus from Tlamacazapa to Acapulco. Most vendors will earn this back on a good day.

Many beach vendors in all three tourist centers make it a point to return to their villages of origin as much as they can afford to do so. Noé (PV-21), a 35-year-old married vendor from Toluca, state of México, returns to his hometown every six months or so, taking a 12-hour-long bus ride. He has been in Puerto Vallarta for nine years. He lives in his parents' home in that city. Noé sells sunglasses that he buys in the Federal District, where he stops on his return trip from Toluca. Estebán (PV-3), also from Toluca, visits his place of origin every year. He has lived in Puerto Vallarta for 15 years. Sebastian (PV-T6), from the same small city, says he tried to go back every two weeks or so, primarily to visit relatives. He has also been in Puerto Vallarta for 15 years, and has owned his own house there for eight. He has been a vendor for 25 years, previously in Mazatlán and in Acapulco, for five years each place.

The expense of the journey can keep some vendors from returning to their places of origin as much as they might wish. Gilberto (PV-8) says he cannot contemplate returning to his small town in Guerrero from Puerto Vallarta because the round trip costs 3,000 pesos (a little less than US $300). He used to come and go for a period of 10 years but settled permanently in Puerto Vallarta in 2001. A number of vendors from Guerrero who work in Puerto Vallarta complained about not having enough money to return to visit their hometowns.

Nonetheless, there are places of origin that vendors in Puerto Vallarta return to annually. For example, eight of the nine female vendors interviewed there from Analco, Guerrero, return to their hometown every March or April (depending on the month in which Easter falls) for the Festival of the Resurrection. They say Analco is not too far away. The one woman who does not return annually says it is because she has young children in school. It is much more difficult to return to one's hometown on the mainland from the peninsula of Baja California. Thus, most vendors from San Juan Tetelcingo, Guerrero, who worked in Cabo San Lucas had not returned to their villages of origin for periods ranging from two to five years, despite there being a Festival of the Resurrection that attracts vendors from there who work closer by.

In any case, for many vendors there are multistranded connections with their villages of origin, where parents, siblings, relatives, ritual kin (*compadres*) and friends may still reside or at least be copresent during annual festivals. These vendors can be conceived of as living in a transnational, and trans-ethnic, social space. For others, the migration is more permanent, and most married vendors have one or more children born in the tourist centers where they ply their trade.

Conclusion

Processes of globalization have marginalized peasants and contributed to the growing population of beach vendors, among others engaged in informal income-generating activities. Yet, the beach vendors are exercising agency in the face of these processes of globalization by seeking out spaces to pursue their trade. If competition becomes too great in one place, many will move on. The vast majority have learned enough English to make a sale to American and Canadian tourists. Many continue to have strong links with their villages of origin, whereas others have migrated in a more permanent fashion and have few return visits to their hometowns. Economic recession has impacted their welfare in three ways: increasing competition as more and more people arrive to vend on the beach; lower numbers of tourists; and lesser spending power of those tourists who do come. All three impacts have driven down prices of their merchandise and the volume of their sales. Meanwhile, however, they continue to sell their wares in what can be considered hybrid transnational social spaces.

It is difficult to assess whether this subsector of the informal or semi-informal economy is pro-cyclical, expanding when the formal economy does, or countercyclical, expanding when the formal economy contracts. In some aspects it is pro-cyclical: as tourism, with its infrastructure of beachfront hotels expands, more unemployed people will envision the opportunity to vend on the beach. This is especially true if they have relatives or other network members who are vendors. In other aspects it is countercyclical, as in the case of former construction workers who, when the economic recession caused building projects to be shelved, turned to beach vending. It can also be considered countercyclical if peasant farming is taken into account. As more peasants are dispossessed or marginalized (i.e., as the peasant economy contracts), a more numerous labor force seeks work where it can find it.

Notably, without tourism, "the largest service industry in the world" (Clancy 1998, 128), there would be no beach vendors. This has two meanings. First, on the supply side, the marginalization of peasants and other workers has led to an inflow of people seeking a livelihood. Among their options are to vend on the beach, an option only in tourist centers. Second, on the demand side, if there were no tourists to sell to, there would be no possibilities for taking part in this form of informal or semi-informal self-employment. Their interface with the international tourists composes a transnational social space, which vendors enter to work and leave to go back to their villages of origin, whether in a circular pattern or for occasional visits during holidays.

Notes

1. Carte, McWatters, Daley, and Torres (2010) show how local perceptions of global processes affect the rural to urban migration to tourist centers of the Mayan

peasants of the Yucatan Penninsula. They explore how neoliberal economic restructuring with its negative effects on agricultural livelihoods and its promotion of tourism development has led these peasants to *perceive* their opportunities for gaining a livelihood. Perceptions of decline in the viability of agricultural pursuits occurred since the implementation of neoliberal reforms such as the modification of Article 27 of the 1917 Mexican Constitution that led to the privatization of ejido parcels and the implementation of NAFTA, which led to undercutting the subsidies and price supports for local produce, especially corn. Perceptions of better opportunities for income-generating activities in the tourist poles such as Cancún led many peasants to migrate there in search of employment, whether formal or informal. The importance of Carte, McWatters, Daley, and Torres's study, and its relevance to the present chapter is that global economic processes affect local spaces and that local perceptions of these processes lead people to change their behavior.

2. Little (2004, 36 passim), adopting the concept from Bruner (1996, 1999), envisions the marketplace in Antigua, Guatemala, as a kind of "touristic border zone" where indigenous Maya and national and international tourists meet and interact, and thus represents a space in which the global and the local interact in complex ways.

3. Appadurai (1996, 193) conceived of tourist locations as "translocalities" that though located within a particular nation-state were produced and reproduced through the activities of "various types of circulating populations with kinds of locals." The idea of cities as translocalities was adopted and developed by Michael Peter Smith (2001) partially in reaction to theories of globalization that held homogenization was the outcome of global economic processes. Although Smith's contention that every city will represent a unique formation of transnational processes both from above and from below (see Smith and Guarnizo 1998), I still prefer the term transnational social spaces as concerns tourist centers because of the contact between various "circulating populations" from within and without Mexico.

4. Merrill (2009, 254) underscores the variability in tourist-host interactions: "U.S. citizens might behave as cultural unilateralists hell-bent on possessing and dominating the Latin other or as cultural multilateralists, willing to respect, negotiate, and exchange cultural differences. Latin Americans, elites and commoners, might indiscriminately accept North American norms and bow to North American demands. Or they might resist, negotiate, and contain influences while simultaneously forging and expressing their own cultural identities."

5

De Facto Residential Apartheid

Casa Kai, Pedregal. Majestically situated on a cliffside, directly above the Pacific Ocean, Casa Kai is a custom designed 5 level masterpiece. 2 full swimming pools, 3 waterfalls, 6 bedrooms, 7+2 half baths, media room, custom designed furniture, state of the art Italian kitchen, custom glowing Onyx bar. Eco-friendly elements include solar power, SMART technology, new growth wood and organic materials. A work of art. Asking: $10,900,000 USD

—Tokase Properties, *Los Cabos Real Estate*, Winter 2011

Casa las Olas-Palmilla. Oceanfront. This fully furnished casual oceanfront estate is located in the prestigious community of Caleta, Palmilla. With 6,800 A!C sq. ft. this spacious bi-level estate features 4 expansive suites and oversized baths. The home is perched on a cliff featuring an infinity edge pool cascading down to a larger pool located on the lower level. Includes a fully-appointed gourmet kitchen, and a dining area that comfortably seats 8-10. Offered at $7,300,000

—Snell Real Estate, *Los Cabos Real Estate*, Winter 2011

Villa 34. Amazing villa, worthy of the Architectural Digest cover, and the home to a world class art collection with statues and sculptures from all over the world. The main house has 2 large master suites and a separate 4th bedroom or maids quarters in the casita. Lots of outdoor entertaining space with a rooftop dining area. All the bells and whistles that would impress your Celebrity/Hollywood clientele! Must see to believe! $3,700,000 USD

—Coastal Properties of Los Cabos,
Los Cabos Real Estate, Spring/Summer 2011

Casa Verde, Pedregal. Nested on the hills of Pedregal de Cabo San Lucas, Casa Verde offers breathtaking Pacific view and the sound of waves. Two swimming pools, Jacuzzi, palapa, fire pit, water features, outdoor BBQ, 2 living areas, game room, caretakers quarters, 5 deluxe suits and 6 and a half bathrooms. Marble floors, granite countertops, A/C throughout the Villa are some of the characteristic [sic] *of this Cabo home. Perfect to entertain guests and family. Offered at $2,900,000 USD*

—Coldwell Banker, *Los Cabos Real Estate*, Spring/Summer 2011

Villa de Amanacer-Palmilla. Ocean & golf view. This home is located on the Ocean Hole of Palmilla's Jack Nicklaus signature course within the gated community of Palmilla Norte. Property is approximately 1/3 acre with room for a casita/5th bedroom. This 4 BR, 4 BA two level boasts 2 master suites, one on each level. Both suites overlook Palmilla Bay. Offered at $1,900,000.

—Snell Real Estate, *Los Cabos Real Estate*, Spring/Summer 2011

These are some of the properties listed in the 2011 editions of *Los Cabos Real Estate*, a glossy, photograph-filled magazine aimed at English-speakers that advertises properties in the municipio of Los Cabos. Most homes advertised in this widely available and free magazine range between US $1 million and US $5 million, though there are houses for as low as $299,000 and for more than US $10 million. Houses are selling for less than they did in 2008, prior to the world economic recession. The excerpts are about houses located in Pedregal (Cabo San Lucas) and Palmilla (San José del Cabo)—two of the most expensive neighborhoods in the *municipio* of Los Cabos. Even houses as low as US $299,000 are far beyond the reach of the beach vendors, however. They tend to find housing on invaded lands, some still unregularized, as is the case of most house lots in El Caribe and Arenal, others on lands that once belonged to ejidos and were negotiated for settlement with the ejidatarios, as in the case of Los Cangrejos, Lomas del Sol, and Mesa Colorada (*Dirección Municipal de Transparencia* 2011*a*). In the unregulated *colonias* (named neighborhoods) or irregular settlements there are initially no electrical or running water services, and people have no titles to the lots they live on. Over time they may be "regularized" by the state or local government, and for a price titles extended and services provided. It has been observed that "The deficiencies in infrastructure and services (houses without piped water, floors and roofs constructed of inadequate materials) are even more marked in the big tourist centers than in Mexico's largest cities, such as Mexico City, Guadalajara, and Monterrey, where they are known to be quite serious" (Brenner and Aguilar 2002, 515).

Notably, in 2010, of a total of 66,588 habitations in the municipio of Los Cabos, 6.7 percent did not have electricity, 21.6 percent had no running water, and 12.8 percent had houses with dirt floors. In the same year in the municipio of Acapulco de Juárez, of a total of 205,485 habitations, about 2 percent (1.97) did not have electricity, 25.2 percent had no running water, and 12.9 percent had houses with dirt floors. The statistics for Puerto Vallarta are as follows: of 68,677 habitations, 3.6 percent had no electricity, 7.5 percent had no running water, and 12.9 percent were houses with dirt floors (derived from INEGI 2011*a*). It appears from these statistics that on some indexes Puerto Vallarta, with a more diversified economy, is more consolidated than Los Cabos or Acapulco. Electricity is the first service extended in new colonias, and the relatively high percentage of residences without electricity in Los Cabos shows the newness of many of its settlements, whether established by invasion or recently divided into lots on ejido lands. The high percentage of homes with only dirt floors is an index of provisional, unconsolidated usually self-built housing.

In this chapter we will first look at the residential apartheid that exists in the three tourist centers of Cabo San Lucas and Puerto Vallarta, with some reference to Acapulco. Then, we will review the expropriation and illegal invasion of ejido lands in Acapulco. Finally, we will explore the origins and conditions of three of the colonias where the beach vendors live in Cabo San Lucas. It must be kept in mind that there is a wide diversity in the economic and residential situation of U.S. migrants to heterogeneous tourist destinations in Mexico. Schafran and Monkkonen (2011), for example, divide the communities in which migrants, whether snowbirds, retirees, or younger migrants, live into four types. In some cases migrants from the U.S. live in the heart of the city, or alternatively, in gated communities on the periphery. Both these patterns are found in Puerto Vallarta (Schafran and Monkkonen 2011, 241). Living in the heart of the city ensures integration with the Mexican population. In Los Cabos, living in mega-resort gated compounds "likely to be almost completely removed from Mexican space" is common (Schafran and Monkkonen 2011, 242). From my stay in Los Cabos, I find that the gated community pattern may be the most usual along with ungated but quasi-segregated planned residential neighborhoods and followed by Schafran and Monkkonen's (2011, 242–43) fourth category, that of residence in RV and trailer parks. Here I will be looking primarily at the extremes, with gated communities and compounds where foreigners live contrasted with the settlements in which the poor and low-waged laborers or the (semi-)informally self-employed are found.

Socio-spatial and Economic Apartheid

In colonias such as El Caribe, Lomas del Sol, Tierra y Libertad, Los Cactus, Los Cangrejos, Arenal, and others in Cabo San Lucas, beach vendors reside with or beside construction workers, domestic servants, restaurant cooks and waiters, carpenters, mechanics, gardeners, chambermaids in tourist hotels, and other workers in low-wage formal, semiformal, and informal employment. These residential areas, lacking in one or more basic services such as electricity, running water, a sewerage system, and never blessed with paved roads, are far from the tourist zone and out of sight to tourists. They represent one aspect of what I have elsewhere called de facto "socioeconomic apartheid" (Wilson 2008). Other scholars who have examined tourist development in Los Cabos—including San José del Cabo, Cabo San Lucas, and the tourist corridor connecting them—have also noted this aspect of spatial apartheid. López-López et al. (2006, 372) remark upon the "extreme differentiation and segregation of space" in Los Cabos, underscoring the isolation of the tourist zones from the colonias populares, many of which are or began as irregular settlements established by the organized invasion of ejido lands or private property. Examining "borders within," Gámez and Ángeles (2010, 12) focus on the case of Lomas del Sol, which they call Colonia el Sol:

> Colonia el Sol may be characterized as a kind of tourism-induced Soweto. A good part of its 27,000 inhabitants work for, but do not have access to, some of the most exclusive and expensive resorts in the world, or labor directly or indirectly to sustain and maintain them and the new tourist-oriented residential complexes. Many of these workers come from the poorer states of Mexico's south, like Oaxaca, Guerrero, and Chiapas, and do jobs that BCS [Baja California Sur] natives and many middle class immigrants disdain, such as construction work and the lower-end occupations of the "hospitality industry."

The proliferation of irregular settlements and of working class colonias on expropriated ejido lands that are segregated from golf courses, luxury hotels and resorts, and expatriate residential areas has been noted for a wide variety of Mexican tourist centers, including not only Los Cabos, but also Cancún, Huatulco, Ixtapa-Zihuatenejo, Rosarito, Manzanillo, Cozumel, Puerto Peñasco, Acapulco and Puerto Vallarta (Brenner and Aguilar 2002; Bringas Rábano 1999; Enriquez Acosta 2008; González Romero et al. 2008; Guilette 2007; Pérez-Campuzano 2010; Torres and Momsen 2005).

Defining this de facto apartheid as "socio-spatial segregation," Pérez-Campuzano (2010, 171) underscores the fact that unskilled workers live in marginal housing in the peripheral areas of Puerto Vallarta. The infrastructure there is sorely lacking as compared to that in the city center where more highly qualified workers live in more consolidated housing. In both cases, however, living conditions pale beside the luxury of tourist hotels and condominiums and second homes owned by expatriates and wealthy Mexicans (González Romero, Pérez-Bourzac, and Rivera Borrayo 2008, 33). González Romero,

Pérez-Bourzac, and Rivera Borrayo (2008, 3–31, 33) examine the real estate speculation in Puerto Vallarta that has pushed the prices of land so high that the local population—unable to afford such prices—is forced to establish irregular settlements in order to procure a living space.[1] Such real estate speculation also exists in Los Cabos, as can be divined from the advertisements in *Los Cabos Real Estate* presented at the beginning of this chapter; it has also been part of the historical development of Acapulco (Gomezjara 1979, chap. 10). The competition for land between rural to urban migrants attracted to the tourist growth poles, on the one hand, and tourism enterprise developers in search of profits along with expatriates and wealthy Mexicans seeking second homes on the other hand, has fueled this socio-spatial segregation.

This spatial segregation is also apparent in Acapulco where unserviced colonias have grown up beneath the hills surround the city (Bringas Rábago 1999, 22), far from the luxury hotels marking the tourist zones of Acapulco Dorado and Acapulco Diamante. Bringas Rábano (1999, 42) calls these Acapulco colonias "belts of misery" ("*los cinturones de misería*"). As in Los Cabos and Puerto Vallarta, beach vendors in Acapulco live in the colonias that form these belts.

Acapulco: The Expropriation of Ejido Lands

There is more documentation about the expropriation of ejido lands in Acapulco in the interests of tourist development than for any other tourist center. Chapters in Francisco A. Gomezjara's (1979) *Bonapartismo y Lucha Campesina en la Costa Grande de Guerrero* and María Teresa Vázquez Castillo's (2004) *Land Privatization in Mexico: Urbanization, Formation of Regions and Globalization in Ejidos* explore this phenomenon in depth. Gomezjara (1979) shows that ejido lands were taken over at the instance of federal, state, or municipal governments for two principal reasons: on the coastal areas for tourism development projects such as golf courses and hotels, and in the interior to provide housing for rural-to-urban migrants, many of whom played (and play) a large role in the construction of maintenance of the tourist economy. Thus Acapulco Tradicional with its Caleta and Caletilla Beaches, Acapulco Dorado with its Icacos Beach, and Acapulco Diamante with its Playa Diamante were all built on expropriated ejido (communally owned and often individually tenured) lands. In 1932, indigenous lands were expropriated to form part of Acapulco Tradicional, and in 1945 there were more expropriations encompassing Caleta and Caletilla Beaches. In 1940, the lands of the Icacos ejido were expropriated and privatized. In 1980 lands of several ejidos were appropriated in the interests of developing Acapulco Diamante (Vásquez Castillo 2004, 129).

Ejido lands in Acapulco and its surroundings were also expropriated in league with local political parties such as the *Partido Socialista de los Trabajadores* (Socialist Worker's Party), local municipal officials, and even state and federal government officials to provide for in-migrants to this tourist growth pole (Gomezjara 1979, 206–28). Government officials also took advantage of these new settlements to acquire properties for themselves. The in-migrants would provide the low-wage labor force to service the tourist industry as construction workers, chambermaids, hotel and restaurant cooks and waiters or waitresses, bartenders, and vendors of tourist souvenirs, some ambulant, some in fixed stalls, some on the beach; and also, as Gomezjara (1979, 238–41) underscores, as male and female prostitutes.

The expropriation of ejido lands in Acapulco tended to be violent: often the army was called in to dislodge the ejidatarios; their houses were often burned to the ground; they were beaten, jailed, and otherwise mistreated; and many received no compensation despite official promises that they would (Gomezjara 1979, chap. 10; see also Vásquez Castillo 2004). In other cases, after land invasions ejidatarios petitioned the government to regularize the settlement so that they could receive some sort of income for their lands–income derived from selling lots to the invaders (Vásquez Castillo 2004, 64–65).

In a third scenario, land was neither expropriated by the government for tourist development and human settlement nor invaded by homeless, but sold illegally. Prior to the 1992 amendment to the Mexican Constitution permitting the sale of ejido lands, ejidatarios illegally sold house lots to the incoming migrants and the local poor (Vásquez Castillo 2004, 135–36). In all three cases, as Vásquez Castillo (2004, 45) underscores, " . . . the conversion of *ejido* lands to urban use provided affordable land to low-income groups in urban areas. Most of the population were landless Indians and poor *Mestizos* who had been displaced from their rural lands and migrated to cities, but once there could only afford land on the urban periphery." The pattern of land invasions, whether of ejido, federal, or private property, has occurred on the peripheries of numerous cities in Mexico, including, for example, Mexico City and Mexicali (e.g., Vélez-Ibañez 1983; Wilson 1992), and also on the peripheries of its tourist centers.

Ciudad Renacimiento, Acapulco

In Acapulco the beach vendors interviewed live in a large number of colonias, with clusters in only two. Four men live in Colonia Emilio Zapata and five men and six women in Ciudad Renacimiento. Most of those living in Ciudad Renacimiento had been born in Acapulco (five women and two men), or had migrated to that tourist center 30 or more years previously (three men).

Ciudad Renacimiento was established in 1980 on 763 hectares of ejido lands by FIDEACA (*Fidecomiso para el Desarrollo Económico y Social de Acapulco*, Trust for the Economic and Social Development of Acapulco), which had been created in 1975 partially in the interests of relocating marginalized populations living on the hillsides around the city (*Sur Acapulco* 2006). The aim was to provide a poor population of approximately 100,000 people with basic services such as electricity and running water—services that could not be provided on the rough terrains that they had invaded and where they previously lived (Noreña Ramirez and Romero Hernández 2009).

If one googles "Ciudad Renacimiento Acapulco," most of the articles that come up are about violence committed there: shootings, decapitations, and kidnappings, some as recent as July 2011. Following in number are advertisements for the sale of houses, which range from US$20,000 to $60,000. Four factors explain the presence of this relatively high-priced housing: 1) cheaper houses and those that are not handled by a real estate agency do not appear on Internet; 2) Ciudad Renacimiento was established 30 years ago, and as is true in most colonias populated by the poor, original unconsolidated housing has become highly upgraded over time by some of the residents; 3) the inflationary land prices in Acapulco have affected even the colonias established for the poor; and 4) as the colonia evolved, more middle-class people sought properties there. The high number of houses for sale may show the desire of people to remove themselves from the violence that affects this settlement.

Below are some snapshot summaries of vendors who live in Ciudad Renacimiento. All worked on Icacos Beach and reported that the settlement was about an hour away from there by bus.

Elizabeth (ACA-9IC) is a 31-year-old married woman born in Acapulco to parents born in Ahuacatitlán, Guerrero. Both her father and mother are beach vendors. She says she has been a vendor for 28 years. She lives with her husband in her parents' house in Ciudad Renacimiento. She sells saris and bathing suits.

Silvia (ACA-10IC) is a 24-year old single vendor born in Acapulco to parents born in Acapulco. She has been a vendor for four years. Her father has a fixed stall in one of the Acapulco markets from which he sells bathing suits, saris, and sundresses. She lives with her parents in their house. She sells semiprecious stone necklaces that she assembles.

Bettí (ACA-15IC), age 26, was born in Acapulco to parents born in Acapulco. She has been a beach vendor for 10 years. Her father is a beach vendor. She lives with her common-law husband in her parents' house in Ciudad Renacimiento. She sells necklaces she assembles from semiprecious stones, pearls, and shells.

Irma (ACA-21IC), is a 25-year-old vendor born in Copanatoyac, Tlapa, Guerrero, where her father was also born. Her mother was born in Acapulco. Her mother is an ambulant street vendor. Irma has been a beach vendor for two years. She lives with her common-law husband in a room they rent in Ciudad Renacimiento for 600 pesos a month. She sells sand buckets, rubber balls, and life jackets for children.

Monica (ACA-23IC), a single mother aged 37, was born in Acapulco to parents born in Acapulco, both of whom were beach vendors. She has owned her own house in Ciudad Renacimiento for 15 years. She sells coconut tanning oil.

Martha (ACA-24IC), a 29-year-old single mother born in Acapulco to parents born in Acapulco, lives with her parents in their house in Ciudad Renacimiento. Both of her parents are beach vendors. She has been a vendor for 22 years, since she was seven years old. She sells shell necklaces, bathing suits, and coconut tanning oil, among other wares.

Leonardo (ACA-7IC), married and age 31, was born in Acapulco to parents born in Telohuapan, Guerrero. He has been a beach vendor for 20 years. Both his father and mother are beach vendors. He rents a room in Ciudad Renacimiento for 700 pesos a month. His parents have a house there. He sells silver jewelry from Taxco.

Joel (ACA-8IC) age 17 and single, was born in Acapulco to parents born in Iguala, Guerrero. He has been a vendor since he was eight years old. Both of his parents are beach vendors. He lives in their house in Ciudad Renacimiento. He sells silver jewelry from Taxco.

Matias (ACA-10IC), age 63 and widowed, arrived in Acapulco when he was 10 years old. He and his parents were born in Valle de Galeano, Guerrero. His father was an ejidatario there. Matias has been a vendor for 17 years, and previously repaired wrecked cars. He has owned his own house in Ciudad Renacimiento for 30 years—since the time the colonia was established. He is a commission seller of sodas, beer, and food.

Lázaro (ACA-12IC), aged 70 and separated, migrated to Acapulco 40 years ago. He has been a vendor for 35 years and previously worked as a stevedore. His father was an ejidatario in San Domigo Armento, Oaxaca, where Lázaro and his parents were born. He has owned a house in Ciudad Renacimiento for 20 years. He sells sunglasses in the summer, serapes and T-shirts in the winter.

Hugo (ACA-28IC), married and age 60, has lived in Acapulco for 30 years and has been a vendor for 25. Previously he worked as a helper putting in air conditioning and in construction. His father was an ejidatario en San Marcos, Guerrero, where Hugo and his parents were born. He has owned his own house in Ciudad Renacimiento for 17 years. He sells silver jewelry and rosaries.

The Colonias of Cabo San Lucas

Water is a scarce resource in the arid desert environment of Los Cabos. It has been noted that, "While the locals are forced to store water in containers for domestic use, in residential neighborhoods [such as those where expatriates and better-off Mexicans live] they have pools and large gardens with a disproportionate use of water . . ." (Lizárraga Morales 2010, 88). Although some of the *colonias* where the beach vendors live have water services available, in El Caribe, Tierra y Libertad and Arenal, water in 2011 was only available by a fee paid to the driver of a circulating water truck. The provision of piped water thus has some aspects of apartheid: the rich have it, the poor often do not.

Most of the colonias where the beach vendors interviewed in Cabo San Lucas live were once ejido lands. All of those established on ejido lands were formed after changes in the Agrarian Reform Law that permitted their sale. In some cases, a political party—whether associated with the municipal government or not—negotiated with the ejidatarios to sell their land to the new settlers. This is the case with Los Cangrejos. In other cases the lands were invaded, and with governmental intervention, arrangements were made for the settlers to pay back the ejidatarios. In a few cases much of the land has been invaded and still not regularized. In El Arenal and Tierra y Libertad invaders occupy all lots. In El Caribe, some ejidatarios had already sold plots of land to people who settled there beginning in 2000; most lots were invaded after 2006, however, and still have not been regularized. This means that no electrical or running water services can be contracted for. Nonetheless, in 2011 the Federal Electricity Commission (*Comisión Federal de Electricidad*) offered to extend electrical services to unserviced colonias if the residents paid 50 percent of the costs of installation (González S., 2011). Power lines are often pirated, however, and the driver of a circulating water truck deposits water—for a fee— in barrels placed in front of houses. Below are some sketches of three of the colonias where beach vendors live.

El Caribe

In the relatively new invasion, El Caribe, the ejidatarios had previously sold off 10 x 20 meter lots to private owners, and these lots were subsequently titled. Squatters, however, occupied most of the unoccupied lots in an invasion that took place in 2006. The result has been that on any one block, there may be titled lots beside invaded lots, and houses with electrical service beside houses without. Eighteen of the beach vendors interviewed live in this colonia. A description of the colonia from my May 2011 field notes, when I visited Erica (CSL-30P) and Héctor (CSL-15P) there, is given below.

"Erica and Héctor moved to El Caribe little more than 4 years ago after renting a room in Lomas del Sol *tercera etapa* (third stage) upon arriving in Los Cabos. A friend of Héctor's, from the same small town in Guerrero (an hour from Chilpancingo by bus) had taken part in the invasion. He contacted Héctor saying he should come to Los Cabos, and eventually transferred the lot to them for 2,000 pesos (about US $200 at that time). There is no electricity or running water provided by the municipio to the houses that were erected after the invasion, although the houses that were there previously have these services. Erica tells me that residents without electricity just hook up to the electric wiring, and do not have to pay a bill. A water truck circulates to put water in plastic barrels in front, but inside, of the invaded lots. Except for the humble mostly unfinished cement-block houses and the *tiendita* (small store) where I go to buy tortillas—all of which existed prior to the invasion—housing is temporary and fragile. Erica's house, for example, is one large room with a partition for the kitchen, made out of rusting corrugated metal sheets. She, Héctor, Héctor's brother (who like Héctor sells sunglasses on the beach), and Erica and Héctor´s three sons, all live there. The bathroom, to the rear of the lot, is unroofed and made of corrugated metal sheets as well. All of the sheets have small holes. There is a toilet, but it cannot be flushed without pouring a bucket of water into it. They bathe from a big blue plastic barrel of water located inside the bathroom, with plastic bowls to pour the water over themselves.

"The large room the family lives in and the kitchen have dirt floors. In El Caribe, one house was made of relatively small sheets of plywood, one of discarded tin cans pounded into small sheets and with a covering made from black plastic garbage bags. Several houses were made of discarded wood, including two with small *tiendas* (stores) run from portions of them. The few houses made of more substantial material, such as cement blocks, are one room and unfinished (i.e., not plastered). The walls and roof of Erica's house have many small holes in the rusting corrugated sheets from which they are made and I ask if it is a problem when it rains. Erica says when there is a storm everyone in the invasion must go into shelters. She and her family usually go to a school in a nearby colonia, Las Palmas, when there are hurricanes.

"There is only an elementary school in El Caribe, and is as unconsolidated and fragile as most of the housing. The roads, unpaved except for the entrance (which also boasts a traffic light), are uneven and deeply rutted. There are small stores every three blocks or so, parts of extremely fragile wooden housing. There are many trees and large cactus plants in El Caribe which lend beauty to the colonia dotted by provisional and ill-constructed houses. In most colonias, people do not invest in materials for more substantial housing until the lots are regularized, as until that time, the government may decide to remove them."

Of all the colonias I visited, El Caribe had the least-developed infrastructure, the most-fragile self-built housing, and a general lack of any type of business except for small grocery stores. This is a typical trajectory, however, and over time, housing will be consolidated and businesses opened. Meanwhile, it is the colonia that most contrasts with the expatriate neighborhoods and the tourist center hotels.

Among the vendors, beside Erica and Héctor, who live in El Caribe are the following:

Elisa (CSL-29P) is a 29-year-old married woman born in Huatletlauca, Puebla. She speaks Nahuatl. She came to Cabo San Lucas with siblings when she was 10 years old and has been a vendor since that time. She and her husband have their own house in El Caribe. She sells dresses she makes and used to also braid hair.

Carolina (CSL-31P) is a 29-year-old married woman who was born in Tecoman, Colima. She speaks Nahuatl. She migrated to Cabo San Lucas five years ago and took part in the invasion of lands in El Caribe. She has been a vendor for 15 years, previously in Puerto Vallarta. She sells dresses and saris she acquires at wholesale prices from a downtown store.

Enrique (CSL-5) is a 40-year-old married Nahuatl-speaking man from Tlamacazapa, Guerrero. He has lived in Cabo San Lucas for 12 years and has a lot with wooden house he constructed in El Caribe. Previously he lived in rental housing. He has been a vendor for 25 years, previously in the Federal District, Cuernavaca, Acapulco, and Mazatlán. He sells silver jewelry from Taxco.

Salvador (CSL-6) is a 37-year-old married Nahuatl-speaking man from San Juan Tetelcingo, Guerrero. He migrated to Cabo San Lucas 12 years prior to the interview in October 2010 and took part in the invasion of El Caribe. Previously he lived in rental housing. He sells hand-painted ceramic plates and bowls.

Los Cangrejos

Los Cangrejos consists of two stages (*dos etapas*), the first having been established in 1999 and the second in 2000, both on ejido lands. Six of the beach vendors interviewed live there. I visited the colonia in May of 2011 with a friend of mine who has lived in the second phase for the past six years. Eloisa bought her 10 x 20 meter lot for 100,000 pesos (about US $10,000). She tells me the lots originally cost 17,000 pesos but are currently selling for 200,000 pesos. A friend of Eloisa's, who has done construction work on her sister's house in the second stage of Los Cangrejos, tells me that political parties were involved in procuring the lands from ejidatarios to form the two stages of the colonia. In the end the PT (*Partido del Trabajo*, Labor Party), a left-wing political party, arranged with the ejidatarios to divide and sell the lots.

Los Cangrejos now has electrical and water services, though it did not for some years after its establishment, and running water has only been available since 2007. It has no paved roads but boasts an ample, well-built, and colorful secondary school. Most houses are semi-consolidated, constructed of cement blocks. Most also have rooms that are still under construction. A few of the houses are plastered and painted. The colonia buzzes with all kinds of business, from humble *paleteros* (ice-cream salesmen) pushing their carts on the dusty streets, to medium-sized mechanic workshops, small stores, a large *tortilleria* with at least three pickup trucks that are driven around the colonia to sell tortillas door-to-door, Eloisa tells me. Los Cangrejos boasts its own PEMEX gas station. There is also a parking lot for the small buses that connect the colonia with Soriana's (a large supermarket about three miles south) or go downtown. Three of the vendors interviewed who live in Los Cangrejos (first stage) have been living in Los Cabos for more than 20 years. The most recent arrival has been in Cabo San Lucas for five years. Those who have resided longest in the city were probably among the pioneering settlers of Los Cangrejos. Although it is a poor and working-class colonia, it has far more advanced housing for most of its residents than El Caribe. This is partially because titles to the lots are available. Once possession of a lot is assured, colonia residents begin to invest in improvements in their housing.

Among the vendors who live in Los Cangrejos are the following:

Claudia (CSL-33P) and her husband, Fortunato (CSL-16P) migrated to Los Cabos 25 years ago. They were born in the town of Ahuatitlán, Guerrero, and initially migrated to Acapulco. They own a cement-block house with a tin roof in Los Cangrejos and have lived in that colonia since its first phase was established in 1999. Both sell women's and children's sundresses that Claudia makes from Indonesian cloth. They both were previously vendors in Acapulco, though Fortunato only intermittently, as he prefers to work in construction. Of their three sons, Juan Carlos (CSL-7), age 35 and married, rents two rooms on another lot in Los Cangrejos. He sells silver jewelry from Taxco. Another son, Marcos, lives in Lomas del Sol.

Leandro (CSL-12) is a 29-year-old married Nahuatl speaker from Monte Alegre, Guerrero. He has lived in Cabo San Lucas since 1995 and presently owns a house in Los Cangrejos. Before buying a lot in that colonia he lived in rental housing. He has been a vendor for eight years, previously working in construction in Cabo San Lucas. He currently sells tablecloths, and previously sold ironwood statues.

Graciela (CSL-18P) is a 27-year-old married woman who was born in San Juan Tetelcingo, Guerrero. She moved with her parents to Cabo San Lucas 10 years prior to the January 2010 interview. She has been a vendor since arriving. She sells semiprecious stone necklaces that she assembles.

Lomas del Sol

Lomas del Sol is the oldest and most consolidated of the colonias where the beach vendors interviewed in Cabo San Lucas live, despite it being viewed as a kind of Soweto. Eleven of the beach vendors who were formally interviewed and three who were informally interviewed lived in this colonia. Erica and Héctor also began their life in Los Cabos by renting a room there. Although the Department of Transparency of San José del Cabo (personal communication 2011*b*) claimed the colonia was established in 1996 and not by invasion, when I passed through the colonia in that very same year it was populated by residents living in makeshift self-built housing. Many of its residents then worked as garbage pickers on the municipal dump that was then located beside the colonia. Lomas del Sol was established on ejido lands that were divided into 2,797 lots, and thus is one of the largest colonias in Cabo San Lucas. It consists of three stages.

In September of 2011, the face of the colonia had completely changed. It was filled with small businesses and dotted here and there with relatively luxurious housing. There is also, however, much semi-consolidated housing, with rooms made of cement blocks that had not been plastered or painted, or had some portion of them that had not. On the main road in Lomas del Sol, first stage, there were two structures offering rooms for rent. One was two stories high, with the second floor painted a turquoise green, and the first floor of unpainted cement blocks (see figure 5.2). Several of the beach vendors rent rooms or did rent rooms in Lomas del Sol.

A paved road connecting two main highways, Route 19 to Todos Santos and Leona Vicaria, traverses the first stage of Lomas del Sol. A paved road extends from the first to the third stages as well, although cross streets are still unpaved. Lomas del Sol has far more traffic than Los Cangrejos, which boasts only unpaved roads. Lomas del Sol has a number of formal businesses, including dentists' and doctors' offices—even more than Los Cangrejos with its PEMEX and tortilleria. It has a well-built secondary school (as does Los Cangrejos) just off the main road running through the colonia. It also has far more informal businesses than Los Cangrejos, with many small stores selling new and secondhand clothing and a number of places selling tacos or homemade food. Unlike the other two colonias it boasts a public library. Internet cafes dot the two main boulevards. On Saturdays there is a tianguis with about 30 semi-fixed stalls, most selling clothing. Although housing is as consolidated or more so than in Los Cangrejos, there still exist relatively unconsolidated houses, especially on the side streets. Very few, however, are of the fragile self-built construction found in El Caribe. Despite its relative well-being, the housing in the colonia, with very few exceptions, does not compare to that in gated and other named communities where well-off Mexicans and expatriates live. That many of its residents have ties to the tourism sector is shown by the mid-afternoon arrival of hotel buses, the names of the hotels inscribed on their sides, carrying employees back to their residences in Lomas del Sol.

Among the vendors who live in Lomas del Sol are the following.

Natalia (CSL-32P), a 49-year-old married Nahuatl-speaking woman was born in Temalac, Guerrero. She came to Cabo San Lucas in 1996. She has been a vendor since arriving and sells women and children's sundresses that she fashions from Indonesian cloth. She has owned a small house in Lomas del Sol for 10 years previous to the October 2010 interview.

Fernando (CSL-1P), a 26-year-old single man from San Martín, Guerrero, migrated to Cabo San Lucas only two months prior to my interview with him in October 2010. He has never been a vendor elsewhere but worked as an agricultural day laborer in his pueblo of origin. He rents a room in Lomas del Sol with a friend of his from San Martín. He sells women's and children's sundresses that he buys from a friend.

Daniel (CSL-18P), a 35-year-old man who lives in free union, migrated to Cabo San Lucas 15 years ago. Born in Tlamacazapa, Guerrero, he speaks a little Nahuatl. He lives with a woman on a lot she owns in Lomas del Sol, on which Daniel has built a small room. Daniel has also worked intermittently, when not employed in construction, as a vendor on the outskirts of the Federal District. He sells handwoven name bracelets that he makes, and leather bracelets that he buys. His only brother in Los Cabos, who sells the same wares Daniel does on the beach, lives in rental housing in Lomas del Sol.

Marcos (CSL-13P) is a 30-year-old man, born in Acapulco, Guerrero. He is separated from his common-law wife and lives alone in a corrugated tin room he erected on his lot in Lomas del Sol. He has owned the lot for eight years, and migrated to Cabo 16 years prior to the interview. His parents, Claudia and Fortunato, live in Los Cangrejos. Marcos sells silver jewelry from Taxco, as does his brother Juan Carlos.

Other Forms of Social Apartheid

Along the tourist corridor in Los Cabos, where hotels are often isolated from one another by rock formations extending out into the ocean, access by the public, and hence by the vendors, is not permitted. Often hotel guests are required to wear plastic bracelets provided by the hotel to prove they are lodged there. People who do not wear a bracelet will be immediately stopped and questioned by hotel security guards about their presence there. This also is common in hotels in Acapulco Diamante, on Medano Beach in Cabo San Lucas, and on the beach in San José del Cabo. There is public access to the beach in these three places, however.

Beach restaurants are off-limits to the vendors as well. Once while I was at a restaurant on Medano Beach a vendor I knew came over to talk to me. I invited him to sit down and have a soda. He did so only on my second invitation. Waiters were suddenly too busy to attend to us, and the restaurant security guard came over and stood less than 10 feet away. After some minutes the vendor said he had to join some friends and left. The beach restaurants in Cabo San Lucas are essentially off-limits to the vendors whether for purposes of making sales or as consumers (when in their white uniforms), though this is less the case in Acapulco and to some extent in Puerto Vallarta.

Notably, Mexican federal law guarantees public access to all beaches. Yet it has been noted for Los Cabos that in hotels like "Solmar, Finistierra, Melía Cabo Real, Westin Regina, Palmilla and Twin Dolphin . . . it is only possible to reach the beach by passing through the hotel . . . [A]lthough constitutional order declares the beaches public domains, the hotel is private property and access to it may be prohibited, especially to the local population" (López-López, Cukier, and Sánchez Crispín 1999, 10). This kind of social apartheid has been present for a long time. Writing in the late 1970s, Evans (1979, 314) points out that in Puerto Vallarta's tourist zones there are "hotel condominiums and expensive residential areas which restrict public access to the beach and appear to benefit no one but affluent nationals and foreigners." Writing of all five tourist poles developed after 1974, Bringas Rábago (1999, 10, translation mine) notes that "The services the [tourist] hotel offers are reserved only for the use of its clients and the same happens with the beaches that are in front of them, even though by law these cannot be privatized since they are considered a public good." Cancún exhibits the same, if not more acute form, of socio-spatial apartheid: "For most of Cancún's residents the tourist zone on the island of Cancun is an exclusive place of conspicuous tourist consumption to be experienced only from a bus window, a kitchen, an unkempt hotel room, or through the prism of some other subservient role" (Torres and Momsen 2005, 317). Thus residential apartheid is not the only form of socioeconomic apartheid found in tourist centers in Mexico.

Conclusion

Residential apartheid in the tourist centers under examination is not bipolar and divided only between tourist hotels and second or retirement homes on the one hand and settlements graced by unconsolidated housing for the poor on the other. Rather there are lower-middle and middle-middle classes composed of Mexicans and foreigners that describe the middle of a continuum between the highly financed and fully serviced tourist and gated communities and the initially underserviced settlements housing the poor. The extremes, however, deserve attention in the interests of showing the great inequalities of wealth and well-being in these transnational social spaces. Marble or ceramic tiled floors as compared to dirt or cement floors; a granite-topped integrated kitchen in contrast to a freestanding gas stove fueled by replaceable canisters; one or more fully equipped bathrooms, some adorned with a Jacuzzi as contrasted to a scrap-wood structure with a shower fixture attached to a hose (if there is running water): These are some of the contrasts in housing. There is also a residential apartheid apparent in the separation of space between the well-off and the tourists on the one hand and the poor and those engaged in low-waged formal employment or informal or semi-informal self-employment on the other. The poor may be less isolated than the well-off as they enter tourist zones to work as chambermaids, bellboys, cooks, waiters and maintenance staff in the hotels and also as vendors on the beaches in front of these hotels. They also enter the gated communities of the well-off as, among other things, domestic servants, housepainters, gardeners, and for electrical, plumbing, and pool maintenance. In these roles they enter the spaces of the "other" while seldom does the "other" visit their spaces.[2]

Residential Apartheid: *Colonias* Where the Beach Vendors Live

FIGURE 5.1
Typical housing on lots occupied by squatters, El Caribe, 2011

FIGURE 5.2
Rental housing in the more consolidated Lomas del Sol, 2011

Notes

1. Using the theory of relative deprivation as a motivation for migration as developed by Oded Stark and his colleagues (e.g., Stark and Taylor 1991; Stark and Wang 2000). Guilette (2007) shows how the arrival of affluent tourists and expatriate retirees in the tourist center of Huatulco, Oaxaca, had led to transnational migration by locals. Given the high price of land because of tourism development, and comparing their economic situation to that of tourists and retirees, some local residents are pushed into the migration stream to the United States in order to send remittances designated to buying land and building a house.

2. However, there are some expatriates who work for charitable organizations in Los Cabos—especially those concerned with children's welfare—who do occasionally visit some of the poor colonias.

6

Indigenous Vendors

Among the vendors interviewed there were 86 from small towns and villages in the state of Guerrero, 63 (73.3 percent) of whom spoke an indigenous language; and 15 from the state of Oaxaca, of whom 13 (86.1 percent) spoke an indigenous language. Sixty of the indigenous language speakers from Guerrero spoke Nahuatl, and 12 of those from Oaxaca spoke Zapotec. Some of their stories will be presented below.

Research in small towns and villages in the state of Guerrero has documented the entry of Nahuatl-speaking artisans and sometimes resellers into the informal or semi-informal subsector of ambulant vending, whether on the streets of major cities such as Tijuana, Monterrey, Guadalajara, and Oaxaca, or on the beaches of such sun and sea resorts as Cancún, Puerto Escondido, Manzanillo, Mazatlán, Cabo San Lucas, Acapulco, and Puerto Vallarta (e.g., Good Eshelman 1988, 37; see also Canabal Cristiani n.d., 2–3; Cowen 2005; Good Eshelman and Barrientos López 2004, 14; González Chévez n.d., 29–30; Morales Aguilar 2007, 5–7; Schryer 2010*a*, 58). Almost all of these studies were based in villages from which vendors originated. Most have also focused on the Alto Balsas region in Guerrero—composed of 23 pueblos and ranchos (Good Eshelman and Barrientos López 2004, 6), and on artisan-vendors, with the amate bark painters given much attention. My research looked at the destinations where they sell, and as mentioned previously is based on formal interviews of 166 beach vendors, 60 in Cabo San Lucas, 51 in Puerto Vallarta, and 55 in Acapulco. Of these, 58 (34.9 percent) were Nahuatl speakers from Guerrero, one of the three poorest states in Mexico.[1] There was participant-observation involving many more beach vendors in those cities as well as in

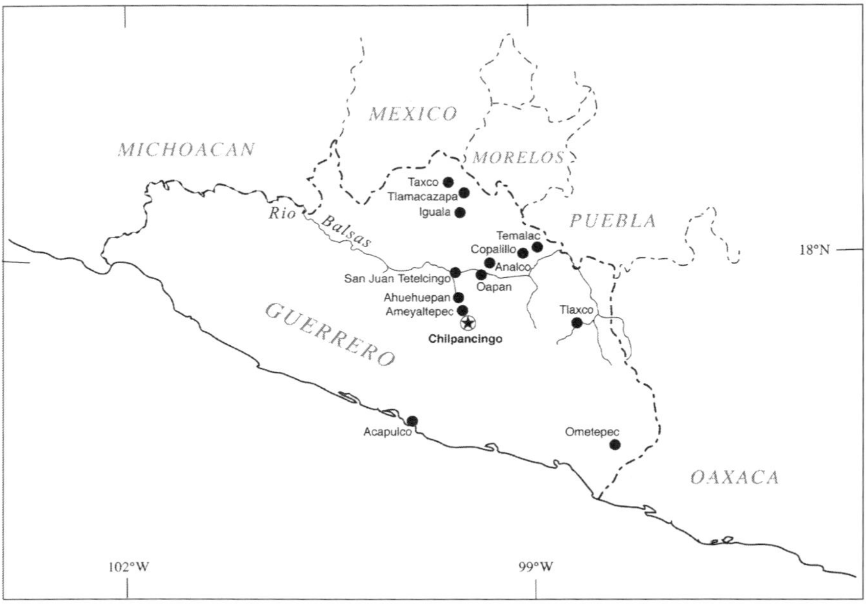

Guerrero

San José del Cabo, and vendors on the marina in Cabo San Lucas. There was also a relatively large sample of vendors from Oaxaca. Of the fifteen, ten were from Mitla. All ten of those spoke Zapotec, as did two others from Oaxaca. I will first present the stories of Nahuatl speakers from four towns in Guerrero, and then summarize some interviews of the sample from Oaxaca. Notably, none of the beach vendors in the three tourist centers seemed to use their ethnicity in their pursuit of an income, unlike the case of other globalized tourist spaces in Mexico and elsewhere in Latin America where vendors stress their indigenous identity to attract the attention of tourists (e.g., Babb,2011; Canclini 1995, chap. 5; Hellier-Tinoco, 2011; Little 2004, 2008; Simon 2009).

Nahuatl Speakers from Four Towns in Guerrero

The majority of Nahuatl-speaking vendors from Guerrero who were formally interviewed come from three towns: Tlamacazapa, near Taxco; San Juan Tetelcingo, about an hour by bus from Chilpancingo; and Analco. Thirteen vendors from Tlamacazapa were interviewed, including eight in Acapulco, two in Puerto Vallarta, and three in Cabo San Lucas. Only one of them was a woman, and she was interviewed in Acapulco. Eleven vendors were from San Juan Tetelcingo. The sample born in San Juan Tetelcingo includes only one man, interviewed in Acapulco, and 10 women. One woman from that pueblo was interviewed in Acapulco and nine in Cabo San Lucas. In addition to the formal interviews, two women from San Juan Tetelcingo were interviewed informally on the beach in San José del Cabo. There were 10 vendors from Analco who were formally interviewed, all in Puerto Vallarta; they included nine women and one man. In addition, one man from Copalillo was formally interviewed in Cabo San Lucas and three more informally in San José del Cabo.[2]

Merchandise Sold

As concerns the wares they sell, the lone woman from Tlamacazapa, interviewed in Acapulco, sells a unique item: handwoven string necklaces, each with a large semiprecious stone pendant, and bracelets woven around a large semiprecious stone. Tlamacazapa is known for its weaving of palm leaves into sombreros and colorful medium-sized handbags. Three male vendors in Acapulco sold these handbags and one sold sombreros. The sombrero seller also sold canvas bags with an Acapulco logo. One man in Acapulco sold unique shark-spine and shell necklaces he and his children make, another handwoven name bracelets that he and his wife make. Hand-woven name bracelets made by the vendor are ubiquitous in all three of the tourist centers and one of the specialties of those from Tlamacazapa. If one's name does not appear among the bracelets being offered, the vendor will offer to make one on the spot. Another man sold T-shirts with an Acapulco logo. T-shirt sellers with a local logo are also ubiquitous in all three tourist centers.

In Puerto Vallarta one man sold woven palm-leaf handbags that he bought from an artisan who lived in a town not far from Tlamacazapa. In Cabo San Lucas, two men sold hand woven name bracelets they make; one also sold leather bracelets that he buys and the other applies tattoos. A third sold silver from Taxco, also an item widely available from beach vendors in all three tourist centers. When I asked one vendor in Cabo San Lucas (Daniel) why he did not sell the woven palm-leaf items for which his town was famous, he replied that they were very heavy and there were problems in transporting them from Tlamacazapa to Cabo San Lucas.

Women vendors from San Juan Tetelcingo and from Analco typically sell semiprecious stone necklaces: they assemble the necklaces with the stones they buy, sometimes interspersing them with river pearls, small shells, or small plastic beads. While some are simply made, others are quite complex and beautiful. Seven of the 10 women interviewed who were born in San Juan Tetelcingo sold these necklaces, one interviewed in Acapulco and six interviewed in Cabo San Lucas. In Cabo San Lucas one worked on the marina and five on Medano Beach. Two sold sunglasses, of whom one also braids hair, and one sold ceramic whistles in the form of turtles. The only man from San Juan Tetelcingo who was formally interviewed sells hand-painted ceramic plates and bowls in Acapulco. Another man, informally interviewed in Cabo San Lucas, sells semiprecious stone necklaces that he and his wife assemble.

All of the vendors who were from Analco, including nine women and one man, were vendors in Puerto Vallarta. This may show that their networks have not yet expanded to include Cabo San Lucas, despite the presence there of vendors from nearby towns. All nine women sell semiprecious stone necklaces they assemble. Their sources for the stones, however, are variable. Several buy the stones in Taxco, another in Iguala, one from a man who lives in the same colonia in Puerto Vallarta as she does, one from a wholesaler who comes to sell them to the vendors on the beach, and one from a man from Taxco who comes to her house every month to sell her the stones. These variable sources for their stones suggest that they might earn more if they formed a buying cooperative and bought in bulk. The man from Analco sells large hand-painted ceramic plates and bowls. Ceramic plates and bowls, sometimes sold as a set and sometimes sold separately, are widely found on all the beaches. Vendors usually buy them in the rough, then paint the designs they wish on them. Although some of the designs are quite standardized, others are unique.

Vending as a Family Tradition

As has been seen previously, ambulant vending, including beach vending, is a family tradition among many of the beach vendors. This is especially true among those who speak an indigenous language. Whereas 12.1 percent of all 166 vendors had 10 or more family members who were vendors, and 43.2 percent had five or more family members who were vendors, 17.5 percent of the Nahuatl speakers from Guerrero had 10 or more family members who were vendors and 63.2 percent had five or more family members who were vendors. Among the nonindigenous language speakers only 9.4 percent had 10 or more family members who were vendors and 31.8 percent had five or more family members who were vendors. That almost one-third of the nonindigenous language speakers had five or more family members who were vendors shows that ambulant vending has become a tradition for nonindigenous peoples as well as for indigenous peoples. Notably, however, several of the nonindigenous language speakers had parents who spoke an indigenous language. In the following sections I will outline some of the characteristics of four of the villages in Guerrero from which Nahuatl speakers originate.

Tlamacazapa

Tlamacazapa, San Juan Tetelcingo, Analco, and Copalillo are known for their high levels of poverty and the low educational levels of their inhabitants. Tlamacazapa, in the municipio of Taxco de Alarcón, had a population of 5, 458 in 2000. Of those, 2,590 were indigenous peoples and 1,247 of the town's residents age five years or more speak an indigenous language There are 1,057 houses in Tlamacazapa, 750 of which (approximately 71 percent) have dirt floors and 405 (38.3 percent) have only one room. Of the population 15 years or older, 2,030 have never attended school and another 1,376 have not completed primary school (*Nuestro México*, 2011a). Tlamacazapa is known for its artisans who weave palm leaves into handbags, sombreros, large and small baskets, and other items. Since 2004 it has had an annual festival to celebrate these artisans. The *Ferie de la Palma* (Palm Fair) consists of a number of events including 1) a contest between palm-leaf weavers, 2) the selection of a queen of the Palm Fair, and 3) a competition between youth in the Nahuatl language. The Nahuatl language competition consists in the presentation of poems and reflections on the history of the pueblo and was initiated in an attempt to halt the loss of fluency in this language among members of the younger generation (Arroyo Reyes 2009). Because of the widespread poverty, the lack of employment and educational facilities, as well as because of local political and religious conflict, many young people are migrating to cities in Mexico (Arroyo Reyes 2009). It is estimated that 50 percent of the children in Tlamacazapa are undernourished and that many women "are anemic due to poor diet, intestinal parasites and frequent pregnancies" (Smith and Marin 2005, 347).

Case Studies of Vendors from Tlamacazapa
Case 6.1

Ramón (PV-14) is a 42-year-old married vendor with three children ages seven, nine and 11. He was born in Tlamacazapa, Guerrero. He speaks Nahuatl, Spanish, and almost no English, he says. He is one of the many Nahautl-speaking beach vendors in Puerto Vallarta, 21 of whom, including nine men and 12 women, were interviewed there. One of his two brothers (of four siblings) goes back and forth between Tlamacazapa and Puerto Vallarta to sell wooden bead necklaces on the beach. His other brother comes and goes between Tlamacazapa and Cancún to sell handwoven name bracelets that he makes to tourists.

Ramón has lived in Puerto Vallarta with his wife and children for 12 years, renting a three-room house for 1,700 pesos a month. A friend of his, a beach vendor from Tlamacazapa who was working in Puerto Vallarta, told him about the opportunities there. Ramón has been a vendor for 25 years. He was an ambulant vendor in Iguala, Guerrero for seven years; Chalma, state of México for five years; and in the downtown Zócalo of the Federal District for two years. He was also a beach vendor for five months or less each place in Zihuatenejo, Guerrero, Mazatlán, Sinaloa, and Puerto Escondido, Oaxaca.

Ramón thinks that Puerto Vallarta is the best place to be a vendor because of higher numbers of tourists and the fact that they often pay him in dollars. He earns 300 to 500 pesos on a good day, 50 pesos or nothing on a bad day, selling wooden bead necklaces and handwoven bracelets and applying tattoos. He buys his merchandise from wholesalers who live in the same colonia he does. He is very satisfied with his life in Puerto Vallarta, and very content with his work as a vendor. If he were not a vendor he would like to be a farmer, noting that when a child he helped his father cultivate corn on his father's small property. He finds that the economic crisis has led to increasing numbers of vendors, many without licenses, due to the lack of other employment. He also notes that there are fewer tourists, and those who come tend to buy less. He says he has seen times that he didn't earn enough money to put food on the table. Although his family social capital, measured by the number of family members who are vendors, is not extensive, Ramón comes from a pueblo that sends vendors to a variety of tourist centers, including Acapulco and Cabo San Lucas among others.

Case 6.2

Rodrigo (PV-13) is a 49-year-old married beach vendor in Puerto Vallarta. He finished primary school and has seven children ranging in ages from five to 21. His eldest son is a beach vendor who applies temporary tattoos. Of his seven surviving siblings, all but one live in Tlamacazapa. His 63-year-old brother is a beach vendor in Acapulco. Besides these family members Rodrigo's father-in-law, five sisters-in-law, and six maternal cousins are beach vendors in Puerto Vallarta. Rodrigo has lived in Puerto Vallarta since 1987 (23 years when interviewed). He does not have his own house but rents a room for 900 pesos a month. He has been a vendor since he was 12 years old. He has previously been a vendor for three years in Acapulco and for two years each in Reynosa and Nuevo Laredo, Tamaulipas, and in the city of San Luís Potosí. Rodrigo has also gone to sell on the beach in Ensenada, Baja California, for two tourist high seasons. Thus he has been both an ambulant street vendor and a beach vendor.

In each place, as well as for the past 23 years in Puerto Vallarta, he has sold woven palm-leaf handbags and sombreros. Rodrigo says that Puerto Vallarta is the best city for sales because there is not much competition, whereas in Acapulco there are many vendors selling the same wares, and it is the worst city for sales. He buys his merchandise from Chilapa, a town near Tlamacazapa. He also sells small handbags that his wife makes. Mauricio has a vendor's license that cost him 7,000 pesos to acquire 23 years ago, and pays 1,700 pesos annually to renew it. He belongs to CROC (*Confederación Revolucionaria de Obreros y Campesinos*, Revolutionary Confederation of Workers and Peasants), a union he says does essentially nothing for the vendors.

If he were not a vendor, Rodrigo says he would manufacture the merchandise he sells: "*nosotros somos puros artesanos*" ("we are all artisans"), he adds. He says the economic recession has affected him because he has no fixed salary, and tourist numbers have fallen. When I remark that there are many people on the beach, he replies that yes, but they are from Puerto Vallarta and don't buy anything. He earns 300 pesos on a good day, but some days nothing.

Case 6.3

Daniel (CSL-18P) is a 35-year-old vendor who lives in free union and has two twin boys age 7, and another son age 6. He finished the second year of primary school and says he could not continue because his parents did not have sufficient money. Daniel says he only speaks a little Nahuatl, though his parents were fluent. His father farms un-owned lands near Tlamacazapa, but, Daniel explains, there is little rain so the land produces little. His father also makes woven palm-leaf handbags and travels to the Federal District to sell them.

Daniel has two brothers and six sisters. Three of his sisters also make handwoven palm-leaf handbags. One lives in Cabo San Lucas, and her husband sells the handbags on the beach. His 37-year-old brother rotates between Tlamacazapa and selling merchandise in a tianguis in the Federal District. His 23-year-old brother is a beach vendor in Cabo San Lucas and sells the same thing Daniel does: handwoven name bracelets that they make and woven leather bracelets that another brother brings them from Mexico City. Five of his sisters' husbands are vendors. Besides his brother-in-law who is a beach vendor in Cabo San Lucas, he has two other brothers-in-law who are beach vendors, one in Acapulco and one in Cancún. Two brothers-in-law are ambulant vendors, one in the state of Veracruz and one in the state of Mexico. They sell woven palm-leaf handbags or woven name and leather bracelets. Thus sales of these three types of merchandise are common among Daniel's family members.

Daniel has been in Cabo San Lucas for 15 years and lives in a house he built on land belonging to his common-law wife in Lomas del Sol. He has been a vendor for 15 years as well, beginning by selling tablecloths and woven name bracelets on Sundays while working the rest of the week in construction and living in the state of Mexico, in a town near the Federal District. He has also worked in construction in Cabo San Lucas, helping to finish the Puerto Paraíso mall, the Hilton and the Melía, among other sites. When he lived in Tlamacazapa he helped his father farm. Daniel has a vendor's license and belongs to CTM. He is very much against giving out more licenses, he told me, when I attended a meeting of the vendors in September of 2010. He resents the growing competition. He dates the falloff of sales from the time after 9/11 occurred and fewer tourists came to Cabo.

Daniel says he earns about 250 pesos in profit on a good day, nothing on a bad day, and that his income is not sufficient to upgrade his housing. He liked living in Cabo San Lucas at first, but not so much now because the competition from other vendors is making it difficult for him to make sales. If he could study anything, however, it would be English so that he could communicate better with the American tourists. He would also like to become fluent in Nahuatl, saying he speaks only a bit. I have seen him address other vendors in Nahuatl though. If he were not a vendor he would like to be a fisherman—so his family would be assured of having food—or return to Tlamacazapa and open a business. He laments the fact that his children have never seen their grandparents.

Case 6.4

Ramona (ACA-13IC) is a 24-year-old married woman with three children who comes to Acapulco seasonally to vend on Icacos Beach. She has done this for only two years. Her mother is a beach vendor and sells items made of woven palm leaves on the beach in Acapulco Diamante. All of Ramona's five sisters and one brother come to Acapulco from Tlamacazapa to vend on the beach during high tourist seasons. They all sell semiprecious stone necklaces and/or handwoven name bracelets. Ramona's husband is an ambulant vendor of name bracelets on the boulevard La Costera. They have their own house in Tlamacazapa and rent a room for 700 pesos a month while in Acapulco. Ramona also has sisters-in-law who vend necklaces on the beach in Acapulco Diamante. Ramona has been a vendor for 10 years, previously selling name bracelets in Taxco. She earns 500 to 600 pesos on a good day and 50 to 100 on a bad day during the high tourist seasons. Ramona has never been to school. She explains that her father died when she was a child—she is the youngest of her sibling group—and her mother had no money to send her to school. If she could study anything she would like to learn to read and write. Ramona is very content with being a vendor, saying it is better to work for oneself than to be employed by a bad boss. She has never worked at anything besides vending, but has apparently heard bad things about waged employment from her peers and paisanos.

San Juan Tetelcingo

San Juan Tetelcingo, in the municipio of Tepecoacuilco de Trujano, had 909 inhabitants in 2000. Of these, 891 were indigenous peoples. Of those age five years or more, 807 spoke Nahuatl. There are 247 houses of which 124 (50.2 percent) have dirt floors and 53 (21.4 percent) consist of only one room. Of the population 15 years or older, 406 are illiterate (*Nuestro México*, 2011b).

San Juan Tetelcingo received much nationwide and international attention, when, in the early 1990s, the federal and state governments initiated a plan to build a hydroelectric dam in that town. If the installation of the dam had been successful, it would have flooded 18 pueblos in the Alto Balsas region. Members of these pueblos formed an organization called *Consejo de Pueblos Nahuas de Alto Balsas* (CPNAB, Council of Nahua Pueblos of Alto Balsas) to fight for the cancellation of the plan (Celestino 2005; Cowen, 2005, 124-27; Schryer 2010*a*, 2010*b*). Schryer (2010*a*, 61) points out that the movement led to the construction of a common regional identity that heretofore had not existed, and claims that this identity has since been endorsed by indigenous intellectuals and anthropologists. After defeating the governments' plans to build the dam, CPNAB was ravaged by infighting and factionalism.

Vendors from this town are found in luxury hotels on Playa del Carmen, near Cancún. They sell their artisan work, especially ceramics, from movable carts and under palapas provided to them by the hotels (Morales Aguilar 2007, 8). They also provide ceramic pieces for tourists to paint themselves. No other group of artisans from Guerrero has entered this particular luxury hotel niche.

Case Studies of Vendors from San Juan Tetelcingo
Case 6.5

Manuel (ACA-15IC), the only man interviewed from San Juan Tetelcingo, sells hand-painted sauce bowls (*salseras*) on Icacos Beach in Acapulco Dorado. Age 48, he has been a widower for 10 years. He has three sons and two daughters. Manuel has been a vendor seasonally in Acapulco for 15 years and previously was an ambulant vendor in the Federal District for 18 years. He says his sales were higher in the Federal District, where he sold his wares in the downtown historic center, the Zócalo. Manuel's deceased father cultivated corn, sesame seeds, and watermelon on borrowed lands. Manuel, his mother, his eldest daughter, age 20, and a 16-year-old son make the ceramic sauce bowls that he sells. All of his siblings, including three sisters and one brother, make and paint sauce bowls—each on their own account. His eldest brother, age 55, sells these bowls at wholesale prices to other vendors. His 38-year-old sister sells them on the beach in Acapulco. He also has two maternal cousins who make and sell the same merchandise. His 18-year-old married daughter sells necklaces on the beach in Zihuatenejo.

Manuel completed only primary school but has always wanted to be a doctor and practice in his hometown where there are no medical facilities—to improve the town; he says. He has previously been a sharecropper cultivating corn, sesame seeds, and watermelons and if he were not a vendor he would like to be a farmer. Manuel tells me that people from San Juan Tetelcingo are migrating to find work to Ontario, California, and as vendors to Mazatlán, Puerto Vallarta, Los Cabos, and other tourist centers.

Case 6.6

Catalina (CSL-8P) is an 17-year-old single vendor who finished secondary school. She has four sisters, three of whom are older than she is, and of whom two are also beach vendors in Cabo San Lucas. She has lived in Cabo San Lucas for the past 15 years, having been brought to this city by her parents, who are also beach vendors. She lives with them in their house in Colonia Arenal. Catalina says she has been a vendor for five years. She sells semiprecious stone necklaces and braids hair. She has a vendor's license that cost her 10,000 pesos with an annual fee of 1,000 pesos. She does not belong to a union or organization. Catalina has never worked at anything else and likes being a vendor because of the flexible hours but finds it tiring to walk up and down the beach. If she could study anything she would like to finish preparatory school and then study business with a view to working in a tourist hotel.

Graciela (CSL-18P) whose interview was summarized in the chapter on levels of contentment, is also from San Juan Tetelcingo.

Analco

Analco, in the municipio of Mártin de Cuilapan, had 505 inhabitants in 2000. There were 104 houses; 88 (84.6 percent) had dirt floors. Of those inhabitants age 15 and over, 230 have never gone to school. Of those age five and over, 481 speak Nahuatl (*Nuestro México* 2011*c*). Despite its small size Analco is known for its production of elaborately embroidered blouses.[3]

None of the beach vendors sell these, however, most probably because they cannot expect a fair price on the beach.

Case Studies of Vendors from Analco
Case 6.7

Esther (PV-6) is a 22-year-old single vendor who finished primary school. Both of her brothers and all three of her sisters are beach vendors in Puerto Vallarta, as is she. Her two brothers sell silver jewelry, two sisters sell semiprecious stone necklaces as does Esther, and one sister sells dresses. Esther has lived in Puerto Vallarta, accompanying her siblings to that city, for five years. She has been a beach vendor since arriving. She says she earns 500 pesos on a good day but nothing on a bad day. She is happy to be a vendor because she can earn her own money, but complains that the economic recession has caused tourist numbers to fall, and those tourists who arrive want to pay a low price for her merchandise. Esther would like to continue her studies but in unsure is what, but knows she would like to work in one of the tourist hotels. She does not belong to a union but has a vendor's license for which she paid 20,000 pesos, with a monthly payment of 100 pesos (or 1,2000 annually).

Flor (PV-7), Carla (PV-11), and Alma (PV-9) are also from Analco. Their interviews were summarized in the chapter concerning levels of contentment.

Case 6.8

Lito (PV-9), married and age 50, completed the fourth year of primary school. He explains that his father was very poor: he farmed his own small piece of private property but later sold it. There was not enough money when Lito was a child to continue sending him to school. Lito has four sons and two daughters ranging in age from 14 to 28. All four of his sons apply temporary tattoos on the beach in Manzanillo (Colima). He has two brothers and three sisters, ranging in age from 32 to 48. His eldest brother is a campesino in Analco. One brother and one sister sell hand-painted ceramic plates and bowls on the beach in Puerto Vallarta, as does he. His sister also sells necklaces. Lito buys the unpainted plates in Manzanillo and the small bowls in a small town in Guerrero; then he, his wife, and his children paint them. He has a brother who is a beach vendor in Manzanillo and another who is a beach vendor in Cancún. They also sell ceramic plates and bowls.

Lito has lived in Puerto Vallarta for 10 years, originally accompanying a brother to that city. He has been a beach vendor since arriving in Puerto Vallarta and previously was a beach vendor in Manzanillo for 25 years. He thinks Puerto Vallarta is the better place to be a vendor, because there are more tourists. He complains, however, about the increasing number of beach vendors, most of whom he says are *piratas* (pirates; i.e., they don't have a vendor's license). He has a vendor's license that one of his brothers passed on to him. Lito says the union to which he belongs, CROC, helps the vendors renew their licenses. He points out that helping involves assembling the necessary paperwork and representing the vendors in front of the municipal authorities.

Lito's wife lives in Manzanillo with their offspring, and he visits them every two or three weeks. He rents a room in Puerto Vallarta for 750 pesos a month but thinks of returning permanently to Manzanillo to be with his family. He estimates that he can earn up to 1,000 pesos on a good day (though I suspect this is total earnings, not profit). He sells his large plates for 250 pesos, earning about 30 pesos each piece, the medium-sized ones for 100 pesos, earning 40 pesos each piece, and the small ones he sells two for 100 pesos, earning 20 pesos on the sale. He is little satisfied with living in Puerto Vallarta because he is separated from his family but very content with being a vendor because he earns enough to support their household. If he were not a vendor he would have liked to work in a bank or a hotel—somewhere in the shade. Notably, the overwhelming complaint of both male and female vendors was working under the hot sun.

Copalillo

Copalillo, located in the municipio of the same name, has 6,387 inhabitants. Nahuatl- and Maya-speaking peoples number 6,013. Of those over five years-old, 5,107 speak an indigenous language. There are 1,148 houses in Copalillo, 820 (71.4 percent) of which have dirt floors, and 137 (11.9 percent) consist of only one room. As concerns schooling, 1,514 people over 15 years old have never attended school, and 1,624 others have completed less than primary school (*Nuestro México* 2011*d*). An article in a widely read newspaper *El Mileneo* (Anónimo, 2008) revealed that Guerrero is the state in which most houses do not have running water and Copalillo is the municipality with the most houses without this service. For their water supply people are dependent on a circulating water truck (*pipa*) which pumps water into barrels (*tambos*) located in front of their houses. It is estimated that people pay one-third of the daily minimum wage for this service.

González Chévez (n.d., 29) writes that the migration from Copalillo to Puerto Vallarta and adjacent Nuevo Vallarta began in the 1980s. It was initiated after the marriage of a woman from that town to a man from Temalac, a pueblo with a longer history of migration to tourist centers. The beach vendors from Temalac specialized in selling silver jewelry from Taxco and ironwood statues, originally carved by the Seri Indians in the state of Sonora.

Those people who later migrated from Copalillo joined those from Temalac to sell on the beach; beach vending became a specialty of the majority of Nahuatl speakers from Guerrero who migrated to the Puerto Vallarta region (González Chévez n.d., 31, 33). Migrants from the village of Temalac are now present in Cabos San Lucas: three of five of the vendors interviewed from that town were interviewed there, and two were interviewed in Puerto Vallarta. Only three, however, spoke Nahuatl. Among the vendors from Temalac who were interviewed are Álvaro (PV-11), a Nahuatl speaker whose story is presented in the chapter on family legacy.

Only one man from Copalillo was formally interviewed, in Cabo San Lucas. However, a family cluster from Copalillo was interviewed informally in San José del Cabo. Their stories will be discussed after presenting the case study.

Case 6.9

César (CSL-9) is a 36-year-old married vendor. He has no children. His father makes hammocks, as does his eldest brother, age 41. His father also farms three hectares of private property that he owns. César has five sisters and one brother. Only one of his siblings, a sister age 37, lives in Cabo San Lucas. Her husband sells hammocks on the beach. Another sister is a beach vendor in Las Barras, Nayarit, and sells necklaces.

César lives in Lomas del Sol and pays 1,000 pesos a month in rent for one room. He has been in Los Cabos for five years, and been a vendor for 18. He sold hammocks in Taxco for five years and name bracelets in Puerto Vallarta for three. He has also vended hammocks for periods ranging from one to six months in the following cities: Ciudad Juárez and Chihuahua (Chihuahua), León (Guanajuato), Lázaro Cardenas (Michoacán), Poza Rica (Veracruz), and Nuevo Progreso (Tamaulipas). Although originally he sold hammocks in Cabo San Lucas as well, for the past two years he has sold ironwood statues. Wholesalers buy them in the Valle de Kino, Sonora, and come to sell them at a house in Colonia Arenal. He says he earns 500 pesos in profit on a good day. For a large statue of a marlin or a turtle he pays 250 pesos and sells it for 400 pesos.

César belongs to an organization called *Pácifico Mar de Cortez*—a grassroots organization formed by the vendors to protect themselves against authorities who might confiscate their goods. He has a provisional license, for which he pays 1,300 pesos annually, but says that it can be taken away from him at the end of the year (i.e., not renewed). He previously worked as a sharecropper for four years in his hometown of Copalillo but said that economic survival as a sharecropper was precarious. If he were not a vendor he would like to be a campesino. He remarks that although there are ejido parcels in his hometown, none are available because all ejido lands have previously been distributed. If he could study anything it would be to become a lawyer. What he likes about vending is getting to know the tourists; what he does not like about vending is the harassment by tax collectors, who once put him in jail and fined him 300 pesos.

In Acapulco I came across four men, working in twos, from Copalillo. One man would carry one end of the red, blue, yellow, or green hammocks and the other man would hold the other end. Both pairs of men said they did not have time for formal interviews when I told them it would take a minimum of 45 minutes. They wanted to walk down the beach and attempt to make a sale, they told me. All four were hammock makers, an artisanry their town is famous for (Good Eshelman and Barrientos López 2004, 8, 13). Not all vendors from Copalillo sell hammocks, however. Informal interviews with a cluster of three family members from Copalillo on the beach in San José del Cabo were conducted; two sold silver from Taxco, one from a briefcase, and one from a short wooden club that he could hide within his shirt if the authorities arrived—he had no vendor's license. Another man, Mauricio, sold ironwood statues of dolphins, turtles, frogs, whales, and other fauna. I was surprised to see ironwood once again being sold by a man from Guerrero since the Seri Indians of Sonora were the original ironwood sculptors. Mauricio acknowledged that origin but said he gets his unfinished statues from his father and an uncle who currently live in Rosarito, Baja California, and fabricate them there. They send him the statues via bus and then he lacquers them. He will also engrave the buyer's name, or the place of sale, or whatever the buyer may want on the base of the statue. When I mention that I understand that Copalillo is famous for its hammocks, Mauricio's face lights up, and he says he too can make hammocks.

Mauricio's brother sells silver from Taxco from a large briefcase that can be opened up to display his wares. Both Maurcio and his brother have vendor's licenses. Their recently arrived uncle, Santos, does not, however. Santos was born in Copalillo but moved with his family to San Felipe, a tourist center in the state of Baja California, when he was 13 years old and lived there for 30 years. He was a beach vendor in San Felipe as well but says that the competition has become very tough. Mauricio dresses in ordinary street clothes, unlike the licensed vendors who must wear white. When I asked him why he did not wear white so that everyone would think he had a license, he replied that the authorities were checking to see that all vendors had their licenses in order. He comes to the beach with his six-year-old son, after his son gets out of school, and presents himself as though he is taking a day out at the beach. Mauricio carries the filigreed bracelets he sells on a short wooden club because, he says, he can rapidly tuck it into his shirt if the authorities arrive—thus pretending that he is not vending. He has applied for a license, and when I see him in April of 2011, Mauricio says that he hopes when we meet again he will be wearing white. When I returned in May, I did not find him there. I found out in July 2011, from a vendor from Mazatlán working on Medano Beach in Cabo San Lucas, that no new licenses would be issued, however. The licensed vendors had demonstrated in front of the municipal building located in San José del Cabo, asking the authorities not to give out any more licenses than the 698 that were already authorized. Nonetheless, by early 2012 Santos had his vendor's license and was wearing white and selling his Taxco silver from a briefcase.

Zapotec-Speakers from Oaxaca

Mitla, Oaxaca, and its surrounding valley and mountain towns have long been engaged in trade; Beals (1975) identifies the networks of trade as a "peasant marketing system." He shows that there were traveling traders taking part in a regional and extra-regional marketing system since pre-Columbian times and that this system continued during the Spanish Colonial period and up through the 20th century (Beals 1975, 37–8, 265–66). Fieldwork in Mitla in the early 1930s led Parsons (1936, 10) to conclude that "half of the able-bodied men are traveling men, *viajeros* . . . commercial travelers, *comerciantes ambulantes*, muleteers or 'men behind,' *arrieros*. Little boys accompany their fathers or older brothers, and now and again a woman goes along with father or husband or even on her own." Beals (1975, 148), in a study of traders in eastern and central Oaxaca, found both men and women were involved in long-distance travels. Some of them sold wares to tourists in Oaxaca City. It can be postulated that, having become accustomed to dealing with tourists in Oaxaca, it was an easy step to deal with tourists in the sun and beach centers such as Acapulco, Puerto Vallarta, and Los Cabos.

Beals (1975, 9) adopts an indigenous Oaxacan perspective in dividing types of vendors into the *propio*, that is, "the producer-vendor who sells his own product" (or products cultivated or manufactured by household members) and the *regatón*, that is, "the trader . . . who buys and sells for a profit." Only two of the vendors interviewed from Oaxaca can be considered propios: they sell "typical Oaxacan clothing" members of their families make. Most would be classified as regatones, though their profit margins are small despite the fact that they tend to buy their wares or the inputs for assembling their wares from wholesalers.[4]

In this study, fifteen vendors from the state of Oaxaca were interviewed, including six men and nine women. Ten were from Mitla, including four men and six women. The rest were from small villages. Two of the men from small villages spoke no indigenous language, including Lázaro (ACA-12IC), whose story was told in the chapter on levels of contentment. One 32-year-old woman in Puerto Vallarta, who begged me to interview her because she needed the 50 pesos I was offering for each interview, speaks Triquí. Cecilia's (PV-21) family had moved to the Federal District many years previously, where she was a vendor since she was 14 years old. She arrived in Puerto Vallarta less than a year ago, joining a brother who works collecting garbage for the municipality. Her mother, one of her two brothers, and four of her five sisters are street vendors in the Federal District.

Twelve of the vendors, including four men and eight women speak Zapotec, including all of those born in Mitla. However, one 40-year-old woman who had migrated with her parents from Mitla when she was only four years old said she spoke only a little. Of the six men from Oaxaca, one was interviewed in Acapulco (Lázaro), two in Cabo San Lucas, and three in Puerto Vallarta. Of the nine women, seven were interviewed in Puerto Vallarta and two on the marina in Cabo San Lucas. No women from Oaxaca were formally interviewed on the beach in Cabo San Lucas, though I understand from the male vendors from Oaxaca that there are some there.

Three of the six men from Oaxaca sold what they called "typical Oaxacan clothing," including shirts, blouses, pants, or dresses. Two were from Mitla. One said his wife and a daughter made the clothing and another said his siblings made it. Both were from Mitla and both were interviewed in Puerto Vallarta. A man from Mitla who has been a vendor for 20 years has for the past five sold T-shirts with a Puerto Vallarta logo. Of the six women from Mitla, four sold dresses they made. Three of them used cloth imported from Indonesia. Two sold necklaces they assembled from semiprecious stones. Both bought these stones from a man who came to the Bahía de Banderas beach in Puerto Vallarta each month to sell them to the vendors. In total there were seven women vendors from Oaxaca working on the beach in Puerto Vallarta. Four of the vendors from Oaxaca sold their wares in Cabo San Lucas. Of these, two were women and two men. One 25-year-old man sold typical Oaxacan clothing and one silver from Taxco. Both women sold ceramic flutes on the marina.

Case Studies of Vendors from Oaxaca
Case 6.10

Virginia (PV-16) is a 36-year-old married vendor with three children, ages 10, 15, and 19. She finished primary school and speaks Zapotec, Spanish, and a little English. She was born in Mitla. Virginia has lived in Puerto Vallarta for 16 years. She and her family of orientation live in a rented house for which they pay 1,300 pesos each month. She joined a brother, also a beach vendor, and her parents, who had preceded her. Virginia has five sisters and two brothers; all but one sister are beach vendors. Her eldest sister, ages 48, is a vendor in Mitla; a 43-year-old sister is a beach vendor in Puerto Escondido; and two sisters and two brothers are beach vendors in Puerto Vallarta, as is she. All but the sister in Puerto Escondido, who sells necklaces, vend saris and sundresses made of cloth imported from Indonesia.

Virginia buys the cloth at wholesale prices from a downtown store and sews it into sundresses. She earns 500 pesos on a good day, receiving 30 pesos for each sundress, and says she earns up to 200 pesos even on a bad day. Her husband is also a beach vendor and sells the same wares. She has been a vendor for 11 years and is very content with her work because no one tells her what to do and she can choose her own hours. She has never done any other work. If she could study anything she would finish secondary school and work as a cashier in a large store. Virginia has a vendor's license that cost her 12,000 pesos and pays 1,300 pesos annually to renew it. She belongs to an organization—though its name is not given—that helps the vendors renew their permits and calls meetings to see what actions can be taken whenever any of them are faced by problems at work.

Case 6.11

Ernestina (PV-17) is a 25-year-old vendor born in Mitla who speaks Zapotec, Spanish, and, she says, very little English. She has never attended school. Ernestina has two children and is separated from her husband. She has one brother and two sisters. Her brother lives in Mitla, and her sisters in Puerto Vallarta. One is a housewife and the other, age 27, is a beach vendor selling the same wares that Ernestina does: semiprecious stone necklaces. Ernestina buys the stones from a man from Guerrero who comes to the beach every month or so to sell them to the vendors, then assembles the necklaces. She earns 300 pesos on a good day, making a profit of 30 pesos on each necklace, and nothing on a bad day. She has lived in Puerto Vallarta for 20 years, residing in her parents' house, and has been a vendor for six. She likes vending because she can earn her own money. She complains only about the heat and the low numbers of tourists. If she could study anything, she would like to learn to read and write. If she were not a vendor she would like to work in a (tourist) hotel as a receptionist or even cleaning rooms ("*en un hotel de recepcionista o hasta de limpieza*").

Case 6.12

Pedro (PV-18) is a 35-year-old vendor from Mitla who speaks Zapotec, Spanish, and a little English. He has two daughters, ages 16 and 9; and one son, age 14. Despite the fact that Pedro finished only primary school, his eldest daughter is going to enter preparatory school this year (2010) and his son is entering the last year of secondary school. It is notable how much more highly educated the children of beach vendors tend to be, in comparison to their parent. Pedro has lived in Puerto Vallarta for 15 years and has been a vendor since arriving. He sells "typical" (his word) Oaxacan blouses that he acquires from a brother and three sisters in Mitla who make them. He has three sisters and two brothers. One brother is a beach vendor in Cabo San Lucas and also sells these blouses. Pedro's wife and two paternal aunts and one paternal uncle also sell these brightly colored, hand-sewn blouses on the beach in Puerto Vallarta. He earns 300 pesos in profit on a good day, receiving 30 to 50 pesos for each blouse over its cost, depending on what his clients will pay. On a bad day he may sell only one blouse and earn 50 pesos. Pedro has also worked in construction but prefers vending, partially because, he says, he can earn more. What he doesn't like about vending is harassment by the restaurant owners, who don't like the vendors to come around (*"las molestias de los restauranteros que no quieren ver a los vendedores"*).

Case 6.13

Amalia (CSL-28M), married and age 38, was born in a small town in Oaxaca. She speaks Zapotec and Spanish (no English mentioned). Amalia sells animal-shaped flutes on the marina in Cabo San Lucas, working only on the days of the week that the cruise ships come in. She finished secondary school, and has only one son, age 15, who is currently studying. Amalia came with her husband to Cabo San Luca five years ago, joining a husband's male cousin who at that time was vending hand-painted ceramic plates on Medano Beach. Her husband works in the laundry room of a hotel. Amalia has been a vendor for about a year, and like the majority of vendors on the marina has no license and does not belong to a union or organization. She estimates that she earns 100 pesos on a good day, nothing on a bad day. She is among the lowest earners of all the vendors in Cabo San Lucas. Amalia says she is very sick or might seek other work, though she does not name anything in particular. If she could study anything it would be computer skills. She does not like being so far away from her family of procreation and finds vending tiring and stressful because often there are no sales. Notably, when I visited the marina in the summer of 2011, there were only two or three ambulant vendors and by the spring of 2012 there were none. The municipality had cracked down on those vendors without licenses and furthermore, fixed stalls had been set up as tourist attractions.

Case 6.14

Moises (CSL-4) is a married 34-year-old vendor from Mitla who finished primary school and speaks Zapotec, Spanish, and a little English. His father is an artisan who weaves tablecloths and also a campesino who farms his two hectares of private property. He has one son, age nine. Moises has four brothers and one sister, all of whom live in Mitla. His sister is a seamstress, and all of his brothers weave tablecloths. Moises has never sold tablecloths, however. When I ask him why, he says the tourists do not want to pay a just price for them. They want to pay only US $10 (about 120 pesos), when the tablecloths should be selling for 300 pesos. In Puerto Vallarta, where he was a vendor for 18 months, he sold leather belts and wallets. Upon his arrival in Cabo San Lucas, four years ago, he sold serapes. In the past year or so, he has sold silver jewelry from Taxco. His wife buys the jewelry in Taxco at wholesale prices and sends it to him; she and their son live in Mitla. He goes back to Mitla every two years. While in Cabo San Lucas he rents a room in Colonia Tierra y Libertad for 1,000 pesos a month. He hopes to return to Mitla in another two years and continue his work of weaving tablecloths.

Moises says he has no relatives who are vendors. He joined a maternal cousin when he migrated to Cabo San Lucas. Moises says Cabo San Lucas is a better place to vend than Puerto Vallarta, and that many beach vendors are leaving the latter city to come to the former. He explains that there are more American tourists in Cabo San Lucas and that in Puerto Vallarta most tourists are locals who do not buy anything from the vendors. Moises is not very satisfied with his life in Cabo San Lucas or with being a vendor, because sales are low. He affirms that there are many vendors from Mitla on Medano Beach.

Moises belongs to the PRD- (*Partido de la Revolución Democrática*, Party of the Democratic Revolution) affiliated organization called *Siete de Febrero* (Seventh of February) but claims they do nothing for the vendors. They had promised the vendors to put in public bathrooms on the beach but none were forthcoming. He has a vendor's license that cost him 12,000 pesos with an annual renewal fee of 1,300 pesos. If he could study anything it would be English, to better be able to communicate with the tourists.

Case 6.15

An incomplete interview with a vendor I call Ernesto (PV-18alt) revealed the discrimination vendors are sometimes subjected to because of their indigenous origins. Although the interview is not included in the database or in the tables, I summarize Ernesto's comments here because they show how indigenous vendors can be subjectively and objectively marginalized. Born in Mitla, Ernesto speaks Zapotec, Spanish, a little French, and, he tells me, almost 100 percent English. When I ask if he has gone to the United States, he replies, "I wanted to but didn't because of the discrimination, all the comments I have heard about this." He continues: "Here in Mexico the same Mexicans discriminate against you. If I am from Oaxaca and they are from Guadalajara they say 'you are a fucking Indian.'" ("*Tuvo ganas pero no—por la dicriminación, todos los comentarios que han hecho sobre eso. Aquí en México los mismos mexicanos te discriminat. Si soy de Oaxaca y ellos de Guadalajara ellsos dicen estás 'a fucking Indian.'*" (This latter was said in English). As I was writing this down a friend of his came along and offered him a lift home. The colonia where he lives is about an hour away by bus, he said, so he was anxious to take advantage of the ride in a car. He refused to take the 50 pesos I offered him.

Discrimination against the indigenous population has been discussed by a number of anthropologists, including Friedlander (2006) and Nutini (1997). They both stress that indigenous peoples are overwhelmingly concentrated in the lowest class strata. Friedlander (2006, 209) reports: "In 1990, over 80 percent of the indigenous population was living below the poverty line, as compared to 17.9 percent of the non-Indians. What is more, the higher the density of indigenous people living in a particular *municipio*, the higher the level of poverty." Later, she continues: "Ten percent of the population in Mexico was illiterate in 1990, but over 40 percent of those who spoke an indigenous language—64 percent of women and 36 percent of men" (Friedlander 2006, 209). This is an objective (economic and educational) marginality of indigenous peoples that is coupled by the subjective marginality of being humiliated by non-indigenous peoples, and by the need to defend themselves when asked about their educational levels by interviewers, whether government officials taking one census or another or anthropologists inquiring about their lives.

A Note on Language Retention and Loss

It has been noted that emigration from rural Nahuatl-speaking regions in Central Mexico is leading to a loss of the ability to speak that language: "Internal emigration and increased urbanization suggest that as Nahuas leave their homeland, they will leave Nahuatl behind" (Rolstad 2001, 10). Yoshioka (2010, 10) also holds that rural-to-urban migration affects the viability of indigenous language use, partially because of greater interactions and intermarriage between indigenous and nonindigenous peoples in the cities, and partially because migrants believe Spanish is a more useful language for their children to learn in the new milieu. In Puerto Vallarta, Nahuatl speakers from Temalac, Guerrero—who overwhelmingly work as beach vendors—tend toward endogamous marriage, but once settled in the city, stop communicating in Nahuatl (González Chévez n.d., 33–34). Nonetheless, this pattern language loss is not written in stone. For example, Nahuatl-speaking peoples from the mountain region of Guerrero (*La Montaña*) who migrate to Acapulco, and most of whom also work as street or beach vendors, have established bilingual schools in the *colonias* in which they live (Canabal Cristiani n.d., 7). Bilingual schools are also being established in Nahautl-speaking rural communities (Rolstad 2001).

The loss of fluency in Nahuatl is obvious among some of the beach vendors I interviewed. Although there was no question on the interview schedule as concerns parents' ability to speak an indigenous language, two vendors in Acapulco offered that although they did not speak Nahuatl, their parents did. One was a 70-year-old man born in Tlamacazapa who was brought to Acapulco by his parents at a young age. Martín's (ACA-26IC) father sold woven palm-leaf handbags in the Acapulco airport. Martín expects to remain in Acapulco the rest of his life, and has not returned to Tlamacazapa in the past 30 years. Another was a 35-year-old man born in Apalanic, Guerrero, who has lived in Acapulco for 17 years. Emilio's (ACA-5IC) ties with his village of origin are stronger than Martín's, as he visits Apalanic every two or three months. He says he can understand a few words in Nahuatl. Irma (ACA-M21), a 25-year-old vendor born in Copanatoyac, Guerrero says she understands Nahuatl but cannot speak it, though her mother (but not her father) can. Irma was brought to Acapulco by her parents soon after she was born. Only one of the 20 vendors born in Acapulco, whose parents came from rural communities in Guerrero, speaks Nahautl.

In Cabo San Lucas, Daniel (CSL-18P), born in Tlamacazapa, speaks only a little Nahuatl. (See case 6.3 above.) Age 35, he left Tlamacazapa 23 years ago, living first near the Federal District and for the past 15 years in Cabo San Lucas. He tried to visit his hometown every two years, and among other things, he would like to learn to be fluent in Nahautl. Two paternal cousins who vend on the beach in Cabo San Lucas have different trajectories as concerns language use. Ismael (CSL-T11) was born on a rancho in the state of Puebla and speaks Nahuatl. Age 42, he migrated to Cabo San Lucas 22 years ago after spending 12 years as a beach vendor in Mazatlán. Ismael accompanied parents and siblings to both destinations. His now deceased father was a beach vendor in both tourist centers, and six of his brothers and one of his sisters (of eight siblings), are currently beach vendors in Cabo San Lucas. Ismael returns each year to his hometown. Ismael's cousin (father's brother's son),

Adrian (CSL-T14), whose parents are from a rancho nearby Ismael's place of birth in Puebla, speaks no indigenous language, however. Age 32, he was born in Mazatlán, where he was a beach vendor for three years, then migrated to Cabo San Lucas four years ago. His father had come to Cabo San Lucas about 20 years previously and still works as a beach vendor there. Adrian says he tries to return to Mazatlán, where he has siblings and other relatives, at least once every two years. Both Adrian and Ismael live in Colonia Arenal. Ismael has had his own house there for 12 years, and Adrian and his wife and children live in a house borrowed from a friend. Their story is notable because of the interlinking family networks that span ranchos in Puebla and the tourist centers of Mazatlán and Cabo San Lucas.

In sum, language loss does seem apparent among the beach vendors. Those who migrated away from their villages of origin at an early age do not speak an indigenous language fluently, and those who were born in cities such as Mazatlán or Acapulco to indigenous-language speaking parents have failed to learn the language. Nevertheless, there may be a revitalization, as shown by the establishment of bilingual schools in Acapulco. Some churches in Los Cabos are taking part in outreach to the Nahuatl-speaking population. For example, the Jehovah's Witnesses offer services in Spanish, in English, and in Nahuatl at their Kingdom Hall in downtown Cabo San Lucas. The people of Tlamacazapa, as seen above, are also attempting to maintain Nahuatl among village youth.

Conclusion

Many indigenous peoples have a tradition of vending that stretches back over generations, whether for their families or for members of their communities. In times of high unemployment, resulting from processes of globalization that have been in place for decades, indigenous peoples migrate from their rural villages and *ranchos* to various cities, where they take up informal self-employment, including street and beach vending. More and more enter the migration stream to tourist centers, using networks established by previous migrants, whether family or community members.

Most indigenous peoples in Mexico are objectively marginalized both economically and in terms of the levels of education that they are able to reach. Many also feel subjectively marginalized, and complain of humiliation by fellow Mexicans. Although many children of indigenous parents cannot themselves speak an indigenous language, especially if they were born in cities to which their parents migrated, there may be a revitalization of this language use in the future.

FIGURE 6.1
Nahuatl speakers selling necklaces they assemble, Cabo San Lucas, 2010

FIGURE 6.2
Nahautl speaker selling necklaces she assembles, Acapulco, Icacos Beach, 2010

FIGURE 6.3
Zapotec-speaker selling "typical" Oaxacan clothing his family makes, Puerto Vallarta, 2010

Notes

1. In total there were 63 Nahuatl speakers interviewed. Besides the 58 from Guerrero, there were three from Puebla and one each from the state of México and Colima. There were also interviews with two speakers of Tlapaneco and three of Mixtec from Guerrero.

2. There were also Nahuatl speakers from the following towns in Guerrero: Chipancingo (three) and three towns in the municipio of Chilpancingo (one from each town), Temalac (three), Ahuehuepan (two). There was one vendor each from 11 different pueblos in Guerrero including Tlexmalac, Tlamamacan, San Augustín Guapa, Zumpango del Río, Iguala, Xalitla, Tecoman, and others. In total there were nine vendors from the municipio of Chilpancingo, although three spoke no indigenous language. Of the six Nahuatl-speakers from the municipio of Chilpancingo, two women were interviewed on Medano Beach and one on the marina in Cabo San Lucas, while one was interviewed on Caleta Beach in Acapulco. One man was interviewed in Cabo San Lucas and one on Caleta Beach in Acapulco. Of the three vendors from Temalac who were Nahuatl speakers (of five vendors from that town), one woman was interviewed on the beach in Cabo San Lucas and two men in Puerto Vallarta. Five people

from other states also spoke Nahuatl. One woman and two men interviewed in Cabo San Lucas were from different towns in Puebla, one woman interviewed in Cabo San Lucas was from Colima, and one woman interviewed in Puerto Vallarta was from the state of Mexico. Only two of the 27 vendors born in Acapulco spoke Nahuatl.

3. A number of these elaborately embroidered blouses can be viewed on http://www.Mexicantextiles.co/textilepatterns/analco/slides/analco5.htm.

4. The handwoven woolen textiles described by Wood (2008) and the Oaxacan wood carvings described by Chibnik (2003) were not sold on any of the beaches where vendors were interviewed, although the wood carvings were sold in souvenir shops in Cabo San Lucas and Puerto Vallarta. Though ironwood statues were sold on all of the beaches, most were made by the Seri Indians of Sonora and by Nahuatl speakers from Guerrero; the latter also vended them. The Nahuatl speakers had learned the craft from the Seri Indians, according to a vendor from Copallilo, Guerrero, whom I informally interviewed in San José del Cabo. His father and uncle had set up a workshop manufacturing these statues in Rosarito, Baja California, to where they had migrated from Copalillo. It may be that the Zapotec weavings and Oaxaca wood carvings have become so extensively marketed, both nationally and internationally, that small retailers, such as beach vendors, were superfluous for their sales. This is also suggested by Stephen's (1993) account of Zapotec weavers: the marketing of their wares, after the peso crisis of 1982, was primarily to buyers in the United States.

7
Women Vendors

Self-employment is more important as a source of employment among women workers than among men workers. In 1990/2000, in every sub-region of the developing world a greater proportion of women than men in non-agricultural employment were self-employed . . . In Africa and Latin America, roughly 50 per cent of women in contrast to about 35 per cent of men are self-employed. However, because many more men than women are in the labour force, men comprise a larger share of self-employed non-agricultural workers than women world wide: 64 per cent in contrast to 36 per cent . . . The only exception is Latin America where 51 per cent of self-employed non-agricultural workers are women and 49 per cent are men.

—ILO 2002*b*, 23

NEOLIBERAL STRUCTURAL ADJUSTMENT policies underpinning processes of globalization and implemented in the 1980s throughout Latin America forced women into the informal economy. This was partially because free trade leading to heightened international competition as well as foreign direct investment in various sectors of the economy drove small and medium businesses into bankruptcy (thus leading to male unemployment or underemployment), fostered a lowering of wages (in the interests of attracting foreign investment), and involved the elimination or cutting back of public services (see, e.g., for Mexico, Alarcón-González and McKinley, 1999; González de la Rocha 1995; for Nicaragua, Babb 1996; Fernández Poncela 1996). As formal wage work dried up for men, or as men's earnings became insufficient to support the household, women were forced to take up salaried employment or to embark upon informal income-generating activities that lengthened their work day and induced a pattern of self-exploitation "that sometimes seems limitless" (Fernández Poncela 1996, 52). These neoliberal policies are ongoing, and although there are only two women interviewed who were vendors when economic crisis hit Mexico in 1982, most others have been forced into finding some way to generate income for family survival over the ensuing decades and until the present time.

Women in Mexico often seek out informal or semi-informal self-employment (or home-based work) for at least three reasons. First, because of continual economic crises full-time formal employment opportunities and real wages declined. It must be stressed that the economic crisis of the 1980s led to the adoption of neoliberal structural adjustment policies imposed by the World Bank and the International Monetary Fund that cut back on social welfare subsidies. As a result, more family members had to undertake income-generating activities to ensure family welfare, and these family members included wives and daughters (González de la Rocha 1995). Second, due to the flexibility of hours, women are more easily able to balance informal income-generating activities with domestic chores (Cunningham 2001, 100; Valenzuela 2005, 14; see also González de la Rocha 1994). The flexibility of hours (and days) was one of the primary reasons for feeling positive about being a beach vendor, as revealed in the chapter on levels of contentment. Third, if a woman's husband is employed in the formal economy, he is paying taxes on his salary for the entire family to be covered by benefit packages. If the wife is also formally employed, the family will essentially be doubly taxed (Maloney 2004, 1165; Maloney and Arias 2007, 46). There was only one woman beach vendor whose husband had formal employment (in a tourist hotel), however, so this did not factor into their seeking informal or semi-informal self-employment. There were an additional nine whose husbands worked in construction, which sometimes, though not always, carries formal employment benefits. There were far more (N=53) women whose husbands or common-law husbands were also vendors, thus suggesting that beach vending was or is becoming part of a family tradition.

Most recent research on women vendors in Latin America has dealt with market vendors located primarily, though not exclusively, in various cities in Peru (e.g., Babb 1998; Bunster and Chaney 1989; Seligmann 2004; Weismantel 2001; see also Aliaga Linares 2002). Market vendors usually sell from a fixed or semi-fixed stall while the vast majority of beach vendors are ambulant. Ambulant street vendors are often forced into government-sponsored markets to clear them off the streets (e.g., see Cross 1998*a* on Mexico City). Unlike market vendors, who can bring their children to work with them, beach vendors in the past decade have been discouraged from doing so and seldom do, except perhaps on their days off. The only place I saw children accompanying vendors was during the summer in Acapulco. Only very occasionally in the other two tourist centers can one see a vendor approaching clients with a baby on her back, and these women are usually newcomers and lack a license. They are still unaware of or are ignoring the normative order.

Licenses are usually required for market vendors and are required for beach vendors in Puerto Vallarta and Cabo San Lucas. Licenses are limited in number in both tourist cities. Both market vendors and beach vendors may sell their licenses or pass them on to a relative or friend. Both may sponsor a friend or relative for membership in an organization or union that represents the vendors' interests. In those tourists centers where beach vendors are required to have a license, they are also required to wear white, whereas no uniform clothing is required for market vendors, who may chose to stress their indigenous identity in their dress (e.g., Little 2004; Van den Berghe 1994; Weismantel 2001). Even in Acapulco, where no uniform dress was required, vendors did not stress their ethnic identity. Both market women and women beach vendors may be immersed in a family legacy of vending, often following in the footsteps of their mothers, fathers, or siblings.

Market vendors, especially if they sell foodstuffs such as fresh produce, may have clients who visit them weekly, and may build an ongoing social relationship, however intermittent, with these customers. Whatever they sell, clients may return to their stalls several times a year, often bringing friends. Although three beach vendors, one of whom sold high-end jewelry he designed in Puerto Vallarta, said they had clients who looked them up each year they returned to the tourist center, the dynamics of vender-buyer relationships tend to be different. Long-term social relationships are nonexistent with one-time tourists, and most return tourists arrive only annually or biannually. Most long-term foreign residents tend to ignore the vendors. Contacts are thus more fragile and fleeting between beach vendors and their customers than between market vendors and their clients. There are exceptions, however. Beach vendors who sell prepared foodstuffs and sodas may establish long-term seller-buyer relationships with other vendors or with locals who come to the beach and buy from them regularly, primarily to avoid the high cost of these items on the beach in some of the tourist resorts. Very occasionally return tourists may seek out a vendor from whom they have bought wares in the past.

In Peru more women than men are market vendors. The reverse is true for beach vendors in Mexico. For example, in Cabo San Lucas, men outnumbered women by about five to three on the beach. Most marina vendors in 2010 tended to be women, however. Ambulant vendors on the marina essentially disappeared by mid-2011, having been replaced by vendors with fixed stalls. There may be an ongoing camaraderie between market vendors who occupy neighboring stalls. There is some camaraderie among beach vendors as well, even if unrelated by family or community ties. Those who belong to the same union or organization will see each other at monthly meetings. Yet beach vendors who live in the same colonia may know one another only by sight. There are, of course, ongoing relationships with paisanos, members of the same community of origin. On the beach, if a client asks a vendor for an item which s/he is not selling, s/he may send a friend or relative who is vending the item asked for.

Most women beach vendors, especially indigenous women, tend to walk up and down the beach with a female friend or relative, though some women are lone vendors. Men tend to vend alone, but when resting cluster with male friends and relatives in groups ranging from three to six. When a woman vendor is married to or in free union with another vendor, they may walk the beach alone, but the couple usually rests and eats lunch together. Mother and daughter vendors will do the same, as will sisters or brothers.

Women in the informal economy, including market, street, and beach vendors, may belong to any given civil status. They may be single and earning money for their own needs, or their income may be integral to their parents' or relatives' household economy. They may be married or living in free union and take part in the informal economy as part of a family labor force involved in the same income-generating activities or be working on their own right in order to pursue incomes supplementary to those of their husband's. Women heads of household, including unwed mothers and those who were abandoned, separated, divorced, or widowed, may often supply the bulk, if not all, of their household's income (Wilson 1998, 105). Furthermore, women beach vendors may be considered as marginalized on a number of indexes: their educational levels tend to be low, they often cannot find (though some do not desire) work in the formal economy, and they live in neighborhoods with high levels of poverty (Gámez, Ivanova, and Wilson 2011; Wilson, Gámez, and Ivanova 2012).[1] Nonetheless, for some women earning an income is seen as empowering, by permitting them to contribute to the household economy and perhaps spend money on the items they prioritize (most usually their children).

Much research on women street vendors in Mexico has focused on indigenous peoples. In a relatively early work, Arizpe (1980) looked at migration of Mazahuatl-speaking women vendors from four communities, three in the state of México and one in Querétaro, to Mexico City. While the most common pattern of migration was seasonal, with vendor income being complementary to subsistence farming, widows, single mothers, and those separated from their husbands tended to migrate more permanently, since rights to a farming plot were ceded almost exclusively to men (Arizpe 1980, 60, 76–77).

Martínez-Nova (2003) has examined the situation of Mixtec-speaking women who sell their wares to tourists in Tijuana and have been coming to the border from the states of Oaxaca, Guerrero, and Puebla since the late 1960s. She underscores their vulnerability to harassment by municipal authorities egged on by established merchants who view the street vendors as unfair competition (Martínez-Nova 2003, 252–53). Velasco Ortiz (2007) focuses on Mixtec migrants from Oaxaca who also have been arriving in Tijuana for the past 50 years. She argues that women street vendors have received training for their occupation at their place of origin:

> Women's market activities have historically been of great economic, political, and social importance not only in the Mixtec region but also throughout the state of Oaxaca. The complicated market system that has existed in the region has forked for centuries and has been a part of indigenous culture. At a young age, Mixtec women receive cultural training for commerce . . . (Velasco Ortiz 2007, 354).

She found that of the Mixtec women she surveyed in 1989, of the 38 percent who worked outside the home, 76 percent of those worked as street vendors, selling primarily to tourists. Notably, there has been a vending tradition in the Alto Balsas region of Guerrero as well, from which many of the vendors come and are found especially though not exclusively in Acapulco, as the chapter on ethnicity shows. Not all of the women beach vendors who were interviewed are indigenous, however. Thirty-seven of the 84 women interviewed spoke no indigenous language, though in several cases their parents did.

Although the women vendors interviewed ranged in age from 15 to 72, the vast majority (N=66, 78.6 percent) were between 20 and 50, and most of these had young children who were in school and dependent on their parents for sustenance. González de la Rocha (1994, 66) has pointed out that during a household's expansion phase, when the presence of children "multiplies the need for earnings," women are often forced to earn some kind of income for family survival. They have less pressure to do so, however, once their offspring begin entering the labor market. Women with children, González de la Rocha (1994, 65) holds, are most likely to be found in the informal economy, at least in Guadalajara. In the following pages we will look at women vendors by marital status, in an effort to show the importance of women's earnings to their household's economy.

Case Studies of Single Women without Children

Nineteen (22.6 percent) of the women beach vendors interviewed had never been married or lived in free union. Single women may spend the money they earn on their own needs or, more commonly, contribute their income or large portions of it to their parental household.

Case 7.1

Elena (CSL-30M), interviewed on the marina in Cabo San Lucas, is financing her studies in preparatory school by coming seasonally to vend in that city. Because she has eight siblings, it necessary for her to earn her own money if she wants to continue her schooling. Born in Donica, Querétaro, 20-year-old Elena speaks Spanish, Otomí, and a little English. Three of her five brothers are campesinos in Donica. One brother works as a cook in the United States and one brother and two of her three sisters are vendors in Cabo San Lucas. She resides with her siblings in the colonia Lomas del Sol when in Cabo. Elena joins these siblings during her school vacations, to vend dolls that she makes, and has done so for seven years. Sometimes her mother helps Elena with her expenses, but Elena tends to support herself through her vending activities. She earns 600 pesos on a good day and 100 pesos or nothing on a bad day; she works every day of the week. Elena has never been a vendor elsewhere, but worked as a cook's assistant in Donica. In Donica she earned 500 pesos for a week's work, while she can earn this daily, she points out, by selling her dolls in Cabo San Lucas. She would consider being a cook in a restaurant, however, if she were not a vendor. Elena would like to continue post-preparatory studies in pedagogy. She is very satisfied with being in Cabo San Lucas because she can be with her brother and sisters. She is very content with being a vendor, finding the most negative aspect to be harassment by authorities. Elena has no license to vend and belongs to no union or organization. Although her family social capital might enable her to get a license, the monthly fees would be prohibitive since she vends only seasonally. In total there were interviews with 11 single women without children in Cabo San Lucas.

In terms of financing her educational expenses, Elena's situation is similar to Damian's (ACA-23IC), who is in the second year of marine ecology at a local university in Acapulco. Damian sells clams and oysters by the dozen on Icacos Beach on weekends and during school vacations. He has a maternal aunt who sells the same thing on a nearby beach. Unlike Elena he does not need to migrate seasonally to earn income for his studies, as he lives in the same city in which he is a vendor. These cases are notable because both work in informal self-employment despite their high educational levels and to further their educational careers. Full-time work in formal employment might well interfere with their educational aspirations.

Case 7.2

Karen (ACA-5PD), age 18, is the eldest of her six siblings. She was born in Acapulco to parents who were also born there. She speaks no indigenous language. Karen has finished preparatory school and would like to continue studying to be a nurse. The family is strapped for money, however, so upon finishing preparatory school she took to beach vending only two weeks prior to being interviewed. Her mother and mother's sisters are also beach vendors. Karen, her mother, and her aunts all sell shells and shell ornaments. They pay a diver for the shells and make the ornaments themselves. She earns about 200 pesos on a good day and nothing on a bad day, while working all days of the week. What Karen likes about being a vendor is her ability to help her mother with household expenses. She contemplates no other work than studying to be a nurse. Her father cultivates borrowed lands on the periphery of Acapulco, and the corn he grows is used for family sustenance. Although licenses are not required for beach vendors in Acapulco, Karen works on Playa Diamante where it is propitious to belong to the local beach vendors' organization, Organización de Vendedores de Mayan. Karen has a temporary identification card from that organization, and her mother, who is a member, sponsored Karen's membership. The interview with Karen's mother, whom I call Victoria (ACA-4PD), was summarized in the chapter on levels of contentment. There were interviews with three single women without children in Acapulco.

Esther's (PV-6) story was summarized in the chapter on indigenous vendors. A Nahuatl speaker from Analco, Guerrero, she has finished primary school and would like to work in a hotel. She likes being a vendor because she earns her own money. All three of her sisters and her two brothers are beach vendors in Puerto Vallarta and will help her with her expenses if she has the need. No other women beach vendors interviewed in Puerto Vallarta were single and without children.

Case Studies of Female Heads of Household

Female heads of household may be single mothers or women who are separated, divorced, abandoned, or widowed. Because these women are among the most economically vulnerable, their work may often be forced, with few elements of empowerment. They may find it especially difficult to combine their economic and domestic work. This is especially true because in at least two of the tourist centers it is not allowed for vendors who are working on the beach to bring their children with them. It was made illegal to do so to stop the use of children as vendors in the hopes that they would attend school. Some vendors do bring their children to the beach on their days off.

Looking at the case of Puerto Vallarta, where there have been relatively high levels of female headed households over the past several decades, Chant

(1997*a*, 140) stresses the importance of employment in tourism as factor in the existence of these types of household:

> On the one hand, because tourism offers a range of female job opportunities, lone women, with or without children, who may lack access to the means of survival in other places, are attracted to resort towns. At another level, the scope to earn an independent . . . income means that there is not the same pressure on women to unite with men or remain with existing partners as in places where they have a less favourable position in the labour market.

As mentioned above beach vendors may earn more than the going minimum wage, and their sales to tourists in times of economic normality provide them with a relatively favorable position, as concerns their earnings, in the labor market.

Notably, in 2010, 22.8 percent of households in Los Cabos were female headed, as compared to 26.1 percent in Puerto Vallarta and 31.2 percent in Acapulco (derived from INEGI 2011*b*). The high percentage of female-headed households in Acapulco is partially explained by its low male to female ratio of 93.8 men per 100 women. It also has a long history as a tourist center that provides work for women. Conversely, the relatively lower percentage of female-headed households in Los Cabos can be partially explained by its high male to female ratio of 106.7 men per 100 women. There are simply more men to partner with in Los Cabos than in Acapulco. Many of the men migrated to Los Cabos during the construction boom of the 1990s and stayed on. The male-female ratio in Puerto Vallarta is almost at par with 101.2 men per 100 women. In this section I will present cases of widows, separated or abandoned women, and single mothers. Many are female heads of household, though some have taken refuge in the household of their parents or other relative.

Widows

Three of the women vendors interviewed were widows.

Case 7.3

Bernarda (ACA-16CA) is a 40-year-old widow whose husband died three years ago. She has a 10-year-old daughter who attends primary school and a 12-year-old son who has begun secondary school. Bernarda, who is from Tlapa, Guerrero, has never been to school and says she does not know how to read or write. She speaks Tlapaneco and a little Spanish. Bernarda comes to Acapulco only during her children's school vacations and sells children's beach toys on Caleta Beach. She lives in a room lent to her by a friend while in Acapulco. Bernarda has no relatives who are vendors. Acquaintances of hers advised her that there was work in the city as a beach vendor. She has been a vendor only since her husband died. He worked in construction and was killed in an accident on the job. When Bernarda is in Acapulco she works every day, earning 150 to 200 pesos on a good day and nothing on a bad day. No one helps her with her expenses. She is happier living in Tlapa than living in Acapulco and would prefer not to have to work. Bernarda says she makes few sales, but is very content with her work because she can earn money to sustain her children.

Case 7.4

Alejandra (CSL-21M), born in Acapulco, was interviewed on the marina in Cabo San Lucas. Age 26, she is a widow. Her husband, a construction work, died on the job, leaving her with four children, age nine months to seven years old. Alejandra has lived in Cabo San Lucas for nine years and been a vendor for eight. She has no relatives who are vendors. She finished secondary school and would like to study to be a nurse. If she were not a vendor she would like to stay at home and take care of her children. No one helps her with household expenses, and she has no relatives in Cabo San Lucas. Alejandra sells ceramic turtle-shaped flutes and has earned up to US$ 70 on a good day. She has no vendor's license and complains about harassment from the police. She likes working without a boss, however. She lives in the colonia El Cactus, having taken part in an invasion of lands that established this colonia. Alejandra hopes to remain in Los Cabos the rest of her life. Notably Alejandra is marginalized on a number of indexes. She is a widow needing to support four children, with no help. She has no relatives nearby to aid her in any way. Since she doesn't have a vendor's license she is at risk of having her merchandise confiscated, of being fined, or even being put into jail.

Case 7.5

Matilde (PV-8) is a 27-year-old widow with two children, age three and four, to support. She was born in Analco, Guerrero, and speaks Nahuatl, Spanish, and a little English. Matilde never went to school and if she could study anything she would like to learn to read. One of her brothers brought her to Puerto Vallarta 10 years ago, and Matilde has been a beach vendor since arriving. Her brother then moved on to Acapulco, where all 10 of her siblings are beach vendors. Matilde buys semiprecious stones in Iguala, Guerrero, during her annual returns to Analco during the Festival of the Resurrection. She assembles them into the necklaces she sells on the beach, and this is her favorite part of her work. She earns 200 pesos on a good day, 50 pesos on a bad day. Matilde is very content with her work because she always earns at least a little money. When Matilde was asked what she doesn't like about being a vendor, she replies that even if she didn't like it there was nothing else she could find to do ("*Aúnque no me gustara, no me queda de otra*"). If she could find other work, however, she would like it to be somewhere in the shade. She does have a vendor's license that cost her 20,000 pesos to acquire, with a 1,000 peso annual renewal fee. No one helps her with her expenses, which include 1,000 pesos a month to rent a room. Matilde is marginalized because she is indigenous, by her lack of schooling, by the absence of relatives nearby, and by the need to support, alone, her two young children.

Separated and Abandoned Women

Seven women (8.3 percent) were separated from or had been abandoned by their husbands.

Case 7.6

Mercedes (ACA-7IC) is a 32-year-old vendor who has been separated from her husband for two years. She has a 10-year-old son who is to enter the fourth year of primary school in fall 2010. Born in Acapulco to parents born in Acapulco, Mercedes speaks no indigenous language. She completed primary school and has been a beach vendor for five years. She sells saris made in Indonesia, earning 200 pesos on a good day and nothing on a bad day. Mercedes works every day of the week on Icacos Beach. No one helps her with her expenses. Her mother is deceased and her father works as a beach vendor in Acapulco. Her three brothers, age 39, 45, and 48, live in the Federal District, but she has no contact with them. She has no relatives, other than her father, who are vendors. Her husband left her their house. She would like to study at least as far as preparatory school. When asked what work she would like to do if she were not a vendor, Mercedes replies, "in anything, but I don't know how to do anything else" ("*en lo que sea per no sé hacer otra cosa*"). She complains about the lack of tourists and earning so little that she can barely cover the cost of food.

Case 7.7

Patricia (PV-23) is a 27-year-old vendor from Lázaro Cardenas, Michoacán. She has a five-year-old son. Of her five siblings, her three brothers are beach vendors, also in Puerto Vallarta. Her brothers brought her to that city

10 years ago. Patricia has been a vendor for six years and sells semi-precious stone necklaces. She acquires the stones from a wholesaler who comes to her eldest brother's house every month to sell them. Patricia lives with this 35-year-old brother and his wife. She earns 300 pesos on a good day and nothing on a bad day. Patricia has finished primary school but would like to complete secondary school and work in an office as a secretary. She has a vendor's license that cost her 20,000 pesos to acquire with an annual renewal fee of 1,200 pesos. What she likes about being a vendor is the ability to earn her own money and assure the welfare of her son. She complains about the lack of tourism and consequent low sales, however. Since she lives with a sibling, Patrica cannot be considered a female head of household but is part of an extended family.

Marina's (ACA-25IC) story was outlined in the chapter on the family legacy of beach vendors. Age 46, she was abandoned by her husband, a taxi driver, six years prior to the interview. The youngest of her four children is 22 and the eldest 29, so she need not support them. Her 25-year-old daughter sometimes helps her with expenses. Both Marina and this daughter sell woven handbags made by prisoners, returning all the money except for 20 pesos per piece to these imprisoned men. Marina can be envisioned as a commission seller. She has lived in her own home, which she says she paid for, for the past 10 years.

Single Mothers

The summary of the interview with Magdaelena (ACA-19CA), a 48-year-old single mother with two adult sons, was included in the chapter questioning whether the vendors had wasted lives. Single mothers, whether female-heads of household or incorporated into an extended family, are under great pressure to earn an income. Four of the vendors interviewed were single mothers.

Case 7.8

Martha (ACA-24IC), age 29, is a single mother with four children ranging in ages from six to 12. The three youngest are in primary school and the 12-year-old has entered secondary school. Martha finished primary school. She was born in Acapulco, as were her parents. She would like to have continued on to finish preparatory school. Martha, her parents, and her four brothers and two sisters are vendors on Playa Icacos. She also has a maternal uncle and nine cousins, offspring of mother's sisters, who are beach vendors. Most of these relatives sell coconut tanning oil, as does Martha. Some also sell silver jewelry. Besides coconut tanning oil, Martha also sells sundresses she buys from friends who make them, sand pails, and necklaces made from shells and beads. She says she earns only 120 pesos on a good day because sales are now very low. She attributes these low sales to increases in the number of vendors. Martha says she has been a beach vendor for 22 years, since she was seven years old. She and her children live in her parents' house and have always done so. No one helps her with her expenses, which include buying school supplies for all four of the children. If she were not a vendor she would like to be a policewoman. Neither Patricia nor Martha are as bad off as the widowed Matilde, since they are able to live with relatives. Matilde, on the other hand, must pay rent each month, and thus her economic burden is greater. Furthermore, she has neither the emotional nor child-care support enjoyed by the other women. This may be the reason why she prefers being in her hometown, where she would have such support, rather than in Acapulco. Partnered women, too, will often have more emotional and child-care support, as well as sharing expenses rather than being responsible for all of them.

Case Studies of Partnered Women

The income earned from the vending activities of partnered women often comprises a core input into the household economy. Their money may be earmarked for school supplies and uniforms for the couple's children. A wife's economic contribution may make the difference between living in a rented room and the ability to acquire a lot in a colonia. Her income may also be used to help buy materials to convert fragile self-built housing into more consolidated cement-block housing. A wife's income may also influence the rapidity with which contracts can be made to pay for the extension of electricity or running water to the lot on which the family lives. At other times a wife's income may be necessary simply for family survival.

Case Studies of Married Women

Thirty-eight of the 84 women vendors interviewed were legally married (45.2 percent). Of these 38, 26 (68.4 percent) were married to men who were also vendors. Five (13.2 percent) were married to men who work or have worked in construction.

Case 7.9

Lourdes (ACA-1PD) is a 56-year-old married women with four children ages 25 to 39. She was born in the mountains of Veracruz. Her parents had migrated there from Arcelia, Guerrero, to cultivate corn, rice, beans, squash, and cucumbers on lands lent to them by ejidatarios.[2] Lourdes has been a vendor for 18 years, since her youngest, a daughter, was seven years old. Her husband and eldest son, age 39, are also beach vendors. Her youngest daughter, age 25, and her 37-year-old daughter are in the United States, both without documents. Lourdes also worked in the United States, in the city of New Orleans, as a babysitter when she was 14 and 15. She crossed the border with a visa arranged for her by the family who hired her. The family she worked for eventually returned to Mexico, settling in Acapulco. Meanwhile Lourdes's family had also moved to Acapulco from Veracruz. Her father continued to cultivate borrowed lands, now on the periphery of Acapulco.

Lourdes and her husband have owned their own house for 15 years, three years after Lourdes started working as a vendor and after her older children became independent. Lourdes sells sundresses made of Indonesian cloth that she buys ready made in a downtown store at wholesale prices. Her husband sells silver jewelry. During high tourist seasons such as those of Easter week, Christmas vacation, and summers, she earns 500 pesos on a good day and 150 pesos on a bad day. Lourdes completed only five years of primary school but would have liked to study interior design. If she were not a vendor, Lourdes would like to be a volunteer in an organization (such as an orphanage or a day-care center) that cares for children. Lourdes says she and her husband share household expenses. She is very happy with her life in Acapulco, saying it is not necessary to be rich in order to be happy ("*No necesita ser rica para ser feliz*").

Case 7.10

Julia (CSL-9P) is a 28-year-old vendor with four children, ranging in ages from four months to 12. Her family of orientation is thus in the stage of expansion, with high levels of dependency. The two eldest, ages nine and 12, are presently in school. Julia, born in San Juan Tetelcingo, Guerrero, speaks Nahuatl, Spanish, and a little English. She had lived in Cabo San Lucas only two months at the time of the interview in September 2010. She, her husband, and their children joined her husband's family there. Nonetheless, all of her siblings, including four brothers and three sisters, also live in Cabo San Lucas and are beach vendors there. She and her husband are renting a house in El Caribe, a colonia partially established by invasion in 2006.

Julia has been a vendor for 20 years, previously in Puerto Peñasco, Sonora. She prefers Cabo to Puerto Peñasco because, she says, it was very cold in that latter city. Unlike most women vendors from San Juan Tetelcingo who tend to sell semiprecious stone necklaces they assemble, Julia sells sunglasses and braids hair. This is also what she did in Puerto Peñasco. Unlike many sellers of sunglasses, she does not work for a commission. Her husband makes ceramic pitchers. On a good day Julia earns 200 pesos, on a bad day nothing. She likes her work because of the flexible hours, but says she works every day of the week. Julia has never been to school and if she could study anything it would be to learn to read and write. If she were not a vendor she would like to work in a beauty salon. Despite the presence of small and dependent children, Julia can work because of the aid she can tap from her siblings' and husband's family members. She does not question that she needs to bring income into her household.

Case 7.11

Irene (PV-20) is a 35-year-old vendor born in Mitla, Oaxaca. She finished secondary school and speaks Spanish, a little English, and a little Zapotec. Her husband is a beach vendor in Puerto Vallarta, as is she. Three of her six brothers are beach vendors in Cabo San Lucas. Irene and her husband have two sons, ages 13 and 14. Both are in secondary school. Although they have lived in Puerto Vallarta for 10 years, the couple does not own their own home. They pay 1,800 pesos a month in rent, which Irene says is often difficult to come up with. Irene sells semiprecious stone necklaces and earrings that she makes. She buys the stones from a man from Guerrero who comes to the Playa de los Muertos in Puerto Vallarta to sell them to the vendors on the beach. She has a vendor's license that her husband acquired for her. The annual renewal fee is 1,500 pesos. If she could study anything it would be to become a teacher or a doctor. When asked how content she was with her work, Irene pointed out that the economic crisis has affected everyone very badly. She adds that one does not earn enough to get out of debt or for daily livelihood ("*No gana uno para salir de deudas o para la vida diaria*").

Case Studies of Women Living in Free Union

Fifteen of the 84 women (17.9 percent) were living in free union. Eight of these 15 (53.3 percent) were common-law wives of beach vendors. The partners of four (26.4 percent) were construction workers. Living in free union is often more the woman's choice than man's (Chant 1991). Chant (1991) has noted that in Puerto Vallarta, where there are many jobs available for women in tourism and tourism-related employment, women often choose free union over marriage. This is partially because in free union the man has less control over his partner's activities, and partially because if he fails to support the family or refuses to work his partner is not obligated to maintain him with her own income.

Alma's (PV-9) story was summarized in the chapter on levels of contentment. She, a brother of hers who is a cook, and her common-law husband, a construction worker, help support the household that contains five children ages seven to 15. All of the children are in school. Alma, age 26, was born in Analco, Guerrero, and speaks Nahuatl as well as Spanish.

Cecilia's (PV-21) interview was also summarized in the chapter on levels of contentment. Age 32 and born in San Juan Copala, Oaxaca, she lives in free union with a man who works cleaning a restaurant. Her children range in age from eight to 18. Her 18-year-old son washes dishes in a taco stand and her 17-year-old son sells candy and chewing gum on the beach in Puerto Vallarta. Cecilia has only been in Puerto Vallarta for one year. She left her 13- and eight-year-old daughters with her parents in the Federal District. Both are attending primary school there. Cecilia finished only the second year of primary school.

Case 7.12

Maribel (ACA-2PD) is a 42-year-old vendor born in Acapulco to parents who migrated to that city from small towns in Guerrero. Her father works in construction, and her mother is a beach vendor on Playa Diamante, as is Maribel. Maribel lives in free union and has two children, a boy age 13, who will enter the second year of secondary school in 2010; and a six-year-old daughter who will begin primary school in that year. Maribel has finished primary school, and as is the case with the vast majority of all of the vendors, her children are reaching higher educational levels than their parents. Maribel's common-law husband, three of her four sisters, and one of her three brothers are beach vendors in Acapulco. Maribel has been a vendor for 29 years, first contributing income to her parents' household and later to her family of orientation. She and her partner have owned a house for 14 years.

Maribel sells blouses, some of which she makes and some of which she buys from a wholesaler who comes to the beach to sell them to the vendors. Although she has never had other employment, Maribel likes being a vendor because no one gives her orders (i.e., she has no boss). Because of her positive evaluation of her autonomy as a vendor, she would not take any other job. Maribel works all seven days of the week. She finds two difficulties about her work: she has fewer clients since fewer tourists are arriving this year; and, second, there are far more vendors on the beach than previously, thus increasing competition for the attention of the few tourists there are. Notably, both of her children are of school age, and an infusion of money into the household is necessary to buy their school uniforms and supplies.

Case 7.13

Janet (PV-25) is a 32-year-old vendor born in Mascota, Jalisco. She lives in free union with a vendor who sells silver jewelry from Taxco on the beach in Puerto Vallarta. Janet finished primary school and if she could study anything it would be to become a beautician. If she were not a vendor she would like to open a beauty salon. She met her partner in Puerto Vallarta, where she has lived for 15 years. She has two children, a daughter age 15 who is in the last year of secondary school, and a son age 10 who is in the fourth year of primary school. Janet has been a vendor for five years. She sells silver earrings that her partner acquires for her. What she likes most about vending is its flexible hours. She has no fixed days that she comes to vend on the beach. On a good day she earns 500 pesos, on a bad day 100. Janet has no vendor's license. Although she likes everything about being a vendor, she complains that sales are low because the economic crisis had led to a fall in the number of tourists.

Case 7.14

Erica (CSL-34P) is a 28-year-old woman living in free union who sells sodas, fruit juices, and snacks on Medano Beach in Cabo San Lucas. Her story was partially revealed in the chapter on residential apartheid. Born in a small town in the municipio of Chilpancingo, Guerrero, her father owns 20 hectares of private property that he farms. All of her siblings, including 11 sisters and four brothers are older than she is. All of her brothers are campesinos in their hometown. Erica has completed only one year of primary school and wishes she could continue her studies until completing secondary school. Although she does not mention it, it is most probably due to her having so many siblings that resources were not forthcoming for her to continue her education.

When I interviewed Erica in September of 2010, she had an 18-month-old and a four-year-old son, and was expecting to give birth to another child. Seven years previously she had worked in Anaheim, California, as a hotel chambermaid. It was there that she met her common law husband, Héctor (CSL-16P), who had crossed three times to work in Anaheim putting down wooden floors. Both had crossed the border without documents. Héctor was born in the city of Chilpancingo, Guerrero, the capital of the municipio of Chilpancingo. His father was a campesino who sometimes sharecropped and sometimes rented lands. Hector is also a vendor on Medano Beach, selling uniquely framed sunglasses made in China and Cuban cigars. He sells both on commission but hopes to become independent in some months.

Erica and I got together several times after the interview, and I visited the family in their corrugated tin house in El Caribe. They had bought the lot in

2007 from a friend of Héctor's who had taken part in the invasion of lands that were still not occupied in the colonia. The friend advised Héctor, soon after the couple's return to Guerrero from Anaheim, that there was work in Cabo.

Erica has been a vendor for only one year, and works four or five days a week. She likes earning her own money so she can spend it on her children. What she does not like about vending is having to leave her children under the care of someone else. This is usually her next-door neighbor, since neither she nor Héctor have relatives in Cabo San Lucas. Just before her youngest son was born in January of 2011, Erica decided to take a year off from being a vendor, until he was old enough so that she could confidently leave him in the care of someone else. She and her children often visit Medano Beach when Hector is vending there, however. Héctor hopes to become an independent vendor by the end of 2011, rather than working on a commission basis. He needs capital to do this, however, which is scarce since Erica has stopped working. They were able to buy a secondhand car—their first—in March of 2011, however.

Once, when I was talking to Erica after her third child was born, I jokingly asked, "When will the wedding take place?" Erica told me in no uncertain terms that she had no desire to get married. She explained to me that problems always come up if one is married, whereas if one is living in free union there is more respect between the couple. This was because if the man mistreated his partner (whether emotionally or physically), she could leave him, taking her children with her. Thus living in free union gives women greater influence on family dynamics. If it occurs to the man to mistreat her, she can just walk away. If he objects to her working in public space, she can continue to do so, on her own. Chant (1997*b*, 160), in her study of women in Puerto Vallarta, has noted that it is primarily women who wish to avoid marriage; they prefer living in free union to try out their partners before making a firmer commitment. She explains that men in that tourist center have some notoriety about seeking women who they can live off, and women wish to avoid partnering with a man who will be a sponge.

Conclusion

It has been suggested that wives who bring an income into their households have more egalitarian relationships with their husbands than those who do not. Benería and Roldán (1987, chap. 7), in their study of women home workers in Mexico City, found that in households in which women contributed 40 percent or more of household income, they have more say in household decision making and can demand more respect from their husbands. This finding has been contested, however, with the argument that women's income may challenge men's traditional role as household breadwinner and lead to domestic violence as men try to assert control over their wives (e.g., Casique 2010; Olivera 2006; Staudt 2008, 68–70). The argument can be reduced to the question of whether or not women are empowered by generating an income.

There must be at least some subjective feelings of empowerment among single women who, like Karen, see themselves as contributing to household well-being, or like Elena, who has taken on responsibility for the bulk of expenditures for her own schooling. Married women and women living in free union may or may not feel empowered. Some partnered women, such as Erica, point out that they can spend their money on their children and feel positive about this. Others, such and Maribel and Janet, simply say they enjoy their work. Still others, such as Irene, point out that the economic recession does not permit them to even cover their basic needs, and thus her contributions to the family may be seen as forced, rather than as empowering.

For women who are heads of household or widowed, divorced, or separated and living with relatives in an extended family household, their economic contributions to the family encompass no element of choice. They must sustain themselves and their offspring at any cost, and as Mercedes, may be forced into beach vending by a lack of education that closes off any other avenues of work. They are thus the least empowered and most marginalized of all the women vendors.

The women vendors are objectively marginalized, as are the men, by their economic activities in a time of economic recession (in which no earnings are received on a bad day), by their lower levels of education than men, and by the social and residential apartheid conditions that they share with their families. Women who are raising children alone, whether separated, abandoned, or single mothers, are struggling to survive in an especially precarious and marginalized situation. In some cases women are also marginalized because they are indigenous peoples. Nonetheless their ambulant vending contributes to family poverty reduction and may permit them to have a greater say within their households, if married, living in free union, or living with relatives (Wilson, and Ivanova Gámez 2012; Gámez, Ivanova, and Wilson 2011).

Notes

1. In looking at the informal economy as a whole throughout the developing world, Sethuraman (1998, 3–31, 37–39) found at least four patterns that distinguished women workers from male workers. First, women are more dependent on employment in the urban informal economy than men. Second, there are proportionally more women in the informal economy than their proportional share in the labor force. Third, nonetheless, fewer women in the informal economy are self-employed

and proportionately more are informal wage workers, including home workers, and unpaid family laborers. Fourth, although the self-employed tend to have higher incomes than the informal wage workers, women tend to earn less than men in both subsectors of the informal economy. Women, then, continue to be marginalized to a greater extent than men in their informal income-generating activities.

2. Under the *ejido* regime extant prior to changes in the Agrarian Reform Law in 1992, lands could be confiscated from an *ejidatario* if they remained uncultivated for more than two years. This may have motivated ejidatarios to lend their ejido plots to someone who would cultivate them in the case of the edjidatario's absence or disability or if they had no sons available to cultivate the land for them.

Conclusion

THE SAMPLES OF BEACH VENDORS are so small and nonrandom that generalizations about their migration to the tourist destinations cannot readily be made. My impression, however, is that most in-migrants to the tourist cities are from rural ranchos and pueblos (78.9 percent of the sample). For the 21.1 percent born in cities such as Acapulco, Mazatlán, and the Federal District, almost all of their parents migrated into these cities from rural areas. Most in-migrants to Acapulco come from the rural hinterlands in various states, and most from the state of Guerrero. This is supported by statistics from Mexico's *Instituto Nacional de Estádistica, Geografía e Informática* (INEGI 2011*c*) that reveal that only 2.7 percent of the population of the municipio of Acapulco de Juárez came from out of the state of Guerrero in 2000. The five principal out-of-state sending areas were the Federal District (25.4 percent of in-migrants), the state of Mexico (15.4 percent), Oaxaca (10.3 percent), and Michoacán (7 percent). Listed as being from another country were 9.8 percent. In Puerto Vallarta, on the other hand, 30.6 percent of its population as from outside the state of Jalisco (see Wilson 2008, table 6, 44). Of these in-migrants 4.4 percent were foreigners. Data retrieved in the 2000 national census show that in Los Cabos 46.7 percent of its population was from outside the state of Baja California. The data also reveal that there are a wider variety of states that send migrants to Los Cabos than to Puerto Vallarta, however (INEGI 2004). On the one hand, in Puerto Vallarta, four sending states and the Federal District send 68.4 percent of the Mexicans born outside the state of Jalisco. The five most important places of origin of in-migrants are Nayarit (26.1 percent), Guerrero (18 percent), the Federal District (13.7 percent),

Michoacán (9.4 percent), and Guanajuato (4.3 percent). The migration networks from these places of origin have become well developed and perhaps exclusionary.

On the other hand, in Los Cabos in-migrants seem to be arriving in an exploratory fashion from almost all regions of the Republic. Thus Guerrero (11.4 percent), Sinaloa (6.9 percent), the Federal District (4.5 percent), Jalisco (3.4 percent), and Oaxaca (2.8 percent) are the top five origins of in-migrants to Los Cabos, yet they make up only 28.8 percent of the migrants born elsewhere in Mexico. Furthermore, the top 10 sending states (of 32 Mexican states and the Federal District) make up only 37.1 percent of the population born outside of Baja California Sur (Wilson 2008, 45). Notably, the economy in Puerto Vallarta is more diverse than that in Los Cabos. For example, in Los Cabos in 1999 only 6.3 percent of salaried employment was in manufacturing, while 37.5 percent was in hotels and restaurants. In Puerto Vallarta, in contrast, 22.5 percent of the salaried employment was in manufacturing, as compared to 17.8 percent in hotels and restaurants (Schafran and Monkkonen 2011, table 5, 238).

Thus it can be postulated that, with some exceptions, most of the vendors on the three beaches are rural-to-urban migrants (or their parents were) in search of employment opportunities. But are they marginalized? A distinction can be made between objective and subjective marginalization, the former referring to their measurable economic and social positioning, the latter with how they feel about their positioning. Much literature on the informal economy has stressed the objective marginalization of those who find themselves as wage workers or self-employed within it. It is important, however, to map the subjective feelings of those involved. As seen previously, these feelings may be expected to differ between the informal salaried and the self-employed, with the latter feeling more positive about their income-generating activities. Nonetheless, there may be variability even among the self-employed.

Two types of questions may be posed to measure subjective marginality in terms of work. The first type involves asking what the self-employed (in this case vendors) would have studied if they could and what work they would like to do if not a vendor. The second type involves asking people how content they are with their work, what they like about it, and what they do not like about it. The responses of beach vendors to these questions were presented in chapters 2 and 3. It was found that the least-educated women and the most-educated men were among those most content with their work. In total 73.2 percent of men and 67.9 percent of women were very content with being beach vendors.

Some of the vendors were relatively well educated and either could not find jobs in the formal economy, or, in a few cases, did not choose to do so.

Those who would have chosen formal employment are essentially faced with a lack of economic development that could use their skills in the places where they live. Others had very little or no education and would be unqualified and unable to find employment in the formal economy. (Tokman 1998) has identified lack of educational opportunities as one of the principal causes of the great income inequality found throughout countries in Latin America. He holds that "the critical issues go beyond universal coverage of primary education and include strategies for narrowing the gap in educational quality differences based on income levels and introducing complementary programs to compensate for household constraints, which result in unequal opportunities" (Tokman 1998, 217). Mexico has moved in the direction, through the *Progresa* (Progress) program established in 1997 and the *Oportunidades* (Opportunities), which replaced it in 2002. Both programs involve giving cash payments to mothers of poverty-stricken families in exchange for their children's regular school attendance as well as attendance at health clinics.

Given the high levels of contentment with their work and the presence of some well-educated vendors, it remains to explore whether, if better educated, some of those vendors with little education would still have remained vendors. This question becomes more complicated in the case of those who are intermittent vendors, especially if they are also peasants. In that case, their vending is necessary to sustain them in their rural communities of origin. It can be concluded that though beach vendors may be objectively marginalized, they are not all subjectively so—with the exception of those who have never been to school and decry their lack of education and those who are marginalized because of being indigenous peoples or female heads of households.

Many of the vendors, as well, are pulled into (semi-)informal self-employment as vendors as part of a family legacy. Family members will pass on important information about how to deal with tourists, how to add value to materials such as semiprecious stones or textiles, where to acquire merchandise, what union it might be valuable to join, how to acquire a license if this is necessary, and so on. Unemployed family members may be networked in to a specific beach in a given tourist center and if kinship and/or community networks span several tourist centers these provide them the opportunity to try vending in multiple locales. These findings can be generalized to ambulant and street vendors as well, if not to most types of self-employment in petty commerce.

There is objective marginalization in the residential and social apartheid to which the less well-off are subjected. This form of marginalization vendors share with most of Mexico's informal, and even the lower echelons of the formal, working class. Although they are residentially segregated due to the speculation in land in the tourist centers that make properties in the central zones beyond their economic reach, they do have the hope of owning their own house lot and home someday. Over time, houses made of scrap materials are converted into more substantial structures, dirt floors are replaced by cement ones with ceramic tiles sometimes added. Although their housing never reaches the quality enjoyed by the better off, they come to have, if the land is regularized, a home of their own. The process may take many years and depend much on the local government's willingness to regularize invaded lands or negotiate with ejidos or landowners to acquire the spaces that will become the residential colonias, but eventually, much of the time, people are able to own their own homes that eventually, over time, become relatively comfortable. People thus do not feel subjectively marginalized, as they come to control a property rather than paying rent or living with relatives in overcrowded housing. On the other hand, the social apartheid on beaches in front of luxury hotels represents both objective and subjective marginalization since vendors and other poor Mexicans are denied entry in a humiliating fashion.

Indigenous peoples involved in petty commerce are traditionally peasants or offspring of peasants and often come from regions where long-distance petty commerce has gone on for an extended period, sometimes for centuries. Many have a dense family or community legacy of vending, and hence may not feel marginalized by partaking in vending activities. Yet as members of peasant families they have been marginalized not only in this new epoch of globalization but since the Green Revolution was introduced into Mexico after World War II. As indigenous peoples they are also marginalized by racist reactions by the some of the nonindigenous population and by assimilationist policies at various levels of government. Yet, in many cases, they reconstruct community in the tourist centers to which they migrate, and in some places found bi-lingual schools so their children will be able to speak the indigenous language. In some places as well, religious organizations attempt outreach by providing services in indigenous languages.

That women are structurally subordinated worldwide as well as in Mexico has received much attention in the feminist literature. This subordination may take a (neo-)patriarchal or an economic form or an intertwining of both. I did not explore women's subordination as such in the interviews, though their answers to questions about their education and work preferences showed some felt they were marginalized. Some women vendors did indeed feel subjectively marginalized and would have preferred to stay at home with their children. (A few of the older men would also have preferred to retire.) Those who had never been to school also felt marginalized because of their lack of literacy. Yet, some women (including those with little education), though objectively forced to earn an income to maintain themselves and their offspring, or to contribute to the household economy, were nonetheless content with their work. Feeling the pressure to contribute to the economic well-being of their households, they found that petty commerce enabled them to work the hours and days they wished, a situation unavailable in formal employment. Many expressed satisfaction that they were generating an income under their own control.

It may be argued, then, that objective and subjective marginality are not coterminous. Although there is no question that on all indexes—including economic well-being, residential arrangements, ethnicity, and gender—the vendors are objectively marginalized, yet they find spaces for contentment even under conditions of economic recession that affect their daily earnings. Crossing economic, cultural, and often linguistic borders, they come to occupy the transnational social spaces that the tourist centers represent.

There are strong links between the formal economy and the semi-informal or informal economy as represented by the beach vendors. Thus canvas bags and T-shirts are mass-produced in Mexican cities and sent to various tourist centers where wholesalers stamp them with a local logo. Silver, mined and fashioned into jewelry in the Taxco region of Guerrero, is ubiquitous in most tourist centers in Mexico. Ceramic or clay plates may be mass-produced, then hand painted by the vendor and/or his/her family members. There are international linkages as well. The semiprecious stone necklaces may be made of beads mined in Mexico or Asia. Dresses are sewn from cloth imported from Indonesia or India; and vendors sell fans, sunglasses, and other wares made in China. Though some of these items may be produced by informalized labor in the various places of origin, a link with the formal economy is necessary for their importation. The vendor often adds value to the items of international origin. This is the case when cloth from Indonesia or India is cut and sewn into dresses, skirts, or sundresses and when semiprecious stones from Asia are assembled into necklaces or other jewelry by many of the vendors who sell them.

There are, however, also "local" value chains. By this I mean that the vendor or his/her family or community members manufacture the merchandise, in an artisan mode. This is the case of handwoven palm handbags, handwoven name bracelets, "typical" Oaxacan clothing, amate bark paintings, paintings on tiles or paper—all made by the vendors with or without the help of family members. In some of these cases there may be inputs from formal firms—for example, the thread used in woven name bracelets or the tiles upon which one vendor paints. Thus there are both formal-informal linkages, both national and international, and informal-informal linkages, both national and local.

I have argued that the growing numbers of beach vendors over the years can be both a pro-cyclical and countercyclical phenomenon. As tourism expands and more tourist hotels fronting the public beaches are built, the number of beach vendors may increase. Thus their numbers expand with the success of the tourist economy, and their presence is pro-cyclical with regard to that sector of the economy. On the other hand, with general economic slowdown leading to high rates of unemployment, this semi-informal or informal economic activity may also expand and thus be countercyclical. The problem, in times of economic downturn as concerns the informally and semi-informally self-employed in the "retail trade" is the following: "Even if the level of sales does not increase, an 'ease of entry' permits new workers to find a job at the cost of reducing the average income of those who are already working in that sector. More vendors at the main square will increase employment, at the cost of reducing the income that each one receives" (Cortázar 1998, 77). Vendors become pitted against vendors in their struggle for a livelihood. In Los Cabos, for example, vendors with licenses pressured the municipal government to rid the beaches of those without licenses, whose numbers were increasing annually. Thus, it can be seen, there are degrees of marginality: those who have licenses, where these are required, are less marginal than those who do not. The former can be considered semi-informal, and the latter completely informal.

Hopefully, some of the findings about beach vendors can be fruitfully used to analyze the situation of others involved in petty commerce around the world, whether on the streets of cities or on the beaches in tourist centers. The stories about their migrations and their quest for a livelihood are interesting in themselves and form part of the history of the contemporary (objectively) marginalized peoples of the world and their struggles for survival under forces of globalization.

Appendix I

Interview Schedule

1. *¿Cuál es su nombre?* (What is your name?)
2. *¿Es usted . . . ?* Are you . . . ?
   ( ) *soltero/a* (single) ( ) *casado/a* (married) ( ) *juntado/a* (free union) ( ) *viudo/a* (widowed) ( ) *separado/a* (separated) ( ) *divorciado/a* (divorced)
3. *¿Hasta que año de la escuela completó?* (Until what year did you finish school?)
4. *¿Cuántos años tiene?* (How old are you?)
5. *¿Qué lenguas habla?* (What languages do you speak?)
6. *¿Dónde nació?* (*nombre de lugar y estado*) (Where were you born? (name of place and state))
   6.1 *¿Es rancho, pueblo, ciudad?* (subraye). (Is it a rancho, pueblo, city? (underline))
7. *¿Cuántas hijos/hijas tiene?* (How many sons/daughters do you have?)
   7.1 Edad (Age) *¿Año de escuela o en que trabaja?* (Year in school or in what is working?)
8. *¿Dónde nació su papa?* (Where was your father born?)

* 9. *¿En que trabaja su papá?* (What work does your father do?)*

**10. *Si la respuesta es en el campo, pregunta si fuera* (If the reply is in on the farm, ask whether he was) ( ) *journalero* (day laborer) ( ) *mediero* (sharecropper) ( ) *teniá propios terrerenos* (had his own lands). (*subraya todos que aplican* (check all that apply).

11. *¿Dónde nació su mamá?* (Where was your mother born?)
12. *¿En qué trabaja su mamá?* (What work does your mother do?)*
13. *¿Ha ido a los Estados Unidos?* (Have you gone to the United States?) *Sí* (Yes) *No* (No). *Si, sí* (If yes).
    13.1. *¿Cuántas veces?* (How many times?)
    13.2. *¿Adónde fue?* (Where did you go?)
    13.3. *¿En que año(s) fue?* (In what year(s) did you go?)
    13.4. *¿En que trabajó?* (What work did you do?)
14. *¿Cuántas hermanas y hermanos tiene?* (How many sisters and brothers do you have?)
    14.1. *¿Cuántas son mayores que Ud.?* (How many are older than you?)
    H o M *Edad* *¿Dónde vive?* *¿En que trabaja?*
    (M or F) (Age) (Where does s/he live?) (What work does s/he do?)
15. *¿Hace cuánto que vive en (Los Cabos, Acapulco, Puerto Vallarta)?* (How long have you lived in (Los Cabos, Acapulco, Puerto Vallarta)?)
16. *¿En que colonia vive? ¿Qué lejos de aquí está?* (What colonia do you live in?) (How far is it from here?)
17. *¿Paga renta?* (Do you pay rent?) *No* (No) *Sí* (Yes)
    17.1 *Si, sí: ¿Le es a veces difícil pagarla?* (If yes, Is it difficult to pay it at times?)
    17.2 *Sí tiene casa, por cuánto tiempo la tiene?* (If s/he owns a house, how long has s/he owned?)
18. *¿Cuánto tiempo piensa quedarese aquí?* (How long do you plan to stay here?)
19. *¿Cómo se enteró de esta ciudad?* (How did you find out about this city?)
20. *¿A quién conoció al llegar? (Si responde tíos pregunta si están hermanos o hermanas de papá o máma, si primos, de que lado de la familia)* (Who did you know here upon arrival?) (If s/he answers aunts or uncles ask if they are brothers or sisters of mother or father, if cousins, from which side of the family)
21. *¿Tiene parientes que son vendedores?* (Do you have relatives who are vendors?)
    Sí (Yes) *No* (No) *Si sí* (if yes)
    21.1 ¿Cuáles? (Which?) ¿Dónde? (Where?) ¿Qué venden? (What do they sell?)
22. *¿Cuándo fue la última vez que regresó a su lugar de origen? ¿Qué cuánto vaya?* (When was the last time you returned to your place of origin? How often do you go?
23. *¿Qué vende?* (What do you sell?)

24. *¿Qué otras cosas ha vendido?* (What else have you sold?)
25. *¿Cuánto tiempo ha sido vendedor/a?* (How long have you been a vendor?)
26. *¿Ha vendido en otras partes de México?* (Have you vended elsewhere in Mexico?)
    Sí (Yes) *No* (No) *Si sí* (If yes)
    26.1 *¿Dónde?* (Where?) *¿Cuánto tiempo?* (For how long?)
    ¿Qué vendió? (What did you sell?)
27. *¿Cuál es la mejor ciudad para vender? ¿Porqué?* (Which is the best city to vend in? Why?)
28. *¿Dónde consigue la mercanciá que vende?* (Where do you acquire the merchandise you sell?)
29. *¿En qué lugar se hizo esa mercancía?* (Where was this merchandise made?)
30. *Más o menos, ¿cómo cuanto le gana a cada pieza lo que vende?* (More or less, about how much do you earn for each item you sell?)
31. *¿Qué le gusta de ser vendedor/a?* (What do you like about being a vendor?)
32. *¿Qué no le gusta de ser vendedor/a?* (What don't you like about being a vendor?)
33. *¿Recibe comisión o se queda con todo el dinero de la venta?* (Do you work on commission or do you retain all of the money from the sale?)
34. *¿Cómo cuánto gana al buen día?* (About how much do you earn on a good day?) *¿Al mal día?* (On a bad day?)
35. *¿Cuántas días la semana trabaja?* (How many days a week do you work?)
    ¿Qué horario tiene? (What hours do you work?)
36. *¿Pretenece a una sindicato u organización?* (Do you belong to a union or organization?) *Sí* (Yes) *No* (No).
    36.1 *Si sí ¿Cuál?* (Which one?)
    36.2 *¿Qué tiene de bueno?* (What is good about it?)
    36.2 *¿Qué tiene de malo?* (What is bad about it?)
37. *¿Tiene licensia para vender?* (Do you have a vendor's license?) *Si sí* (If yes)
    37.1 *¿Cuánto le costó?* (How much did it cost you?)
    37.2 *¿Cuánto cuesta al año?* (What is the annual renewal fee?)
38. *¿Qué otros trabajos ha tenido?* (What other work have you done?) *¿Dónde?* (Where?)
39. *¿En que trabaja su esposa/o? (O pareja?)* (What work does your spouse do? (Or companion?))

40. *¿Le ayudan sus hijos/as a vender?* (Do your sons/daughters help you to vend?)
41. *¿Gana uno más en (Cabo San Lucas, Acapulco, Puerto Vallarta) que en otros lados? Porque será?* (Does one earn more in (Cabo San Lucas, Acapulco, Puerto Vallarta) than in other places? Why would that be?)
42. *Cuando se enferma, ¿dónde se atienden usted y su familia?* (When you get sick, where do you and your family go for medical care?)
43. *Si pudiera, ¿qué le gustaría estudiar?* (If you could, what would you like to study?)
44. *¿Le ayuda alguien con dinero para sus gastos? ¿Quién?* (Does anyone help you with your expenses? Who?)
45. *¿Qué tan satisfecho está con su vida en (Cabo San Lucas, Acapulco, Puerto Vallarta)?* (How satisfied are you with your life in (Cabo San Lucas, Acapulco, Puerto Vallarta?) ( ) *Nada satisfecho* (Not at all satisfied) ( ) *Poco satisfecho* (Little satisfied) ( ) *Muy satisfecho* (Very satisfied) *¿Porqué?* (Why?)
46. *¿Qué tan contento está con su trabajo?* (How content are you with your work?)
47. ( ) *Nada contento* (Not at all content) ( ) *Poco contento* (Little content) ( ) *Muy contento* (Very content). *¿Porqué?* (Why?)
48. *Si no fuera vendedor/a ¿qué le gustaría hacer?* (If you were not a vendor, what would you like to do?)

**49. *¿Le ha affectado la crisis económica? ¿En que forma?* (Have you been affected by the economic crisis? In what way?)

**50. *¿En su opinion, hay más o menos vendedores este año en comparación con el año pasado? ¿Por qué sería?* (In your opinion, are there more or less vendors this year in comparison with last year? Why would that be?)

---

* Question added after first 81 interviews (30 in Cabo San Lucas and 51 in Puerto Vallarta) were analyzed. Questions answered on 84 interviews.

** Question added after the first 30 interviews with women vendors in Cabo San Lucas. Questions asked of 136 vendors.

Appendix II

List of Vendors Interviewed

Women, Acapulco (PD=Playa Diamante, IC=Icacos Beach, CA=Caleta Beach)

Interview No.	Age	Marital Status	Place of Birth	Indigenous Language	Years Vendor	What Sold
ACA-1PD	56	married	Suchitl, Veracruz	no	18	dresses she buys/Indonesian cloth
ACA-2PD	42	free union	Acapulco, Guerrero	no	29	blouses she buys
ACA-3PD	17	single	Acapulco, Guerrero	no	3	dresses she buys/India
ACA-4PD	37	free union	Acapulco, Guerrero	no	31	shells & shell ornaments
ACA-5PD	18	single	Acapulco, Guerrero	no	1	shells & shell ornaments
ACA-6IC	37	separated	Chapultlahua, Guerrero	Mixteco	16	saris/Indonesian cloth & bathing suits
ACA-7IC	32	separated	Acapulco, Guerrero	no	5	saris/Indonesian cloth
ACA-8IC	21	married	Acapulco, Guerrero	no	3	blouses & dresses/India
ACA-9IC	31	married	Acapulco, Guerrero	no	18	saris/Indonesian cloth & bathing suits
ACA-10IC	29	single	Acapulco, Guerrero	no	4	semiprecious stone necklaces
ACA-11IC	50	married	Tlaxco, Guerrero	Mixteco	30	pails, water pistols, bracelets
ACA-12IC	30	free union	Tlaxco, Guerrero	Mixteco	20	handwoven bracelets & braids hair
ACA-13IC	24	married	Tlamacazapa, Guerrero	Nahuatl	10	woven bracelets & necklaces w/stone
ACA-14IC	38	married	San Juan Tetelcingo, Guerrero	Nahuatl	20	shell & pearl necklaces

ACA-15IC	26	free union	Acapulco, Guerrero	no	10	semiprecious stone, pearl, shell necklaces
ACA-16CA	40	widowed	Tlapa, Guerrero	Tlapaneco	3	pails
ACA-17CA	53	divorced	Acapulco, Guerrero	no	41	dresses Indonesian cloth & bathing suits
ACA-18CA	72	married	Acapulco, Guerrero	no	7	earrings, headbands, barrettes
ACA-19CA	48	single mother	Arcelia, Guerrero	no	20	bananas in crème sauce
ACA-20CA	26	married	Nezcala, Guerrero	Nahuatl	18	semiprecious stone & shell necklaces
ACA-21IC	25	free union	Copanatoyac, Guerrero	Nahuatl	2	pails, balls, life jackets for children
ACA-22IC	60	married	Monterrey, Nuevo León	no	30	sodas, fruit drinks, homemade food
ACA-23IC	37	single mother	Acapulco, Guerrero	no	27	coconut tanning oil
ACA-24IC	29	single mother	Acapulco, Guerrero	no	22	coconut tanning oil & shell necklaces
ACA-25IC	46	abandoned	Acapulco, Guerrero	no	12	woven handbags made by prisoners
Men, Acapulco (PD=Playa Diamante, IC=Icacos Beach, CA=Caleta Beach)						
ACA-1PD	27	married	Acapulco, Guerrero	no	8	semiprecious stone necklaces
ACA-2PD	48	divorced	Taxco, Guerrero	no	10	magazines & newspapers
ACA-3PD	36	married	Tlamamacan, Guerrero	Nahuatl	30	shark-bone necklaces
ACA-4PD	34	free union	Ahuacatitlán, Guerrero	no	10	doughnuts

Interview No.	Age	Marital Status	Place of Birth	Indigenous Language	Years Vendor	What Sold
ACA-5PD	35	married	Apalanic, Guerrero	little Nahuatl	20	cotton candy
ACA-6IC	68	widowed	Madinatepec, Guerrero	Tlapaneco	40	filigreed silver bracelets & rings/Taxco
ACA-7IC	31	married	Acapulco, Guerrero	no	20	silver necklaces, bracelets, rings/Taxco
ACA-8IC	17	single	Acapulco, Guerrero	no	9	silver chains, bracelets, rings/Taxco
ACA-9IC	59	married	Valle de Galeana, Guerrero	no	51	silver-plated & silver bracelets/Taxco
ACA-10IC	63	widowed	Valle de Galeana, Guerrero	no	17	sodas, seafood (commission seller)
ACA-11IC	51	married	Acapulco, Guerrero	no	20	rubber sandals, canvas bags
ACA-12IC	70	separated	Santa Domingo Armento, Oaxaca	no	35	sunglasses, T-shirts, serapes
ACA-13IC	57	married	Tlamacazapa, Guerrero	Nahuatl	10	woven palm-leaf handbags
ACA-14IC	48	married	Zacatepec, Morelos	no	41	dresses, T-shirts
ACA-15IC	48	married	San Juan Tetelcingo, Guerrero	Nahuatl	23	hand-painted sauce bowls
ACA-16CA	27	married	Tlamacazapa, Guerrero	Nahuatl	12	handwoven name bracelets
ACA-17CA	37	married	Acapulco, Guerrero	no	15	mangoes & fruit cocktails
ACA-18CA	85	widowed	Zumpango del Río, Guerrero	Nahuatl	45	bracelets, earrings of plastic beads & shell
ACA-19CA	39	married	Acapulco, Guerrero	no	27	sundresses wife makes

ACA-20CA	25	single	Taxco, Guerrero	no	13	applies temporary tattoos he designs
ACA-21IC	57	separated	Tlamacazapa, Guerrero	little Nahuatl	37	canvas bags, woven palm-leaf sombreros
ACA-22IC	35	separated	Acapulco, Guerrero	no	15	sunglasses/from China
ACA-23IC	20	single	Las Salinas, Guerrero	no	<1	clams & oysters
ACA-24IC	54	married	Tlamacazapa, Guerrero	Nahuatl	39	handwoven palm-leaf handbags
ACA-25IC	55	married	San Agustín Guapa, Guerrero	Nahuatl	41	starfish & shells
ACA-26IC	70	married	Tlamacazapa, Guerrero	no	40	T-shirts
ACA-27IC	35	married	Tlamacazapa, Guerrero	Nahuatl	23	handwoven palm-leaf handbags
ACA-28IC	60	married	San Marcos, Guerrero	no	25	silver bracelets & rosaries / Taxco
ACA-29IC	16	single	Zumpango del Río, Guerrero	Nahautl	2	semiprecious stone & shell necklaces
ACA-30IC	41	married	Tlaxco, Guerrero	no	27	applies tattoos downloaded from Internet
Women, Cabo San Lucas (Marina)						
CSL-1M	58	married	State of Mexico	no	50	ceramic flutes
CSL-2M	22	married	State of Mexico	no	12	sombreros
CSL-3M	22	single	State of Mexico	no	4	Cuban cigars
CSL-6M	34	married	Acapulco, Guerrero	no	6	ceramic flutes

Interview No.	Age	Marital Status	Place of Birth	Indigenous Language	Years Vendor	What Sold
CSL-13M	23	single	Chilpancingo, Guerrero	Nahautl	5	small statues & chewing gum
CSL-19M	15	single	San Juan Tetelcingo, Guerrero	Nahuatl	<1	semi-precious stone necklaces
CSL-20M	18	free union	Acapulco, Guerrero	no	1	ceramic flutes
CSL-21M	26	widowed	Acapulco, Guerrero	no	8	ceramic flutes
CSL-23M	17	single	Palenque, Chiapas	no	1	ceramic flutes & braids hair
CSL-24M	20	separated	Federal District	no	<1	Cuban cigars
CSL-27M	36	married	Chichicapa, Oaxaca	Zapoteco	15	ceramic flutes
CSL-28M	38	married	San Baltazar Chichicapam, Oax.	Zapoteco	1	ceramic flutes
CSL-30M	20	single	Donica, Querétaro	Otomí	7	cloth dolls she makes
Women, Cabo San Lucas (Medano Beach)						
CSL-4P	25	married	San Juan Tetelcingo, Guerrero	Nahuatl	10	semiprecious stone necklaces
CSL-5P	17	single	San Juan Tetelcingo, Guerrero	Nahuatl	2	semiprecious stone necklaces
CSL-7P	22	single	Chilpancingo, Guerrero	Nahuatl	3	semiprecious stone neck laccs & braids hair
CSL-8P	17	single	San Juan Tetelcingo, Guerrero	Nahuatl	5	semi-precious stone neck laces & braids hair
CSL-9P	28	married	San Juan Tetelcingo, Guerrero	Nahuatl	20	sunglasses & braids hair

CSL-10P	15	single	San Juan Tetelcingo, Guerrero	Nahuatl	<1	turtle statuettes & wind chimes
CSL-11P	43	married	Xalitla, Guerrero	Nahuatl	10	semiprecious stone necklaces
CSL-12P	31	free union	Chilpancingo, Guerrero	Nahuatl	10	ceramic statuettes
CSL-14P	15	single	Iguala, Guerrero	Nahuatl	1	semiprecious stone necklaces
CSL-15P	38	married	Temalac, Guerrero	no	3	homemade food & sodas
CSL-16P	18	single	Acapulco, Guerrero	Nahuatl	8	semiprecious stone necklaces
CSL-17P	26	married	San Juan Tetelcingo, Guerrero	Nahautl	4	sunglasses
CSL-18P	27	married	San Juan Tetelcingo, Guerrero	Nahuatl	10	semiprecious stone necklaces
CSL-22P	28	married	Temalac, Guerrero	no	<1	saris/Indonesian cloth
CSL-25P	20	single	Puerto Vallarta, Jalisco	no	3	homemade food & sodas
CSL-26P	50	married	Michoacán	no	13	T-shirts
CSL-29P	29	married	Huatletlauca, Puebla	Nahuatl	19	dresses she makes
CSL-31P	29	married	Tecoman, Colima	Nahuatl	15	dresses & saris/Indonesian cloth
CSL-32P	49	married	Temalac, Guerrero	Nahautl	14	sundresses she & daughter make
CSL-33P	52	married	Aguatitlán, Guerrero	no	35	sundresses she makes/ Indonesian cloth
CSL-34P	28	free union	Hualahuaca, Guerrero	no	1	snacks, sodas, fruit juices

Men, Cabo San Lucas (Medano Beach)

Interview No.	Age	Marital Status	Place of Birth	Indigenous Language	Years Vendor	What Sold
CSL-1	26	single	San Martín, Guerrero	no	<1	sundresses bought from wholesaler
CSL-2	25	single	Zaachila, Oaxaca	no	5	Oaxacan-style shirts & dresses
CSL-3	20	married	Mazatlán, Sinaloa	no	10	silver jewelry/Taxco
CSL-4	34	married	Mitla, Oaxaca	Zapoteco	10	silver jewelry/Taxco
CSL-5	40	married	Tlamacazapa, Guerrero	Nahuatl	25	silver jewelry/Taxco
CSL-6	37	married	San Juan Tetelcingo, Guerrero	Nahuatl	24	ceramic & wooden plates & bowls
CSL-7	35	married	Acapulco, Guerrero	no	16	silver jewelry/Federal District (DF)
CSL-8	18	married	San Antonio, Guerrero	Nahuatl	1	rosaries of shell, crystal, & wooden beads
CSL-9	36	married	Copalillo, Guerrero	Nahuatl	18	ironwood statues
CSL-10	19	single	Tlamacazapa, Guerrero	Nahuatl	11	handwoven name bracelets & tattoos
CSL-11	42	married	Santa Cruz Tetelpincinto, Puebla	Nahuatl	34	sundresses bought from wholesalers
CSL-12	29	married	Monte Alegre, Guerrero	Nahuatl	8	tablecloths
CSL-13	30	separated	Acapulco, Guerrero	no	12	silver & enameled jewelry/Taxco/DF
CSL-14	32	married	Mazatlán, Sinaloa	no	10	blankets, serapes, & applies tattoos

CSL-15	41	married	Santa María de las Flores, Guerrero	no	30	silver jewelry/Taxco
CSL-16	55	married	Ahuatitlán, Guerrero	no	17	dresses wife makes/ Indonesian cloth
CSL-17	21	single	Tepezisintla, Puebla	Nahuatl	8	sundresses
CSL-18	35	free union	Tlamacazapa, Guerrero	little Nahuatl	15	leather & handwoven name bracelets
CSL-19	40	married	Federal District	no	23	silver bracelets/Taxco
CSL-20	55	married	San Juan Tetelcingo, Guerrero	Nahuatl	7	wind chimes w/painted ceramic fish
CSL-21	35	married	Xalotlaco, State of Mexico	no	12	crocheted handbags & applies tattoos
CSL-22	29	single	Mazatlán, Sinaloa	no	5	blankets
CSL-23	19	single	Mazatlán, Sinaloa	no	1	T-shirts
CSL-24	46	married	Acambaro, Guanajuato	no	15	canvas bags
CSL-25	32	married	Queszalapa, Guerrero	no	20	enameled & silver jewelry/ Taxco
CSL-26	30	free union	Chilpancingo, Guerrero	no	1	sunglasses/China & Cuban cigars
Women, Puerto Vallarta						
PV-1	31	married	Tlajomulco, State of Mexico	Mazahuatl	5	woven name bracelets & braids hair
PV-2	43	married	Xitlala, Guerrero	no	10	saris & sundresses/ Indonesian cloth
PV-3	38	free union	Zihuatenejo, Guerrero	no	30	seafood, ceviche, & sodas

Interview No.	Age	Marital Status	Place of Birth	Indigenous Language	Years Vendor	What Sold
PV-4	28	married	Analco, Guerrero	Nahuatl	11	semiprecious stone necklaces
PV-5	25	married	Analco, Guerrero	Nahuatl	5	semiprecious stone necklaces
PV-6	22	single	Analco, Guerrero	Nahuatl	5	semiprecious stone necklaces
PV-7	24	married	Analco, Guerrero	Nahuatl	5	semiprecious stone necklaces
PV-8	27	widowed	Analco, Guerrero	Nahuatl	10	semiprecious stone neck laces & braids hair
PV-9	32	free union	Analco, Guerrero	Nahuatl	5	semiprecious stone neck laces & braids hair
PV-10	25	married	Analco, Guerrero	Nahuatl	10	semiprecious stone necklaces
PV-11	27	married	Analco, Guerrero	Nahuatl	10	semiprecious stone necklaces
PV-12	32	free union	Analco, Guerrero	Nahuatl	12	semiprecious stone necklaces
PV-13	25	married	San Miguel, Guerrero	Nahuatl	4	semiprecious stone necklaces
PV-14	32	married	San Agustín, Guerrero	Nahuatl	4	semiprecious stone necklaces
PV-15	54	separated	Mitla, Oaxaca	Zapoteco	25	dresses/Mexican cloth
PV-16	36	married	Mitla, Oaxaca	Zapoteco	11	dresses/Indonesian cloth & braids hair

PV-17	25	separated	Mitla, Oaxaca	Zapoteco	6	semiprecious stone necklaces
PV-18	48	married	Mitla, Oaxaca	Zapoteco	15	dresses/Indonesian cloth
PV-19	40	married	Mitla, Oaxaca	little Zapoteco	10	dresses/Indonesian cloth
PV-20	35	married	Mitla, Oaxaca	little Zapoteco	6	semi-precious stone neck laces & earrings
PV-21	32	free union	San Juan Copala, Oaxaca	Triqui	18	animal magnets, woven hair bands
PV-22	44	free union	Tacambaro, Michoacán	no	10	fans/China & braids hair
PV-23	27	separated	Lazaro Cardenas, Michoacán	no	6	semiprecious stone necklaces
PV-24	54	single mother	Federal District (D.F.)	no	16	braids hair
PV-25	32	free union	Mascota, Jalisco	no	5	silver earrings/Taxco
Men, Puerto Vallarta						
PV-1	35	married	Toluca, State of Mexico	no	20	sunglasses, masks
PV-2	40	married	Toluca, State of Mexico	no	10	silver jewelry/Guadalajara
PV-3	23	married	Toluca, State of Mexico	no	4	puppets, sequined handbags
PV-4	51	married	La Magdalena, State of Mexico	no	25	silver jewelry he designs
PV-5	37	married	Santiago Tilapa, State of Mexico	no	15	silver jewelry/Taxco
PV-6	42	married	Cuautepec, Guerrero	no	23	silver-plated jewel & money clips/Taxco

Interview No.	Age	Marital Status	Place of Birth	Indigenous Language	Years Vendor	What Sold
PV-7	43	single	Ahuehuepan, Guerrero	Nahuatl	9	ceramic wind chimes, fish, & burros
PV-8	79	widowed	Xiclala, Guerrero	Nahautl	70	baby toys made of wood & plastic beads
PV-9	50	married	Analco, Guerrero	Nahuatl	35	hand-painted ceramic plates & bowls
PV-10	65	married	Temalac, Guerrero	Nahuatl	15	bedspreads
PV-11	40	married	Temalac, Guerrero	Nahuatl	21	blankets, tablecloths
PV-12	49	widowed	Tlaxmalac, Guerrero	Nahuatl	28	handwoven hammocks
PV-13	49	married	Tlamacazapa, Guerrero	Nahuatl	37	handwoven palm-leaf handbags
PV-14	42	married	Tlamacazapa, Guerrero	Nahuatl	25	wooden bead necklaces, applies tattoos
PV-15	61	married	Ahuehuepan, Guerrero	Nahuatl	30	ceramic wind chimes, pitchers
PV-16	42	married	Tenanguillo, Guerrero	no	15	silver-plated bracelets/Taxco
PV-17	59	married	Ometepec, Guerrero	no	13	fruit: cut-up mango, pineapple, etc.
PV-18	35	free union	Mitla, Oaxaca	Zapoteco	15	Oaxacan-style blouses
PV-19	49	married	Mitla, Oaxaca	Zapoteco	20	T-shirts
PV-20	55	married	Mitla, Oaxaca	Zapoteco	15	Oaxacan-style shirts, blouses, pants
PV-21	52	free union	Federal District (D.F.)	no	22	silver-plated & copper jewel & keychains

PV-22	36	married	Ciudad Sagún, Hidalgo	no	18	deserts: cheesecake, flan
PV-23	49	married	Arandas, Jalisco	no	40	sunglasses/from China & D.F.
PV-24	57	married	San Pedrito, Michoacán	no	15	sombreros from Guanajuato
PV-25	55	free union	Monterrey, Nuevo León	no	5	hand-painted porcelain tiles
PV-26	42	married	Tlaxcala, Tlaxcala	no	25	baseball caps

Bibliography

Alarcón-González, Diana and Terry McKinley. 1999. "The Adverse Effects of Structural Adjustment on Women in Mexico." *Latin American Perspectives* 26(3): 103–17.

Aliaga Linares, Lissette. 2002. *Sumas y Restas: El Capital Social Como Recurso en La Informalidad.* Lima: Alternativa.

Ángeles, Miguel, Alba E. Gámez, and Antonina Ivanova. 2009. "On the Impact of Tourism on the Economy of Baja California Sur, Mexico: A SAM Approach." *Sustainable Development and Planning* 4(2): 183–790.

Anónimo. 2008 (November 18). "Copalillo, el lugar de los tambos . . . y del alcalde con pipas." *El Milenio.* Available at http://impreso.milenio.com/node/8054019.

Appadurai, Arjun. 1990. "Disjuncture and Difference in the Global Cultural Economy." *Public Culture* 2(2): 1–24.

Appadurai, Arjun. 1996. *Modernity at Large: Cultural Dimensions of Globalization.* Minneapolis: University of Minnesota Press.

Arias, Omar S. 2007. "Infomality, Earnings, and Welfare." In *Informality: Exit and Exclusion,* Guillermo E. Perry, William F. Maloney, Omar S. Arias, Pablo Fajnzylber, Andrew D. Mason and Jaime Saavedra-Chanduvi, contributors, 79–100. Washington, D.C.: The World Bank.

Arizpe, Lourdes. 1979. *Indígenas en la Ciudad de México: El Caso de las "Marias."* México, D.F.: Secretaría de Educación Pública.15

Arroyo Reyes, José. 2009. "5a.Ferie de la Palma, Tlamacazapa 2009." *El Diario de Taxco.* http:eldiariodetaxco.com.

Babb, Florence E. 1996. "After the Revolution: Neoliberal Policy and Gender in Nicaragua." *Latin American Perspectives* 23(1): 7–20.

Babb, Florence E. 1998 (1989). *Between Field and Cooking Pot: The Political Economy of Market Women in Peru,* rev. ed. Austin: University of Texas Press.

Babb, Florence E. 2011. *The Tourism Encounter: Fashioning Latin American Nations & Histories*. Stanford: Stanford University Press 105–124.

Balán, Jorge, Harley L. Browning and Elizabeth Jelin. 1973. *Men in a Developing Society: Geographic and Social Mobility in Monterrey, Mexico*. Austin: University of Texas Press.

Basch, Linda, Nina Glick Schiller, and Cristina Szanton Blanc. 1994. *Nations Unbound: Transnational Projects, Postcolonial Predicaments and Deterritorialized Nation-States*. Basel: Gordon and Breach.

Beals, Ralph L. 1975. *The Peasant Marketing System of Oaxaca, México*. Berkeley: University of California Press.

Benchwick, Greg and John Hecht. 2009. *Puerto Vallarta & Pacific Mexico*. Oakland, Calif.: Lonely Planet Publications.

Benería, Lourdes and Martha Roldán. 1987. *The Crossroads of Class & Gender: Industrial Homework, Subcontracting, and Household Dynamics in Mexico City*. Chicago: University of Chicago Press.

Berger, Dina. 2006. *The Development of Mexico's Tourism Industry: Pyramids by Day, Martinis by Night*. New York: Palgrave Macmillan.

Berger, Dina. 2010. "Good Will Ambassadors on Holiday: Tourism, Diplomacy, and Mexico-U.S. Relations. In *Holiday in Mexico: Critical Reflections on Tourism and Tourist Encounters*, edited by Dina Berger and Andrew Grant Wood, 107–29. Durham: Duke University Press.

Berger, Dina and Andrew Grant Wood, eds. 2010. *Holiday in Mexico: Critical Reflections on Tourism and Tourist Encounters*. Durham: Duke University Press.

Bhimji, Fazila. 2010. "Struggles, Urban Citizenship, and Belonging: The Experience of Undocumented Street Vendors and Food Truck Owners in Los Angeles." *Urban Anthropology* 39(4): 455–92.

Bhowmik, Sharit K. 2010. "Introduction." In *Street Vendors in the Global Urban Economy*, edited by Sharit K. Bhomik, 1–19. New York: Routledge.

Brenner, Ludger and Adrían Guillermo Aguilar. 2002. "Luxury Tourism and Regional Economic Development in Mexico." *The Professional Geographer* 54(4): 500–20.

Bringas Rábago, Nora L. 1999. "Políticas de desarrollo turístico en dos zonas costeras del pácifico mexicano." *Región y Sociedad*. 11, (017): 3–51.

Bromley, Ray. 1978. "Organization, Regulation, and Exploitation in the So-called Urban Informal Sector: The Street Traders of Cali, Colombia." *World Development* 6(9/10): 1161–71.

Bromley, Ray. 2002. "Street Vending and Public Policy: A Global Review." *The International Journal of Sociology and Social Policy* 20(1/2): 1–28.

Brown, Alison. 2006. "Challenging Street Livelihoods." In *Contested Space: Steet Trading, Public Space, and Livelihoods in Developing Cities*, edited by Alison Brown, 3–16. Warwickshire, UK: Intermediate Technology Publications.

Bruner, Edward M. 1996. "Tourism in the Balinese Border Zone." In *Displacement, Diaspora, and Geographies of Identity*, edited by Smadar Lavie and Ted Swedenburg, 157–79. Durham: Duke University Press.

Bruner, Edward M. 1999. "Return to Sumatra: 1957, 1997." *American Ethnologist* 26(2): 461–77.

Bunster, Ximena and Elsa M. Chaney. 1989. *Sellers & Servants: Working Women in Lima, Peru*. Granby, Mass.: Bergin and Garvey Publishers.

Butler, Edgar W., James B. Pick, and W. James Hettrick. 2001. *Mexico and Mexico City in the World Economy*. Boulder: Westview Press.

Canabal Cristiani, Beatriz. n.d. "Mujeres indígenas migrantes: el caso de la region de la Montaña de Guerrero, México." http://www.egeneros.org.mx/admin/archivos/mujeres_indigenas_migrantes_cristiani.pdf.

Canclini, Nésto García. 1995. *Hybrid Cultures: Strategies for Entering and Leaving Modernity*. Minneapolis: University of Minnesota Press.

Carr, Marilyn and Martha Alter Chen. 2001. *Globalization and the Informal Economy: How Global Trade and Investment Impact on the Working Poor*. WEIGO: Women in Informal Employment Globalising & Organising. http://natlex.ilo.ch/wcmsp5/groups/public/---ed.emp/documents/publications/wcms_122053.pdf.

Carte, Lindsey, Mason McWatters, Erin Daley, and Rebecca Torres. 2010. "Experiencing Agricultural Failure: Internal Migration, Tourism and Local Perceptions of Regional Change in the Yucatan." *Geoforum* 41: 700–710.

Casique, Irene. 2010. "Factores de empoderaiento y protección de las mujeres contral la violencia." *Revista Mexicana de Sociología* 72(1): 37–71.

Castellanos, M. Bianet. 2010. *A Return to Servitude: Maya Migration and the Tourist Trade in Cancún*. Minneapolis: University of Minnesota Press.

Castells, Manuel and Alejandro Portes. 1989. "World Underneath: The Origins, Dynamics, and Effects of the Informal Economy." In *The Informal Economy: Studies in Advanced and Less Developed Countries*, edited by Alejandro Portes, Manuel Castells, and Lauren A. Benton, 11–37. Baltimore: Johns Hopkins University Press.

Celestino, Eustaquio. 2005 (June). "El projecto hydroceléctrico San Juan Tetelcingo, Guerrero ¿cancelado o suspendido?" *Diario de Campo* 33: 53–57.

Chant, Sylvia. 1991. *Women and Survival in Mexican Cities: Perspectives on Gender, Labour Markets and Low-Income Households*. Manchester: Manchester University Press.

Chant, Sylvia. 1997*a*. "Gender and Tourism Employment in Mexico and the Philippines." In *Gender, Work, and Tourism*, edited by M. Thea Sinclair, 129–79. New York: Routledge.

Chant, Sylvia. 1997*b*. *Women-Headed Households: Diversity and Dynamics in the Developing World*. New York: St. Martin's Press.

Chibnik, Michael. 2003. *Crafting Tradition: The Making and Marketing of Oaxacan Wood Carvings*. Austin: University of Texas Press.

Chossudovsky, Michel. 2003. *The Globalization of Poverty and the New World Order*, 2nd ed. Montréal: Global Reach.

Clancy, Michael. 1998. "Commodity Chains, Services and Development: Theory and Preliminary Evidence from the Tourism Industry." *Review of International Political Economy* 5(19): 122–148).

Clancy, Michael J. 1999. "Tourism and Development: Evidence from Mexico." *Annals of Tourism Research* 26(1): 1–20.

Clancy, Michael J. 2001*a*. *Exporting Paradise: Tourism and Development in Mexico*. New York: Pergamon.

Clancy, Michael J. 2001*b*. "Mexican Tourism: Export Growth and Structural Change since 1970." *Latin American Research Review* 36(1): 128–50.

Cornelius, Wayne A. 2001. "Death at the Border: Efficacy and Unintended Consequences of U.S. Immigration Control Policy." *Population and Development Review* 27(4): 661–81.

Cortázar, René. 1998. "Globalization and Job Creation: A Latin American Perspective." In *Poverty and Inequality in Latin America: Issues and New Challenges*, edited by Víctor E. Tokman and Guillermo O'Donnell, 75–90. Notre Dame, Ind.: Notre Dame University Press.

Cowen, Tyler. 2005. *Markets and Cultural Voices: Liberty vs. Power in the Lives of Mexican Amate Painters*. Ann Arbor: University of Michigan Press.

Cross, John C. 1998*a*. *Informal Politics: Street Vendors and the State in Mexico*. Stanford: Stanford University Press.

Cross, John C. 1998*b*. "Co-optation, Competition and Resistance: State and Street Vendors in Mexico City." *Latin American Perspectives* 25(2): 41–61.

Cross, John C. and Marina Karides. 2007. "Capitalism, Modernity and the 'Appropriate' Use of Space. In *Street Entrepreneurs: People, Place and Politics in Local and Global Perspective*, edited by John Cross and Alfonso Morales, 19–35. New York: Routledge.

Cross, John C. and Sergio Peña. 2006. "Risk and Regulation in Informal and Illegal Markets." In *Out of the Shadows: Political Action and the Informal Economy in Latin America*, edited by Patricial Fernández-Kelly and Jon Shefner, 49–80. University Park: Pennsylvania State University Press.

Cunningham, Wendy. 1996. "Breadwinner Versus Caregiver: Labor Force Participation and Sectoral Choice over the Mexican Business Cycle." In *The Economics of Gender in Mexico: Work, Family, State, and Market*, edited by Elizabeth G. Katz and Maria C. Correia, 85–132. Washington, D.C.: The World Bank

Datatur. 2011. "Reporte de llegada de pasajeros en aeropuertos del país." Acapulco, Los Cabos, and Puerto Vallarta, 2005, 2006. 2007, 2008, 2009, 2010. http://datatur.sectur.gob.mx/wb/datatur/dat_reports.

Davis, Benjamin, Guy Stecklov, and Paul Winters. 2002. "Domestic and International Migration from Rural Mexico: Disaggregating the Effects of Network Structure and Composition." *Population Studies* 56(3): 291–309.

de Soto, Hernando. 1989. *The Other Path: The Invisible Revolution in the Third World.* New York: Harper & Row.

Despres, Leo A. 1990. "Macrotheories, Microcontexts, and the Informal Sector in Three Brazilian Cities." In *Perspectives on the Informal Economy*, edited by M. Estellie Smith, 97–122. Lanham, Md.: University Press of America.

Dirección Municipal de Transparencia. San José del Cabo, Baja California Sur. 2011*a* (September 14). "Información sobre colonias en Cabo San Lucas." Personal communication.

Dirección Municipal de Transparencia. San José del Cabo, Baja California Sur. 2011*b* (6 August). "Información sobre hoteles en Cabo San Lucas." Personal communication.

Duneier, Mitchell. 1999. *Sidewalk*. New York: Farrar, Straus & Giroux.

elijuarez. 2008 (December 24). "La crisis impacta a Baja California Sur." *El Milenio*. http://impreso.milenio.com/node/8513158.

Enríquez Acosta, Jesús Ángel. 2008. "Las Nuevas ciudades para el tursimo. Caso Puerto Peñasco, Sonora, México." *Scripta Nueva: Revista Electronia de Geografía y Ciencias Sociales* 12: 1–16.

Evans, Nancy H. 1979. "The Dynamics of Tourist Development in Puerto Vallarta." In *Tourism: Passport to Development?*, edited by Emanuel de Kadt, 305–20. New York: Oxford University Press.

Everitt, John, Bran H. Massam, Rosa M. Chávez-Dagostino, Ródrigo Espinosa Sánchez, and Edmundo Andrade Romo. 2008. "The Impact of Tourism on Puerto Vallarta, Jalisco, Mexico." *The Canadian Geographer* 52(1): 83–104.

Fernández Poncela, Anna M. 1996. "The Disruptions of Adjustment: Women in Nicaragua." *Latin American Perspectives* 23(1): 27–48.

Friedlander, Judith. 2006 (1975). *Being Indian in Hueyapan*, Second ed. New York: Palgrave Macmillan.

Gámez, Alba and Manuel Ángeles. 2010. "Borders Within: Tourism Growth, Migration and Regional Polarization in Baja California Sur (Mexico)." *Journal of Borderland Studies*. 25(1): 1–18.

Gámez, Alba E, Antonina Ivanova, and Tamar Diana Wilson. 2011. "Género y Comerico Informal en Destinos Turístocos. El Caso de las Vendedores de Playa en Los Cabos, Baja California Sur, México." *TuryDes (Revista de Investigación en turismo y desarrollo local.* 4(9): 1–31. http://www.eumed.net/rev/turydes/.

Gámez, Alba E., Tamar Diana Wilson, and Antonina Ivanova. 2011. "Las mujeres en la migración interna y el empleo informal en Baja California Sur, Mexico." *La Ventana: Revista de Género*, Universidad de Guadalajara.

García, Martha. 2007. "Migraciones del Alto Balsas." *Regiones: Suplemento de antropología* 30: 2–4.

Glick Schiller, Nina. 2003. "The Centrality of Ethnography in the Study of Transnational Migration: Seeing the Wetlands Instead of the Swamp." In *American Arrivals: Anthropological Engages the New Immigration*, edited by Nancy Foner, 99–128. Santa Fe: School of American Research Press.

Glick Schiller, Nina, Linda Basch, and Cristina Blanc-Szanton, eds. 1992. *Towards a Transnational Perspective on Migration: Race, Class, Ethnicity, and Nationalism Reconsidered.* New York: The New York Academy of Sciences.

Gomezjara, Francisco A. 1979. *Bonapartismo y Lucha Campesina en la Costa Grande de Guerrero*. México, D.F.: Editorial Posada.

González, Marco, Javier Torres Medina, and Omar Jiménez. 2008. *La república informal: El ambulantaje en la ciudad de México*. México, D.F.: Porrúa.

González Chévez, Lilian. n.d. "Anclajes y transformaciones culturales de un pueblo nahua en transición: El caso de Temalac, Guerrero." http://phpwebhosting.com/%7Emigration/modules/seinarioe/gonzalezlilian.pdf.

Gónzalez Chévez, Lilian. 2005. "De Temalac a Waukegan: Flujos culturales en una comunidad indígena transnacional." *Diario del campo: Supplemento* 30: 9–12.

González de la Rocha, Mercedes. 1994. *The Resources of Poverty: Women and Survival in a Mexican City*. Oxford: Blackwell.

González de la Rocha, Mercedes. 1995. "The Urban Family and Poverty in Latin America." *Latin American Perspectives* 22(2): 12–31.

González Romero, Daniel, María Teresa Pérez-Bourzac, and Elizabeth Rivera Borrayo. 2008. "El turismo y sus penumbras: Puerto Vallarta, Un lugar turístico en la encrucijada de la planeación." *Urbano*. 11, (18): 24–34.

González S., Verónica. 2011 (May 4). "Dan respuestas a familias asentados en Caribe Bajo." *El Sudcaliforniano*.

Good Eshelman, Catharine. 1988. *Haciendo la Lucha: Arte y Comercio Nahuas de Guerrero*. Mexico, D.F.: Fondo de Cultural Económica.

Good Eshelman, Catharine and Guadalupe Barrientos López. 2004. *Nahuas del Alto Balsas: Pueblos Indígenas del México Contempráneo*. Mexico, D.F.: Comisión Nacional para Desarrollo de los Pueblos Indígenas. http://www.edi.gob.mx.

Gordon, Gary I. 1997. *Peddlers, Pesos, and Power: The Political Economy of Street Vending in Mexico City*. Ph.D. dissertation, Department of History, University of Chicago.

Guilette, Gregory S. 2007. "Migration and Tourism Development in Huatulco, Oaxaca." *Cultural Anthropology* 48(4): 603–11.

Hannam, Kevin. 2002. "Tourism and Development I: Globalization and Power." *Progress in Development Studies* 2(3): 227–34.

Hart, Keith. 1973. "Informal Income Opportunities and Urban Employment in Ghana." *Journal of Modern African Studies* 11(1): 61–89.

Harvey, David. 2007 (2005). *A Brief History of Neoliberalism*. New York: Oxford University Press.

Hellier-Tinoco, Ruth. 2011. *Embodying Mexico: Tourism, Nationalism & Performance*. New York: Oxford University Press.

Hewitt de Alcantara, Cynthia. 1976. *Modernizing Mexican Agriculture: Socioeconomic Implications of Technological Change 1940–1970*. Geneva: UNRISD (United Nations Research Institute for Social Development).

Hiernaux-Nicolas, Daniel. 1999. "Cancún Bliss." In *The Infrastructure of Play: Building the Tourist City*, edited by Dennis R. Judd, 124–42. Cleveland: Cleveland University Press.

IADB (Inter-American Development Bank). 2004. "Infrastructure Program for Tourism Development. Mexico." http://www.iadb.org/exr/doc98/apr/aptur.htm.

ILO (International Labour Organisation). 1972. *Employment, Income, and Equality: A Strategy for Increasing Productive Employment in Kenya*. Geneva: International Labor Office.

ILO (International Labour Organisation). 2002*a*. *Decent Work and the Informal Economy*. Geneva: International Labour Office.

ILO (International Labour Organisation) 2002*b*. *Women and Men in the Informal Economy: A Statistical Picture*. Geneva: International Labour Office.

INEGI (Instituto Nacional de Estadística, Geografía y Informática). 2004. "Población total por municipo de residencia actual y lugar de nacimiento, y su distribución según sexo." http://www.inegi.gob.mx/est/librerias.

INEGI (Instituto Nacional de Estadística, Geografía e Informática). 2011*a*. "Vivienda y urbanización." http://www.inegi.org.mx/sistemas/mexicocifras/default.aspx.

INEGI (Institutio Nacional de Estádistica, Geografía y Informática). 2011*b*. "Población." http://www.inegi.org.mx/default.aspx.

INEGI (Instituto Nacional de Estadística, Geografía y Informática). 2011*c*. "Tabulados basicos." http://www.inegi.org.mx/sistemas/tabuladosbasicos/tabulados/cpv/2000/12mi03.pdf.

Kettles, Gregg W. 2007. "Legal Responses to Sidewalk Vending: The Case of Los Angeles, California." In *Street Entrepreneurs: People, Place and Politics in Local and Global Perspective*, edited by John Cross and Alfonso Morales, 58–78. New York: Routledge.

Levitt, Peggy. 2001. "Transnational Migration: Taking Stock and Future Directions." *Global Networks*. 1(29): 195–216.

Little, Walter E. 2004. *Mayas in the Marketplace: Tourism, Globalization, and Cultural Identity*. Austin: University of Texas Press.

Little, Walter E. 2008. "Living with the Mundo Maya Project: Strategies of Maya Handicraft Vendors." *Latin American Perspectives* 35(3): 87–102.

Lizárraga Morales, Omar. 2008. "La inmigración de jublidados estadounidenses en México y sus prácticas transnacionales. Estudio de caso en Mazatlán, Sinaloa y Cabo San Lucas, Baja California Sur." *Migración y Desarrollo*. 11: 97–117.

Lizárraga Morales, Omar. 2010. "The US Citizens Retirement Migration to Los Cabos, Mexico. Profile and Social Effects." *Recreation and Society in Africa, Asia & Latin America* 1(1): 75–92.

López-López, Álvaro and Álvaro Sánchez Crispín. 2002. "Canales espaciales de articulación en el corridor turístico Los Cabos, Baja California Sur, México." *Cuadernos de Turismo* 9: 53–66.

López-López, Álvaro, Judith Cukier, and Álvaro Sánchez-Crispín. 2006. "Segregation of Tourist Space in Los Cabos, Mexico." *Tourism Geographies* 8(4): 359–79.

Maloney, William F. 2004. "Informality Revisited." *World Development* 32(7): 1159–78.

Maloney, William F. and Omar S. Arias. 2007. "The *Razón de Ser* of the Informal Worker." In *Informality: Exit and Exclusion*, Guillermo E. Perry, William F. Maloney, Omar S. Arias, Pablo Fajnzylber, Andrew D. Mason, and Jaime Saavedra-Chanduvi, contributors, 43-78. Washington, D.C.: The World Bank.

Martí, Judith E. 1994. "Subsistence and the State: The Case of Porfirian Mexico." In *The Economic Anthropology of the State*, edited by Elizabeth M. Brumfield, 316–23. Lanham: University Press of America.

Martínez Nova, Carmen. 2003. "The 'Culture' of Exclusion: Representations of Indigenous Women Street Vendors in Tijuana, Mexico." *Bulletin of Latin American Research* 23(3): 249–68.

Massey, Douglas, Rafael Alarcón, Jorge Durand, and Humberto González. 1987. *Return to Aztlán: The Social Process of International Migration from Western Mexico*. Berkeley: University of California Press.

Massey, Douglas S., Jorge Durand, and Nolan J. Malone. 2003. *Beyond Smoke and Mirrors: Mexican Immigration in an Era of Economic Integration*. New York: Russell Sage Foundation.

Mendiola García, Sandra C. 2008. *Street Vendors, Marketeers, and Politics in Twentieth Century Puebla*. Ph.D. dissertation, Department of History, Rutgers University.

Merrill, Dennis. 2009. *Negotiating Paradise: U.S. Tourism and Empire in Twentieth Century Latin America*. Chapel Hill: The University of North Carolina Press.

Milanovic, Branko. 2003. "The Two Faces of Globalization: Against Globalization as We Know It." *World Development* 31(4): 667–83.

Morales Aguilar, Berenice. 2007. "Productión y comercialización artesana por los migrantes nahuas de San Juan Tetelcingo en Playa del Carmen, Quintana Roo: Classes Paint Your Own." *Regiones: Supplemento de Antropología* 30: 5–8. http://www.elregional.com.mx/suplementos/regiones.php.

Mowforth, Martin and Ian Munt. 1998. *Tourism and Sustainability: New Tourism in the Third World*. New York and London: Routledge.

Noreña Ramirez, Guadalupe Irely and Tonantzin Arcadia Romero Hernández. 2009. "Ciudad Renacimiento: Percepción Urbana." *Renayork*. http://renayork.com/2009/ciudad-renacimiento-percepcion-urbana/.

Nuestro México. 2011*a*. "Tlamacazapa-Guerrero." http://www.nuestromexico.com/Guerrero/Taxco-de-Alarcon/Tlamacazapa/.

Nuestro México. 2011*b*. "San Juan Tetelcingo-Guerrero." http://www.nuestro-mexico.com/Guerrero/Tepecoacuilco-de-Trujano/San-Juan-Tetelcingo/.

Nuestro México. 2011*c*. "Analco-Guerrero." http://www.nuestro-mexico.com/Guerrero/Martir-de-Culiapan/Analco/.

Nuestro México. 2011*d*. "Copalillo-Guerrero." http://www.nuestro-mexico.com/Guerrero/Copalillo/Copalillo/.

Nutini, Hugo G. 1997. "Class and Ethnicity in Mexico: Somatic and Racial Considerations." *Ethnology* 36(3): 227–38.

Nye, Joseph S., Jr. 2004. *Soft Power: The Means to Success in World Politics*. New York: PublicAffairs.

Olivera, Mercedes. 2006. "*Violencia Femicida*: Violence Against Women and Mexico's Structural Crisis." *Latin American Perspectives* 33(2): 104–14.

Parsons, Elsie Clews. 1936. *Mitla: Town of the Souls*. Chicago: University of Chicago Press.

Peña, Sergio. 1999. "Informal Markets: Street Vendors in Mexico City." *Habitat International*. 23 (3): 363–72.

Pérez-Campuzano, Enrique. 2010. "Segregación socioespacial en ciudades turísticas, el caso de Puerto Vallarta, México." *Región y Sociedad*. (49): 143–78.

Perry, Guillermo E. and Willliam F. Maloney. 2007. "Overview: Informality: Exit and Exclusion." In *Informality: Exit and Exclusion*, Guillermo E. Perry, William F. Maloney, Omar S. Arias, Pablo Fajnzylber, Andrew D. Mason, and Jaime Saavedra-Chanduvi, contributors, 1–20. Washington, D.C.: The World Bank.

Perry, Guillermo E., William F. Malhoney, Omar S. Arias, Pablo Fajnzlber, Andrew D. Mason, and Jaime Saavedra-Chanduvi, contributors. 2007. *Informality: Exit and Exclusion*. Washington, D.C.: The World Bank.

Portes, Alejandro. Manuel Castells and Lauren A. Benton. eds. 1989. *The Informal Economy: Studies in Advanced and Less Developed Countries*. Baltimore: Johns Hopkins University Press.

Portes, Alejandro. 1994. "When More Can Be Less: Labor Standards, Development, and the Informal Economy." In *Contrapunto: The Informal Sector Debate in Latin*

America, edited by Cathy A. Rakowski, 112–30. Albany: State University of New York Press.

Portes, Alejandro. 1995. *En torno a la informalidad: Ensayos sobre teoría y mediación de la economía no regulada*. México, D.F.: Porrúa.

Portes, Alejandro. 2000. "Globalization from Below: The Rise of Transnational Communities." In *The Ends of Globalization: Bringing Society Back In*, edited by Don Kalb, Marco van der Land, Richard Staring, Bart von Steenbergen, and Nico Wilterdink, 253–70. Lanham: Rowman & Littlefield.

Portes, Alejandro and Bryan R. Roberts. 2008. "Introducción. La ciudad bajo el libre Mercado." In *Ciudades latinoamericanas: Un análisis comparative en el umbral del nuevo siglo*, 2nd. ed.,edited by Alejandro Portes, Bryan R. Roberts, and Alejandro Grimson, 19–74. Buenos Aires: Prometeo Libros.

Propin Frejomil, Enrique and Álvaro Sánchez Crispín. 2002. "La estructura regional del turismo en México." *Ería* 59: 386–94.

Propin Frejomil, Enrique and Álvaro Sánchez Crispín. 2007. "Tipología de los destinos turísticos preferenciaes en México." *Cuadernos de Turismo*. 19: 147–66.

Rivera, Juan M. 2009. "Multinational Agribusiness and Small Corn Producers in Rural Mexico: New Alternatives for Agricultural Development." In *NAFTA and the Campesinos: The Impact of NAFTA on Small-Scale Agricultural Producers in Mexico and the Prospects for Change*, edited by Juan M. Rivera, Scott Whiteford, and Manuel Chávez, 89–110. Chicago: University of Chicago Press.

Rivera, Juan M. and Scott Whiteford. 2009. "Introduction: Mexican Agriculture and NAFTA—Prospects for Change." In *NAFTA and the Campesinos: The Impact of NAFTA on Small-Scale Agricultural Producers in Mexico and the Prospects for Change*, edited by Juan M. Rivera, Scott Whiteford, and Manuel Chávez, xiii–xxv. Chicago: University of Chicago Press.

Rivera, Juan M., Scott Whiteford, and Manuel Chávez, eds. 2009. *NAFTA and the Campesinos: The Impact of NAFTA on Small-Scale Agricultural Producers in Mexico and the Prospects for Change*. Chicago: University of Scranton Press.

Robinson, William I. 2004. *A Theory of Global Capitalism: Production, Class, and State in a Transnational World*. Baltimore: Johns Hopkins University Press.

Robinson, William I. 2007. "Theories of Globalization." George Ritzer, edited by George Ritzer, 125–30. ed. In *The Blackwell Companion to Globalization*. Oxford: Blackwell.

Robinson, William I. 2008. *Latin America and Global Capitalism*. Baltimore: Johns Hopkins University Press.

Roever, Sally. 2010. "Street Trade in Latin America: Demographic Trends, Legal Issues and Vending Organisations in Six Cities." In *Street Vendors in the Global Urban Economy*, edited by Sharit K. Bhomik, 208–40. New York: Routledge.

Rolstad, Kellie. 2001. "Language Death in Central Mexico: The Decline of Nahuatl and the New Bilingual Maintenance Programs." *Bilingual Review* 26(1): 3–18.

Rothstein, Frances Abrahamer. 2007. *Globalization in Rural Mexico: Three Decades of Change*. Austin: University of Texas Press.

Sackett, Andrew. 2010. "Fun in Acapulco? The Politics of Development on the Mexican Riviera." In *Holiday in Mexico: Critical Reflections on Tourism and Tourist*

Encounters, edited by Dina Berger and Andrew Grant Wood, 161–82. Durham: Duke University Press.

Sanders, Jimy M. and Victor Nee. 1996. "Immigrant Self-Employment: The Family as Social Capital and the Value of Human Capital." *American Sociological Review* 61(2): 231–49.

Sandstrom, Alan R. and Pamela Effrein Sandstrom. 2011. "The Long and Short of Ethnographic Research among the Nahua of Norhern Veracruz, Mexico." *Anthropology and Humanism* 36(1): 25–35.

Sassen, Saskia. 1998. *Globalization and Its Discontents*. New York: The New Press.

Sassen, Saskia. 2000. "Spatialization and Temporalities of the Global: Elements for a Theorization." *Public Culture* 12 (1): 215–32.

Sassen, Saskia. 2005. "When National Territory is Home to the Global: Old Borders and Novel Borderings." *New Political Economy* 10(4): 523–41.

Schafran, Alex and Paavo Monkkonen. 2011. "Beyond Chapala and Cancún: Grappling with the Impact of American Migration to Mexico." *Migraciones Internacionales* 6(2): 233–58.

Schuerkens, Ulrike. 2008. "Transformations of Local Socioeconomic Practices in a Global World: A Theoretical Approach and Some Empirical Evidence from Different World Regions." In *Globalization and Transformations of Local Socioeconomic Practices*, edited by Ulrike Schuerkens, 1–19. New York and London: Routledge.

Schryer, Frans J. 2007 (July). "Continuidades y discontinuidades en la communidad de Ahueheupan: Lengua, trabajo y migración." *Regiones: Suplemento de antropología*. 30: 9–12.

Schryer, Frans J. 2010*a*. "Globalization and *Indígenas*: The Alto Balsas Nahuas." In *Latin American Identities After 1980*, edited by Gordana Yovanovich and Amy Huras, 51–78. Ontario: Wilfrid Laurier University Press.

Schryer, Frans J. 2010*b*. "The Alto Balsas Nahuas: Transnational Indigeneity and the Interactions in the World of Arts and Crafts, the Politics of Resistance, and the Global Labor Market." In *Indigenous Cosmopolitans: Transnational and Transcultural Indigeneity in the Twenty-First Century*, edited by Maximillian C. Forte, 91–126. New York: Peter Lang.

Schafran, Alex and Paavo Monkkonen. 2011. "Beyond Chapala and Cancún: Grappling with the Impact of American Migration to Mexico." *Migraciones Internacionales* 6(2): 233–58.

Seligmann, Linda J. 2004. *Peruvian Street Lives: Culture, Power, and Economy among Market Women of Cuzco*. Urbana and Chicago: University of Illinois Press.

Sernau, Scott. 1994. *Economies of Exclusion: Underclass Poverty and Labor Market Change in Mexico*. Westport: Praeger.

Sethuraman, S. V. 1998. *Gender, Informality, and Poverty: A Global Review*. Geneva: World Bank/WIEGO (Women in Informal Employment: Globalising and Organising).

Silva Londoño, Diana Alejandra. 2010. "Comercio ambulante en el Centro Histórico de la Ciudad de México (1990–2007)." *Revista Mexicana de Sociología* 72(2): 195–224.

Simon, Beatrice. 2009. "Sacamefotos and Tejedoras: Frontstage and Backstage Meaning in a Peruvian Context." In *Cultural Tourism in Latin America: The Politics of*

Space and Imagery, edited by Michael Baud and Annelou Ypeij, 117–40. Boston: Brill.

Smart, Josephine. 1990. "Self-Employment vs. Wage Employment in Hong Kong: A Reconsideration of the Urban Informal Economy." In *Perspectives on the Informal Economy*, edited by M. Estellie Smith, 251–80. Lanham, Md.: University Press of America.

Smith, Michael Peter. 2001. *Transnational Urbanism: Locating Globalization*. Oxford: Blackwell Publishing.

Smith, Michael Peter and Luis Eduardo Guarnizo. 1998. *Transnationalism from Below*. New Brunswick: Transaction Publishers.

Smith, Susan E. and Luis E. Marin. 2005. "Water and the Rural Poor in Latin America: The Case of Tlamacazapa, Guerrero, Mexico." *Hydrogeology Journal* 13: 346–49.

Spatler-Roth, Roberta M. 1988. "The Sexual Political Economy of Street Vending in Washington, D.C." In *Traders vs. the State: Anthropological Approaches to Unofficial Economies*, edited by Gracia C. Clark, 165–87. Boulder: Westview Press.

Stark, Oded and J. Edward Taylor. 1991. "Migration Incentives, Migration Types: The Role of Relative Deprivation." *Economic Journal* 101: 1163–78.

Stark, Oded and Y. Q. Wang. 2000. "A Theory of Migration as a Response to Relative Deprivation." *German Economic Review* 1: 131–43.

Staudt, Kathleen. 2008. *Violence and Activism at the Border: Gender, Fear, and Everyday Life in Ciudad Juárez*. Austin: University of Texas Press.

Staven, Ward. 2005. "Latin American Globalization in Historical Perspective: Human Reality and the First and Second 'Global Eras." *Journal of Developing Societies* 21(3–4): 233–51.

Stephen, Lynn. 1993. "Weaving in the Fast Lane: Class, Ethnicity, and Gender in Zapotec Craft Commercialization." *Crafts in the World Market*, edited by June Nash, 59–84. Albany: State University of New York Press.

Stillerman, Joel and Catherine Sundt. 2007. "Embeddedness and Business Strategies Among Santiago, Chile's Street and Flea Market Vendors." In *Street Entrepreneurs: People, Place and Politics in Local and Global Perspective*, edited by John Cross and Alfonso Morales, 180–200. New York: Routledge.

Stoller, Paul. 2002. *Money Has No Smell: The Africanization of New York City*. Chicago: University of Chicago Press.

Sur Acapulco. 2006. "Documentan la historia de Ciudadad Renacimiento a 26 años de su creación." http//www.suracapulco.com.mx/2006/marzo/04/sociedad.htm.

Tokman, Víctor E. 1998. "Jobs and Welfare: Searching for New Answers." In *Poverty and Inequality in Latin America: Issues and New Challenges*, edited by Víctor E. Tokman and Guillermo O'Donnell, 209–25. Notre Dame: Notre Dame University Press.

Tokman, Victor E., 2001. "Las relaciones entre los sectores formal e informal. Una exploración de su naturaleza." *Revista Economía*. 48: 17–74.

Torres, Rebecca Maria and Janet D. Momsen. 2005. "Gringolandia: The Construction of a New Tourist Space in Mexico." *Annals of the Association of American Geographers* 95(2): 314–35.

Torres, Rebecca and Janet Henshall Momsen. 2006. "Gringolandia: Cancún and the American Tourist." In *Adventures into Mexico: American Tourism beyond the Border*, edited by Nicholas Daven Bloom, 58–74. Lanham: Rowman & Littlefield.

Valenzuela, María Elena. 2005. *Informality and Gender in Latin America*. Working Paper No. 60. Geneva: International Labour Office.

Valenzuela Valdivieso, Ernesto and Átlantida Coll-Hurtado. 2010. "La construcción y evolución del espacio turístico de Acapulco (México)." *Anales de Geografía* 30(1): 163–90.

Van den Berghe, Pierre L. 1994. *The Quest for the Other: Ethnic Tourism in San Cristóbal, Mexico*. Seattle: University of Washington Press.

Vázquez Castillo, María Teresa. 2004. *Land Privatization in Mexico: Urbanization, Formation of Regions and Globalization in Ejidos*. New York: Routledge.

Velasco Ortiz, Laura. 2007. "Women, Migration, and Household Survival Strategies: Mixtec Women in Tijuana." In *Women and Migration in the U.S.-Mexico Borderlands: A Reader*, edited by Denise A. Segura and Patricia Zavella, 341–59. Durham: Duke University Press.

Vélez-Ibañez, Carlos G. 1983. *Rituals of Marginality: Politics, Process, and Culture Change in Urban Central Mexico, 1969–1974*. Berkeley: University of California Press.

Virgen Aguilar, Carlos Rogelio. 2009. "El ciclo de vida de un destino turístico: Puerto Vallarta, Jalisco, México." *Cultur: Revista de Cultrura y Turismo* 3(1): 2–24.

Ward, Evan L. 2008. *Packaged Vacations: Tourism Development in the Spanish Caribbean*. Gainesville: University of Florida Press.

Weismantel, Mary. 2001. *Cholas and Pishtacos: Stories of Race and Sex in the Andes*. Chicago: University of Chicago Press.

Wilson, Tamar Diana. 1992. *Vamos para buscar la vida: Patterns of Outmigration from a Rancho in Jalisco and Inmigration to a Mexicali Squatter Settlement*. Unpublished Ph.D. dissertation, Department of Anthropology, University of California, Los Angeles.

Wilson, Tamar Diana. 1998. "Approaches to Understanding the Position of Women Workers in the Informal Sector." *Latin American Perspectives* 25(2): 105–19.

Wilson, Tamar Diana. 2003. "Is Semi-informalized Self-Employment Counterhegemonic? A Comparison of Irish Jarveys and Mexicali Brickmakers." *Urban Anthropology* 32(3–4): 281–310.

Wilson, Tamar Diana. 2005. *Subsidizing Capitalism: Brickmakers on the U.S.-Mexican Border*. Albany: State University of New York Press.

Wilson, Tamar Diana. 2006. "'I Thought Horses Was the Best Thing Ever': Irish Jarveys in Dublin." *Critique of Anthropology* 26(2): 139–56.

Wilson, Tamar Diana. 2008. "Economic and Social Impacts of Tourism in Mexico." *Latin American Perspectives* 35(3): 37–52.

Wilson, Tamar Diana and Alba Gámez. 2010. "A Consideration of Social and Human Capital Among Beach and Marina Vendors in Cabo San Lucas, Mexico." *Urban Anthropology* 39(4): 425–53.

Wilson, Tamar Diana and Alba E. Gámez. 2012. "Women Beach and Marina Vendors in Cabo San Lucas, BCS, Mexico: Considerations about their Marginalization." *Latin American Perspectives* (forthcoming).

Wood, W. Warner. 2008. *Made in Mexico: Zapotec Weavers and the Global Ethnic Art Market*. Bloomington: Indiana University Press.

World Bank. 2004*a*. "Zihautenejo Tourism Project." http://web.worldbank.org/external/projects.

World Bank. 2004*b*. "Baja California Tourism Project." http://web.worldbank.org/external/projects.

World Bank. 2004*c*. "Tourism Development Project." http://web.worldbank.org/external/projects.

Yoshioka, Hirotoshi. 2010. "Indigenous Language Usage and Maintenance Patterns among Indigenous People in the Era of Neoliberal Multiculturalism in Mexico and Guatemala." *Latin American Research Review* 45(3): 5–34.

Index

About the Author

Tamar Diana Wilson has published articles on tourism and/or the informal economy in *Critique of Anthropology, Latin American Perspectives, Urban Anthropology,* and *Review of Radical Political Economics.* Her first book, *Subsidizing Capitalism: Brickmakers on the U.S.-Mexico Border* (SUNY Press, 2005), was concerned with the family labor force utilization and with the economic contributions of these participants in the informal economy to the growth of Mexicali, Baja California, Mexico. She is a research affiliate with the Department of Anthropology, University of Missouri, St. Louis. She has lived in Mexico since 1988 and in Los Cabos since 1994.